THE ISLANDS SERIES

THE ISLE OF ARRAN

Arran is one of the gems of the British Isles. This new
edition has been revised throughout to include recent
local government and other changes. It is therefore
right up to date. Even the most casual visitor or arm-
chair traveller will find his appreciation enriched by
Mr McLellan's colourful and sympathetic portrait. He
writes as an islander; he captures all the moods of
coast and mountain, of hope and fear as the permanent population dwindles and more cottages become
holiday homes for non-residents. But though this is a
work to be read for pleasure, it is also a reference
book packed with detailed fact on every aspect of the
island's history, industry, communications, natural
history and social life. It will undoubtedly remain the
standard work on the island for many years to come.

THE ISLAND SERIES

*Published in the United States by Stackpole
 Other titles published in the United States by David & Charles Inc
 The series is distributed in Australia by Wren

THE ISLE OF ARRAN

ARRAN

by ROBERT McLELLAN

DAVID & CHARLES

NEWTON ABBOT LONDON NORTH POMFRET (VT) VANCOUVER

ISBN 0 7153 6946 6

Printed in Great Britain by Redwood Burn Ltd
Trowbridge and Esher for David & Charles
(Publishers) Limited Brunel House Newton Abbot
Devon

To Tom Alexander

CONTENTS

ILLUSTRATIONS

8

ILLUSTRATIONS

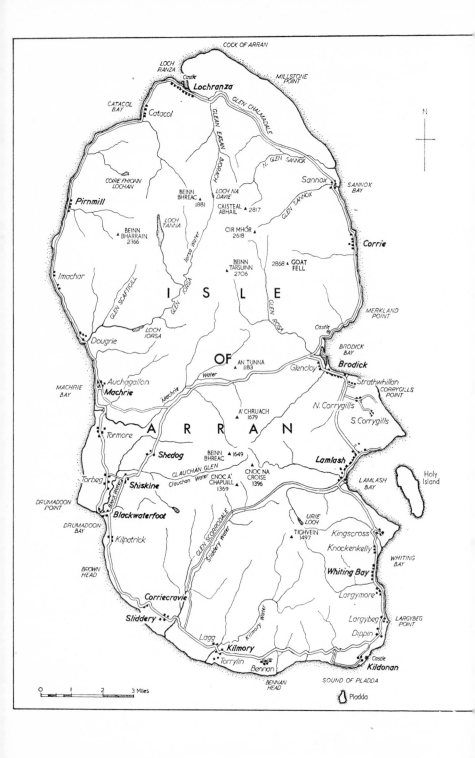

COCK OF ARRAN

LOCH
RANZA
MILLSTONE
POINT

Castle
Lochranza

CATACOL
BAY

GLEN CHALMADALE

Catacol

GLEN EASAN BIORACH

N. GLEN SANNOX

COIRE FHIONN
LOCHAN

Sannox

SANNOX
BAY

Pirnmill

BEINN
BHREAC
1881

LOCH NA
DAVIE

CAISTEAL ▲ 2817
ABHAIL

GLEN SANNOX

LOCH
TANNA

BEINN ▲
BHARRAIN
2366

CIR MHÓR
2618

Corrie

Imachar

GLEN SCAFTIGILL

GLEN IORSA

Iorsa Water

BEINN
TARSUINN
2706

2868 ▲ GOAT
FELL

GLEN ROSA

I S L E

MERKLAND
POINT

Castle

LOCH
IORSA

Dougrie

O F

Castle

BRODICK
BAY

AN TUNNA
1183

Brodick

Water

Glencloy

Machrie Water

Strathwhillan

MACHRIE
BAY

Auchagallon

Machrie

A' CHRUACH
1679

CORRYGILLS
POINT

N. Corrygills

A R R A N

S.Corrygills

Tormore

Shedog

BEINN ▲ 1649
BHREAC

CLAUCHAN GLEN

Clauchan Water

CNOC A'
CHAPUILL
1369

CNOC NA
CROISE
1396

Lamlash

Torbeg

Black Water

Shiskine

LAMLASH
BAY

Holy
Island

DRUMADOON
POINT

Blackwaterfoot

GLEN SCORRODALE

Sliddery Water

URIE
LOCH

DRUMADOON
BAY

Kilpatrick

TIGHVEIN ▲
1497

Kingscross

Knockenkelly

WHITING
BAY

BROWN
HEAD

Kilmory Water

Whiting Bay

Corriecravie

Largymore

Sliddery

Largybeg

LARGYBEG
POINT

Lagg

Kilmory

Dippin

Castle

Torrylin

Bennan

BENNAN
HEAD

SOUND OF PLADDA

Kildonan

0   1   2   3 Miles

Pladda

N

1   LANDSCAPE

ROBERT BURNS is said to have been blind to natural grandeur because he could see Arran almost daily from the Ayrshire farms on which he spent his youth, yet never once mentioned it either in verse or prose. His blindness has been explained either on the ground that he lived before the fashion for scenery developed, or that his agricultural preoccupations compelled him to be more conscious of foreground detail than of the broader sweep of the landscape. But there may be another and more cogent reason why, although he could see Arran frequently in periods of good visibility, he failed to identify it.

The stranger approaching Arran for the first time, and by the common route, by rail from Glasgow to Ardrossan, may first see it as a spectacular range of hills rising beyond the uplands which slope away from the water-meadows by the side of the railway, but he is no more likely than Burns to apprehend its separate identity, for there is no sign from inland Ayrshire of the large stretch of water which lies between it and the coast, and makes it visibly an island. He is likely to be conscious of it only when he reaches the coast. Then its impact can be breathtaking, depending on the weather, time, and season. Too often, when the wind is in the south and rain is falling, the island is invisible, or only a long black smudge beneath a dreary monotony of grey cloud. But let the wind be in the west or north, preferably the latter, and its contribution to the glory of the Firth of Clyde is undeniable. Lying fifteen miles or so across the water, lofty and jagged in the north, undulating in the middle, and sloping to the south, its sides gashed by narrow glens, its coastline broken by the steep bulk of Holy Isle, and given added variety at its southern extreme by the outline of the low islet of Pladda, it dominates every other natural feature in sight, drawing the eye from the water to its summit peaks, then up to the blue of the sky, or into the clouds. Spiritually, as well as in this more literal sense, the sight is uplifting.

This view of the island is the common one. It becomes commonplace when opportunity affords other viewpoints. Sail in Kilbrannan Sound, or in the Sound of Bute, so that you see it from the west or north, and from the water, and you will find the view from the Ayrshire coast totally eclipsed. Walk along the east coast of Kintyre, at dawn in the summer, or to Dunagoil in the south-west of the Isle of Bute, at sunset on a winter evening, and see the northern peaks of the island heightened and glorified by the luminosity of the hidden sun, and you will experience the holiness of the beauty of nature with the wonder and fervour of a Wordsworth.

There might seem to be a case for suggesting that if you are to enjoy the island to the full you must view it from an adjacent area, and possibly from a purely pictorial point of view this may be so. It has been said that Bute is superior to Arran in only one respect, that the view of Arran from Bute surpasses that of Bute from Arran. The Ayrshire coast and Kintyre may also claim this restricted superiority. Bute, seen from the north-east of Arran over 6 miles of water, is a pleasant place, with its light sandy bays, whitewashed farms, patchwork fields, and round heathery hillocks, sitting in an amphitheatre formed by the high hills of Argyll, and affording, in the space between its southern headland and the dark scarps of the Little Cumbrae, the latter relieved by a dazzling white lighthouse, a faint glimpse of the little holiday town of Millport, spread around a bay on the Greater Cumbrae beyond. Ayrshire, too, is not unattractive, a long crescent of coastline studded with industrial towns too far away to be oppressive, and backed by pleasantly varied ranges of faint but shapely hills. Kintyre, only 4 miles to the west of Arran across Kilbrannan Sound, is nearest of all to being dull, lying low and little varied either in contour or colour, just saved from monotony by irregularities at Saddell and Campbeltown Loch, and by the little islet of Sanda, lying off the coast to the south. Yet while none of these areas is really dull, or without great charm when known more intimately, it has to be admitted that Arran offers them their most striking prospect, while they seldom surpass, when viewed from almost anywhere on the island, the interest of the landscape close at hand.

It is 19 miles from the Cock of Arran in the north of the island to Bennan Head in the south, and 10 from Machrie Bay in the west to Corrygills Point in the east, and the island is estimated to cover an area of 165 square miles. The road round the island, which leaves the coast only in the north and south, and very briefly at the promontories of Clauchlands and Druma-doon, is 56 miles long, and the coastline is estimated to be 60. Two roads cross the island from east to west, high over the water-shed, one from Brodick to Blackwaterfoot, and the other from Lamlash to Sliddery, yet the total length of the island roads is short of 90 miles. All fourteen villages lie close to the coast, indeed only Shedog is slightly inland, so the whole of the inhabited part of the island, and much of its unpopulated and wild interior, can be looked over by the motorist in a single day. Even to the pedes-trian it may be said to be accessible, for although it will take him many pleasant years to explore it thoroughly, he can cross even its wildest stretches in the course of a long summer day, and even in a short day in winter can reach a summit and be back before dark.

Because of this handy size, and the fact that it contains most of the features of the Highland and Lowland scenery of Scotland, it has become fashionable to describe the island as a Scotland in miniature, but no part of it resembles the black midland belt which stretches on the mainland from the Clyde to the Forth, and contains nearly all the industry, and most of the population, of mainland Scotland. Nor has any part of the island anything in common with the fertile low farmlands of the Lothians or the eastern coastal counties between the Forth and the Moray Firth. Nowadays regarded as one with the Clyde islands, Arran is, nevertheless, in the west particularly, Hebridean in character, and indeed geologically, historically, and culturally has considerable affinities with the Inner Hebrides, and even with Ireland. Except in the three main villages on the east coast, Brodick, Lamlash, and Whiting Bay, which are fairly typical small coastal resorts, with a suburban character of comparatively recent development, the landscape is of a pattern established after the Clearances of the early nineteenth century, common to the Highlands and Islands and to Ireland. It may be said to be Celtic, although the word would more properly apply to the pattern which the Clearances destroyed. White farmhouses lie irregularly by the little fields of the coastal strip and the lower inland waters, with open hillside

13

behind, and peaks in the distance. There is indeed a Celtic quality in the whole island environment, in spite of changes in social organisation and language, and the influx of much new blood. It carries like Yeats' Ireland a sense of the co-existence with the present of a past so remote as to stretch beyond history into legend. Almost every feature of the landscape has a name in Gaelic or Norse, although Norse was the tongue of a remote episode, and Gaelic, although its accent lingers, is almost forgotten. Everywhere in the upper glens are the ruins of old blackhouses and turf dykes. In the straths or on the shores are the little oblong sites of ancient chapels. On the hilltops round the coast are faint traces of fortification, and on the moors are monoliths, stone circles and chambered cairns. And all this in the same world as the stone-built Victorian hotels and villas, the brick and rough-cast boarding-houses built between the two world wars, and the recent bungalows of pre-cast concrete and coloured tiles, which dominate the main villages; in the same world, too, as the nuclear power station across the Firth of Clyde at Hunterston, the great cooling tower and oil tanks at Ardrossan, the submarines in training on the Firth itself, and the jet planes crossing over between Prestwick and Gander. The contrast creates a perspective, in which past and present alike take their place, under the eye of eternity.

GEOLOGY

This consciousness of the infinity of time, so powerfully evoked by the island, while owing much to the evidence of habitation by a long sequence of peoples of different races and cultures, springs also from the fact that the primal processes of natural creation are almost everywhere visible, either still at work, or in their effects, and this even to those without the slightest knowledge of geology. The eroding influences of frost and wind and running water are obvious, in the denuded sides of the peaks, the masses of tumbled rock in the corrie bottoms, the exposed outcrops in the glens, and the level deposits of mud or sand or gravel through which the larger waters wind to the sea. Even to the uninitiated the U-shaped glens of the northern waters, the hanging tributary corries, the scored rock surfaces, and the existence

14

almost everywhere of precariously balanced gigantic boulders, in shapes and positions inexplicable in terms of common weather erosion or of the force of gravity, combine to suggest, if not the agency of ancient ice, that at least of some powerful force no longer active. And if the 1,000 ft plateau, clearly visible around the northern peaks, fails to suggest marine erosion during a remote period of submergence, the strip of level land around the coast, backed by cliffs full of caves obviously water-worn, arouses at least a suspicion of a not greatly distant past when the sea was at a higher level than today.

It was in fact from the power of the island's striking physical features to arouse wonder and stimulate conjecture that the science of geology made progress in the days of its infancy, for it was to Arran that James Hutton, the father of igneous geology, came at the end of the eighteenth century for evidence in favour of his view that some rocks are not a result of the hardening of sediments accumulated at the bottom of the sea, and then raised into the air by sudden supernaturally ordained convulsions of nature, but were formed by the cooling and hardening of molten material forced up from within the earth by the power of heat. The war between the Plutonists, led by Hutton, and the Neptunists or Wernerians, the latter named after the German mineralogist Werner, who maintained that all rocks were aqueous in origin, was waged to a large extent on Arran soil. Hutton was followed to the island by Jameson and Headrick, both Neptunists, who treated him with a degree of sarcasm which makes them now appear ridiculous, for Hutton's view has prevailed, and it is largely due to his influence that we know now that the striking northern granite peaks of Arran are the eroded remnants of a great mass of molten material which welled up from the fiery interior of the earth, pushing up the existing layers of rock to form a gigantic blister. Protected by the upper layers from the chill of the air the mass cooled so slowly as to produce the large crystals characteristic of granite. Then, cooled and hardened, the great dome-shaped mass was exposed to the air when the layers of older and softer rock above it were eroded away.

The tremendous extent of this erosion is made plain by consideration of another characteristic feature of the island landscape, the basaltic and other dykes which exist in such profusion,

15

particularly in the south, where they are exposed along the coast. These vertical walls of dark rock, running from the inland cliffs along the foreshore and out across the sand to the sea, were explained by Hutton as due to molten material bursting its way through the earth's surface and filling the cracks it made in the process. In this case the material, different in composition from that which formed the granite, cooled rapidly in the chill of the air, producing the almost imperceptible crystals characteristic of basalt. The dykes, harder than the sedimentary rocks through which they were injected, now dominate a shore composed of sand being ground from the softer rocks by the action of the sea.

Yet the dykes, although most obvious where they are exposed along the shore, create most astonishment when they are found cutting across the high ridges which join the granite peaks of the north. The outstanding instance is the dyke which rises in the floor of Ceum na Caillich, or the Witch's Step, a great V-shaped chasm breaking the sharp ridge between Caisteall Abhail and Suidhe Fhearghas, and visually the most exciting feature of the island landscape. This dyke is proof of the tremendous amount of material eroded from the granite dome in the north of the island, between the time of its subterranean cooling and the present day. For if the surface of the land had been as it is today, the molten material which formed the dyke could never have risen to the top of the ridge, but would have escaped and flowed out along the bottoms of the glens. The glens have clearly been excavated since the dyke was formed, and as great a thickness of granite may well have been eroded from above the ridge as has been cleared from the glens below.

The basaltic dykes which cut the northern ridges have clearly been formed somewhat later than the granite, and belong to a subsequent phase of the same great igneous episode. To an earlier phase belong the sills of igneous rock which give the southern half of the island its own dominant features. Prominent around the southern coast, from Drumadoon Point in the west to Clauchlands Point in the east, as at Brown Head, Bennan Head, and Dippen Head, and on the eastern and western sides of Holy Isle, are beetling cliffs of igneous rock of varying composition, originally intruded in their molten state between the layers of soft

16

Page 17: (above) Brodick castle from the south-east, showing the Victorian wing on the left and the Cromwellian battery on the right; *(below)* diagram of Brodick Castle

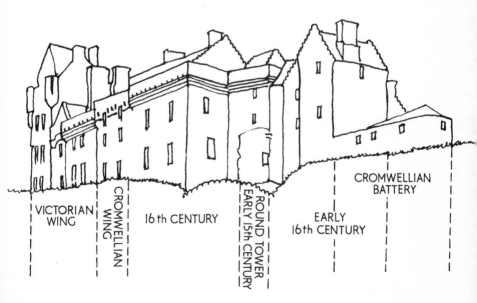

VICTORIAN WING | CROMWELLIAN WING | 16th CENTURY | ROUND TOWER EARLY 15th CENTURY | EARLY 16th CENTURY | CROMWELLIAN BATTERY

Page 18: (above) Cir Mhor from the Mullach Buidhe; one of the peaks of the glacially eroded granite boss in the north of the island; (left) Glenashdale Falls, the largest of the sill waterfalls characteristic of the southern half of the island

sedimentary rock already in existence, and then, after cooling and hardening, exposed to the air by the more rapid erosion of the latter. These horizontal intrusions, or sills, some of them hundreds of feet thick, not only give us the headlands of the coast, but the tabular hills, scarps, and terraces of inland southern Arran, and the waterfall sequences of the southern burns. The water, resisted by the hard rock of a sill, has to flow to its edge, where the force of its fall erodes the softer rock below, until a new sill is reached, where the process is repeated. Where the drop between the sills is considerable so are the waterfalls, and one of these, at Glenash-dale, which falls in two leaps of 40 and then 100 ft, is the most impressive natural feature of the southern landscape.

The igneous episode which produced the northern granite and the almost contemporaneous sills and dykes, and incidentally left traces in the centre of the island, just south of the String road, of a volcanic centre active after the upheaval of the granite, was undoubtedly ancient. The extent of the erosion required to expose its manifestations baffles the imagination. Yet in terms of the time involved in the formation of the earlier rocks visible in the island, it was recent. Much of the investigation which enabled this truth to be determined was conducted elsewhere, but as with the enquiry into the origin of igneous rocks, so too in regard to the meaning of the relative positions of the different rock layers, the island was the scene of significant discovery, and again James Hutton was the pioneer, for it was near Lochranza, in the north-west of the island, that he first distinguished the feature known now to geologists as an unconformity. On the shore near the mouth of the North Newton burn he discovered strata of schist inclined at an angle of over 45 degrees, in contact with strata of sandstone almost equally inclined, but in an opposite direction, so that they came together 'like the rigging of a house'. He saw, too, that the strata of sandstone overlapped the ends of the strata of schist. The significance was that the schist must have been upturned from its original horizontal position before the sand-stone was deposited, and the schist and sandstone subsequently upturned together, to bring them into the position observed. Immense intervals must have followed the deposition of the two sets of strata.

Immense as these intervals must have been, they were but

two of many which preceded the formation of the granite. Consideration of the conditions under which the earlier rocks were formed, the present angle of their stratification, the extent to which they have been altered by heat or pressure or intercalated with material of igneous origin, and the presence or absence of fossil remains, has enabled the many geologists who have studied the island to build up a long history of submergence and deposition, of elevation and denudation, and of igneous explosion and upheaval, long before the granite came into being. Some idea of the ages of time involved may be obtained from the fact that the episode which produced the granite, and the other igneous rocks of the sills and dykes, is estimated as having been the seventh of which the island rocks give evidence. There is no distinct period in the development of the island's structure, from the time of the oldest schists, themselves altered from their original state by tremendous heat and pressure, through the long history of the deposition of the lower and upper old red sandstones, the calciferous sandstones and their associated carboniferous limestones and coal measures, and the lower and upper new red sandstones, without its evidence of a contribution of igneous material. Although these contributions, apart from a thick series of lavas below the calciferous sandstones, are comparatively slight, they do involve, when considered in the light of the time which must have elapsed between them to allow for the deposition of the rocks they separate, a period infinitely greater than that which has elapsed since the final igneous episode which brought the granite into being. Estimates in terms of years are given to support this view. The schists, the oldest rocks on the island, are said to have existed for over five hundred million years. The final igneous episode began only about seventy million years ago.

Recent this episode may have been, but it preceded the existence of the island as a separate entity. At its close Arran was part of an elevated plateau which included most of Scotland, and stood in the Arran region 2-3,000 ft above sea level. This plateau, which had a gentle inclination from the north-west to the southeast, lasted long enough to develop its own drainage system, and the Sound of Bute, Kilbrannan Sound, the Firth of Clyde, and the through-valleys of Arran, may have been originated by the rivers of this period. Most authorities are agreed that the Sound of Bute, and the almost parallel trough running in a south-easterly direction through the north of the island, from Lochranza to Sannox, and now occupied by Glen Chalmadale and North Glen Sannox, had such an origin. There is a conflict of opinion in regard to Kilbrannan Sound and the Firth of Clyde, and to the three great troughs which cut the island from north to south : the first now occupied by Glen Catacol and Glen Scaftigill; the second by Glen Easan Biorach and Glen Iorsa; and the third by Glen Sannox and Glen Rosa, and continuing west of the Clauch-land Hills to pass between King's Cross and Holy Isle. Tyrrell, the author of the standard work on the geology of the island, following Gregory, held the view that these were the result of crustal faulting and cracking. He maintained that the crustal block from which Arran was subsequently shaped rose a few hundred feet, while parallel blocks to the west and east subsided, letting in the sea from the south, and forming Kilbrannan Sound and the Firth of Clyde. This faulting was accompanied by crack-ing across the northern granite, producing the three great north to south troughs. Whichever view is correct, it is at least agreed that Kilbrannan Sound and the Firth of Clyde, and the three troughs in dispute, originated in the period following the close of the final igneous episode.

The newly created island stood long enough at its initial level for considerable denudation to take place, accompanied by the formation of a plain of marine erosion, which was raised by a further upward movement of about 1,000 ft to produce the plateau, already mentioned, which rings the northern peaks. And all this happened before the glacial period, initiated a million years ago, during which Arran nourished an ice sheet of its own, strong enough not only to fend off the main ice streams which filled Kilbrannan Sound and the Firth of Clyde, but in the pro-cess of sculpturing the peaks and glens into roughly their present shape, to deposit huge blocks of the northern granite over the western and eastern fringes, and the whole southern half of the island.

Of the raised beaches visible around the island, at heights of 100, 50, and 25 ft, the two former, which are best displayed near the mouths of the Iorsa and Machrie waters, belong to the close of the glacial period, when the release of water by the melting ice led to a rise in sea level, followed by a fall when the sea itself was reduced by evaporation. Following the close of the glacial period there were three further distinct changes in sea level, the first to somewhat below that of today, the second to a level some 25 ft higher, and the third to that of today. The 25 ft beach, most obvious to the north of Drumadoon Point, between Catacol and Lochranza, and between Corrie and Brodick, was formed after the second of these changes. It is curious that although Arran became an island between the final igneous episode and the glacial period, the severance of Britain from the mainland of Europe did not occur until the period, between 5500 and 3000 BC, during which the 25 ft beach was formed. Arran was, therefore, an island before Britain itself.

Those who wish to study the geology of the island seriously will find it treated extensively in an expanding literature. Because of the importance of Huttonian theory in the early days of the science, and the fact that it was based on so many observations made in Arran, the island became a place of pilgrimage for later geologists, some of them foreign, and many of them eminent, who carried on the work of discovery. Arran is therefore classic ground for the geologist, and because of this, and because it contains within practicable bounds a fairly complete synopsis of the geology of Scotland, with its contrast between the Highland formations in the north and the Lowland in the south, it is now visited every year, usually at Easter, by hundreds of students and their teachers, who erupt from the boarding-houses equipped with knapsack and hammer, to assist nature in the work of erosion.

The evidence of their hammering is most obvious where interest is concentrated into a relatively small area, as in North Glen Sannox, where rocks of an age between that of the schists and the lower old red sandstones, not visible elsewhere, are exposed in the burn a little below the North Sannox bridge; on the Corrie shore and along the north coast of the island between Corloch and the Cock of Arran, where the carboniferous series is well displayed; and to the west of the area of the volcanic centre south of the String road, where certain sedimentary rocks, subsequent in their deposition to the upper new red sandstones, but earlier than the granite, and not visible in any outcrop, are to be found in the form of fragments thrown up by eruption.

In the Corrygills neighbourhood, too, where pitchstone seems to have been first discovered, there is much chipping away of specimens, particularly from the sill exposed about ninety yards downstream from the point at which the South Corrygills road crosses the southern branch of the Corrygills burn, and from the same sill where it crosses the shore to the south-east. Pitchstone, a glassie rock of the same composition as granite, its non-crystalline structure due to extremely rapid cooling, can be found in a variety of colours in sills and dykes throughout the island, but the dark green rock of the sill just mentioned seems to be the most highly prized, having been described by Tyrrell as 'perhaps the finest spherulitic rock in Britain'.

PHYSICAL GEOGRAPHY

Since the close of the glacial period the drainage in the north of the island has been determined mainly by the existence of the through-valleys or troughs, already listed, which were formed during the post-igneous period. These troughs contain the most considerable waters in the island, the longest being the Iorsa, with a run of about 8 miles. There are also minor systems of drainage radial to the two sections of the granite dome split by the central trough. The higher eastern section, which contains the main peaks of Goatfell, Caisteall Abhail, Cir Mhor, Beinn Tarsuinn and Beinn Nuis, all over 2,500 ft in height, sends off feeders westward into Glen Iorsa, north-eastward into Glen Sannox and southward into Glen Rosa. Eastward some shorter burns run to the sea direct, the most striking being the White Water or Corrie Burn, which cascades from Coire Lan just under Goatfell to the plateau below in a great white streak, easily seen from the mainland coast if Arran itself is at all visible. The western section of the granite dome, whose main summits, Beinn Bhreac and Beinn Bharrain, rise to little over 2,000 ft, is drained to the north by the Easan Biorach and Catacol burns, and to the south-west by the Scaftigill burn and Iorsa Water, but in the west sheds many short steep burns direct to the sea, the longest of which is the forked Alltgobhlach.

23

In the southern half of the island the drainage is east and west from a long irregular watershed formed by the ridge joining A' Chruach, Cnoc na Croise, Cnoc Dubh, and Tighvein, all just over 1,000 ft in height, and situated closer to the eastern side of the island than the western. The western waters are, therefore, the longer, and include the Machrie, Black, Sliddery, and Kilmory waters, all with narrow upper glens of a moorland character, opening out as they approach the sea into little straths of alluvial soil. The main eastern waters in the southern half of the island, the Glencloy, Benlister, Monamore, King's Cross, and Glenashdale burns, fall steeply from high moorland to land just above sea level, either some distance inland, in long cascades, or more gradually by a series of sill waterfalls of the kind already described. The principal burn running south from the interior of the southern half of the island, the short Allt Mor, is steep also, with one notable waterfall.

The fresh water lochs of the island are in the main highly situated, and are of three types: longish drift-dammed shallow lochs lying at or near watersheds between the heads of glens, deep glacial rock basins, and small lochans lying among peat. The largest loch in the island, Loch Tanna, which is well over a mile long and just under half a mile broad, is drift-dammed and shallow, as is Loch na Davie, which is perhaps the more curious because the Iorsa Water runs out of it to the south, and the Easan Biorach burn to the north. In dry weather it is almost empty, a waste of black silt littered with white granite boulders. The Urie Loch, in the southern half of the island, seems at first sight to be of this type, feeding the Monamore burn regularly and the King's Cross burn in very wet weather, but the latter only because it is artificially dammed at the Monamore outlet. The finest of the rock basins are Loch Chorein Lochain, lying high between Meall nan Damh and Meall Biorach in the northwest of the island, in a corrie surrounded by steep granite crags, and Loch Garbad, the source of the Allt Mor in the south of the island, surrounded by the scarps of an exposed sill. With the exception of Loch Garbad the rock basins, like most of the other lochs and lochans of the island, lie at heights above 1,000 ft. Loch Iorsa, a widening of the Iorsa Water where it is dammed by drift, is the most considerable loch at a lower level, lying just short of 150 ft above the sea. The lowest loch of any size is Loch a' Mhuilinn, which lies a little to the south of Lochranza, in the extreme north-west, at a height of little over 50 ft. The peat lochans vary considerably in size and are too numerous to detail, but those in the centre of the island, about the headwaters of the Clauchan and Benlister burns, seen on a fine summer day as a foreground to the peaks of the north, are unexpectedly beautiful, their black waters reflecting like a mirror the silky white heads of the bog cotton, which grows so plentifully where surface peat has been removed, whether by man or nature, and the soil below left soggy but unflooded.

The coastline is most deeply indented by bays at the extremities of the through-valleys or troughs which originated in the post-igneous period, less deeply by bays lying at the mouths of waters originating after the uplift of the 1,000 ft plateau. Machrie Bay, in the west, and, continuing clockwise, Catacol, Lochranza, Sannox, Brodick, and Lamlash bays, all lie at the extremities of one or more of the post-igneous troughs, and Lamlash has a special feature in that it contains Holy Isle, a great bulk weathered out of lower new red sandstones and thick igneous sills. The other bays lie at the mouths of waters flowing in the southern half of the island either east or west from the watershed, as at Whiting Bay, entered by the King's Cross, Kiscadale, and Glenashdale burns, and at Drumadoon, entered by the Black Water. Machrie Bay, although entered at its northern end by the Iorsa Water and its tributary Scaftigill, both trough waters, takes its name from the Machrie Water, a lateral from the watershed. It should be said of Machrie Bay also, and of Brodick, which lie opposite each other and give the island its waisted shape, that they owe their existence in part to the fact that the sedimentary rocks which lie between them have resisted denudation less successfully than the great granite dome immediately to the north and the central volcanic area, also largely granitic, immediately to the south.

The bays differ also with the type of rock underlying them, and the ground over which their associated waters have travelled. Machrie Bay, fed at its northern end by waters from the granite and the schists, and in the middle by a water running for a considerable distance over mixed red sandstones, has a white

25

strand of pebbles and sharp sand except at its southern extreme, where the sand is less sharp and tinged slightly with red. At Catacol, where the burn falls rapidly from the granite to flow over hard schists, the beach is of large pebbles, although it should be noted that the sea has piled up here a cairn of rock fragments of the carboniferous series, which outcrops just offshore, under the water. Lochranza, like Catacol, lies over the schists, and its shores are pebbly, although the basin inland from the castle promontory is silting up with a deposit of darkish sand which seems to include material eroded in Glen Chalmadale from the strata of softer clay-slate schists which outcrop there. Sannox, fed by a water from the northern granite which crosses a vein of barytes in its short passage over the lower old red sandstones, has a strand of sharp white sand. At Brodick, where the Rosa and Cloy burns flow over granite but meet the lower new red sandstones in their final reaches, the sand is tinged with red, and is less sharp than at Sannox. At Lamlash and Whiting Bay again the land behind is underlain by the lower new red sandstones, and the sand is red and fine. At Drumadoon, where the Black Water runs to the sea over a sill of felsite, a rock similar to granite in its molten state but cooled rather more rapidly, the sand is golden brown, except at the north end of the bay, where the upper new red sandstones form the base. There are sandy beaches elsewhere than in the bays, notably along the whole southern coast of the island, broken only at Bennan Head. Here the sand, worn by the sea from the underlying upper new red sandstones, is red and soft.

2

NATURAL HISTORY

SOIL AND CLIMATE

THE climate of the island, after the close of the glacial period, changed first to cold and wet, and then, when the sea level had fallen to below that of today, to continental, with warm dry summers and cold winters. During the period of the 25 ft beach the climate was insular, mild and wet, milder and wetter than that of today. As the sea level fell again two further changes followed, to cold and dry, and finally to mild and wet, the climate of today. These changes would be of mere academic interest if they had left no mark on the island's vegetation, but they initiated many of the tree species which have survived into the present. They initiated also the formation of the peat which covers so much of the high inland area, for much of the tree growth encouraged during the dry continental period was destroyed by moss during the subsequent very wet period of the 25 ft beach. This great blanket of peat, which covers the surface of the 1,000 ft plateau around the northern peaks, and its declining extension to the south, determines the vegetation of the most considerable area of the island. Elsewhere the determining factors are the mass of boulder clay deposited during the glacial period at the tail of the Arran ice stream in the southwest of the island, the mixed soils worn from the rocks by the waters and burns and deposited in the straths, the sandy gravels of the 25 ft beach, and of course the climate itself.

The climate is mild because of the warming influence of the Gulf Stream; and wet because of the moisture-laden character of the prevailing south-westerly wind, which blows in from the Atlantic, and being impeded very little by the low land of Kintyre, meets the Arran peaks with its load unshed. The rainfall in the higher central area of the island must average 80-100 in a year. At Dougrie, on the west coast, the average is 46 in, and at Brodick, on the east, it is 65-70 in, so the east is rather wetter than the west, which is to be expected, since the wind unloads

27

its moisture only when the hills are reached. Though the south-westerly wind brings rain, it does so usually in the form of showers, with bright intervals between. The wind bringing most continuous rain, accompanied by overcast skies, is from the south, blowing warmly in July and early August, and mildly and frequently in winter. The east wind in summer brings dry grey weather to the east of the island, but leaves the west under blue sky. In winter, with a touch of north in it, it can bring snow, although usually only to the higher ground. In March it is a cold drying wind, and blows so regularly then that it can be relied upon to prepare the ground for early sowing. The north wind, common in May and June, brings cool sunny weather, and in winter, when it is not infrequent, cold sunny days and frosty nights. The north-west wind, common in November and April, seldom blows below gale force, and brings battering showers of cold rain.

These are impressions based on thirty years spent in the north-east of the island, and may not apply generally, as the deep glens funnel the winds and cause local variations, but they do not seem to be contradicted by official figures, as average daily temperatures show that July is the warmest month, with a maximum of 63-64° F, but that June too has high maximum and minimum temperatures, with the lowest rainfall and the most sunshine. January and February are the coldest months, with an average minimum of just under 36° F. The maximum rainfall occurs between November and January, and the minimum between May and June. Frost can be expected between the middle of November and the middle of March, but is seldom severe.

Wind force and exposure to the sun vary considerably in an island of such rugged relief, with so many steep precipices, corries, scarps, and deep glens. The northern peaks, high southern moorlands, and the west coast, are sometimes violently windswept, as are the glens which open to the west and north and funnel the gales. Snow lies throughout the winter in the corries facing north, and often on the highest peaks, even in bright sunshine. The lonely north coast, the deep fjord-like depression containing Lochranza, the southern slopes of the glens which run from east to west, or west to east, have little or no sunshine for several months in the winter. On the other hand hillsides with a southern exposure, the northern slopes of the glens just mentioned, and the coast around the southern part of the island, enjoy full winter as well as summer sunshine, and where the southern exposure is accompanied by shelter from the prevailing wind, as at Lagg, near the mouth of the Kilmory Water, conditions can be sub-tropical.

VEGETATION

These local variations, in conjunction with the variety of soils, sustain a vegetation wide enough in range to include, among its arboreal curiosities, the Arran service trees at one extreme and palm trees at the other. The service trees are to be found at a height of about 900 ft in Glen Diomhan, a glacial hanging valley which runs north-westward to meet Glen Catacol about 2 miles from the sea; and in the upper reaches of North Sannox burn, about half a mile below Coire na Ceum, under the great chasm of Ceum na Caillich. The trees, which in Glen Diomhan are protected by a Nature Conservancy enclosure, are of two varieties, *sorbus arranensis* and *sorbus pseudo-fennica*. They are related to

Sorbus pseudo-fennica on left with independent basal leaflets; *sorbus arranensis* on right

the rowan, but seem to survive in situations which the rowan could not tolerate, hanging precariously by the tips of their roots to cracks in the granite almost wholly devoid of soil. The leaf of the *arranensis* is broadly ovate in outline, irregularly and sharply lobed, and toothed. The creamy flowers grow in corymbs. The berries are ovoid and bright red, rather larger than those of the rowan. The *pseudo-fennica* differs in that its leaf is pinnate at the base. The trees are certainly capable of growth in less barren conditions than nature has chosen for them, for some have been transplanted into local gardens, but in the high hills the rowan probably excludes them from the more fertile rock crevices. Nature Conservancy drawings and notes may be seen at Catacol farm.

Of the other indigenous trees the rowan, although requiring more soil than the service trees, grows at higher levels, some admittedly stunted specimens having established themselves at 1,500 ft in the corrie north-west of Suidhe Fhearghas, on the steep sides of little ravines inaccessible to grazing animals. Birch grows plentifully, too, on the steep sides of the glens, generally from the level of about 800 ft, and rather lower down is accompanied by hazel. Scrubby oak grows thinly on the lower hillsides, and ash, hawthorn, holly, and gean, are common at the margins of abandoned fields or in formerly inhabited hollows. Alder and willow appear by the banks of the waters as they come closer to sea level, and there are odd clumps of blackthorn. Most of the other trees, which grow around the low-lying cultivated and inhabited areas, are the result of planting, and include sycamore, beech, chestnut, elm, lime, and Scots pine. Several nineteenth-century plantations of spruce or larch grow starkly up some of the hillsides in unnatural squares and oblongs, as in Glenrosa and Glenshurig, at Corrygills, Glenashdale and Whitefarland, and between the lower reaches of the Sannox and North Sannox burns. Some of these are now being felled. In pleasing contrast are the more recent plantings of the Forestry Commission, in Glencloy and on the higher ground in the middle and south of the island, where the choice of trees planted has been varied to suit the soil, and a pattern has resulted which, while differing in its colours from that of the open hillside, has nevertheless a variety dictated by nature.

Where the land is open to grazing animals the trees, as has been indicated, survive only in the steep sides of the glens, or very thinly in areas where stocking has not been intense, as on the hillsides north of Corrie, south of Lochranza, and east of Pirnmill. The grazing animals on the higher ground are the red deer and blackface sheep, the latter an eighteenth-century import, and although the deer are indigenous they are to some extent husbanded for purposes of sport, the island north of the Glenshurig and Machrie waters being fenced off as deer forest and the animals protected from all but stalkers. The deer forest has been managed also, though less so recently, to encourage the red grouse, which feed mainly on heather, normally controlled by burning. So the vegetative pattern of the bare, unplanted hillside, commonly considered natural, is perhaps no more so than that of the new forests, since it, too, is affected by human intervention : that of the shepherd and gamekeeper. It is, however, more familiar to the older generation, and therefore more congenial; and it certainly gives great aesthetic pleasure.

The summits and ridges of the north are mainly of bare rock and coarse granite sand, but the tops of the shoulders encircling the corries nourish a mat of sedges, mosses, and lichens, with rare plants of purple and starry saxifrage, alpine willow, crowberry, cloudberry, and bearberry; the berries exciting to find in such bare surroundings. Heather, chiefly ling, grows among the tumbled boulders in the corries, accompanied by some blaeberry, and continues down the steep slopes below to the level of about 1,500 ft, where, if the ground is less stony, bracken takes its place.

On the moorland of the plateau, sloping from 1,000 ft, ling, bell-heather, and cross-leaved heath, cover the stony ground, bracken the drier patches of the peat, and rushes and bog myrtle the wetter. Bog cotton occurs most plentifully where the peat has been worked, and at the heads of springs are beds of red-stained sphagnum moss, often beautifully starred with little light-green plants of butterwort. The common grass here is moor-grass, *molinia caerulea*, called by its Gaelic name *ciob* on the island, and known elsewhere as flying bent. Its withered leaves, in colour and texture rather like raffia, fly before the autumn winds to lodge in hollows or accumulate by the edges of burns, where they

31

are caught and washed down by the winter spates to clog the inlet pipes of the innumerable domestic water-tanks which stand above the villages.

On the hillsides between the high moorland and the 25 ft beach, where much of the land was formerly cultivated but is now pasture for sheep, the old lea ground still carries a useful herbage of mixed grasses, although the damper patches are being invaded by rushes, and the drier by bracken. Here, in a region of straggling old hedges of hawthorn and holly, the common ground flowers are wild thyme, tormentil, lady's bedstraw, scabious, hawkbit, knapweed, and daisy, with wild white clover where the old black honeybee survives, while in the glens by the burn-sides, among the birches and hazels, are ferns in a profusion of varieties baffling except to the expert botanist, with primrose, wood-sorrel, celandine, wild strawberry, honeysuckle, and foxglove. Lower on the old lea ground are mushrooms, although not in great numbers, and among the birches on more open ground are the edible bolitus and the chanterelle. There are inedible fungi, too, in even greater numbers and varieties, among them the yellow staining mushroom, almost exactly like the edible but turning yellow when rubbed, the lurid bolitus and even the satanic, and the decorative fly agaric, red with white spots, beloved by the illustrators of children's fairy tales, but eaten by the Vikings when they wanted to go berserk.

On the 25 ft beach, if the ground is not enclosed and drained, are marshes of rushes and sphagnum, and clumps of alder, over-hung by the rowans and hazels which cling to the old cliff, and near the high water mark, on the sandy levels, are bushes of whin, golden in early spring and well on through the summer, while in the stretches of black tidal silt are beds of the yellow flag iris.

The hedgerows of the enclosed ground, confined to the lower hillsides in the south of the island, the straths and the 25 ft beach, harbour much the same vegetation as the sheltered lower reaches of the glens, with a plentiful addition of bramble and dog-rose. The more common weeds of the enclosed pasture are ragwort, docken, field thistle, and buttercup, while the more poorly managed arable ground is infested with yarr, or stinking-willie, a plant with a little starry flower against a network of thin, fleshy,

32

almost cylindrical leaves, branching from the stem in whorls. It is sticky to touch and in wet weather emits what the botanical guides describe as 'an unpleasant odour', which is a decided understatement. It is known in the guides as corn spurrey. The crops of the cultivated ground will be considered more fully later in the book, but here it may be briefly noted that they consist mainly of potatoes, for which the island is famous, oats, swede turnips, kail, and grass sown either for hay or silage.

The traditional Arran cottage garden has an apple and a plum tree, some currant and gooseberry bushes, a plot of potatoes, several rows of curly kail, swedes and leeks, a row of lettuces and spring onions, and a hedge of parsley. These suit the soil and weather and require little effort, although the apple tree, unless resistant to scab, is likely to be more rewarding for its blossom than its fruit, and the plum is likely to show gale damage. Some of the larger gardens extend their range to include a row of raspberry canes and a bed of strawberries. The latter thrive in varieties which ripen early in summer, before wet weather brings danger of mould. Flowers are usually confined to the vicinity of the gate, footpath, and front door, and the most memorable are snowdrops, crocuses, and daffodils, which after the mild winter flower unusually early. Hedgerows of the dark red fuchsia *riccartoni* provide most of the colour in summer, outmatching the flowers in the borders, although roses thrive, too, except apparently in the Brodick castle gardens. Magnolias and camellias feature vividly in sheltered corners of gardens attached to some of the older stone villas, and hydrangeas, in an assortment of artificial and not very attractive colours, are to be seen everywhere. The traditional cottage garden is on the decline, and the trim suburban garden, confined mainly to lawn and flowers, is on the increase, and indeed predominates in the main villages.

The palms for which Arran is noted, because they are plentiful and easily seen, and, therefore, mentioned in guide books, are not true palms but palm lilies, of the variety *cordyline australis*, a native of New Zealand. Although associated mainly with Lagg, where they figure in the hotel tea garden, they are to be found in private gardens throughout the island, in the west at Whitefarland and as far north as Lochranza, and in the east notably at Lamlash, and in the Cromla garden at Corrie, where they seed freely. It can be said, if further evidence is needed of the mildness of the winter in the more sheltered corners, that true palms do indeed flourish, specimens from the Mediterranean, of *chamaerops humilis*, and from China, of *trachycarpus excelsa*, having been established at Cromla in the first half of the nineteenth century. Cromla, where the Rev Dr David Landsborough, an early Arran enthusiast, used sometimes to stay with a relative while visiting the island, had its garden enriched by many foreign plants brought to it by the doctor or his sons. Although a minister, he had studied botany at Edinburgh University, and was noted in his time as a naturalist, having added nearly seventy items to the known flora and fauna of Scotland. He lived first at Saltcoats and then at Stevenston, both on the Ayrshire coast, from which he could see Arran almost daily. He visited the island with his family regularly when both the interior and the west were still difficult of access, and encouraged such a taste for strenuous travel in his second son that the latter became noted as an explorer, opening up new routes in then unknown parts of Australia. The doctor himself, while in his 70s, followed a tour of duty as chaplain to the garrison at Gibraltar by a journey round the Mediterranean coast. The more unusual plants in the Cromla garden and in the ground of the Free Church at Corrie, notably several varieties of gum-tree, owe their presence to these various Landsborough explorations.

In the 1850s Princess Marie of Baden, wife of the 11th Duke of Hamilton, laid out the wild garden at Brodick Castle and introduced the rhododendron *ponticum*. Later importations of foreign plants did not occur until the 1920s, when the then Duchess of Montrose, daughter of the 12th Duke of Hamilton, continued the work of her predecessor. At this time, botanical exploration was being carried out in China, Yunnan, Burma, and Tibet, by Farrer, Forest, Ward, and Rock, all of whom contributed to her collection, notable for its rhododendrons. Later introductions by Ludlow and Sherriff contributed some of the finest of the sweet-scented rhododendrons, usually grown in Britain under glass but flourishing at Brodick in the open. The rhododendrons vary from dwarfs of a few inches to huge specimens such as *giganteum* and *magnificum*, which after some 45 years have grown to a height of over 20 ft. Notable for the giant

Page 35: (above) Lagg Inn, with *cordyline australis*, the club palm common in Arran, in the tea garden; *(below)* fishing in North Glen Sannox. The stone bridge has since been widened but without being deprived of its original character

Page 36: (above) An uncovered horned gallery grave of the neolithic period, at East Bennan. In the foreground are the laterals dividing the chamber, with two portal stones beyond and beyond these again, the stones marking part of the semicircular forecourt; (below) remains of a stone circle on Machrie Moor. Within its area was found a decorated tripartite food vessel of the early middle Bronze Age

size of its leathery leaves and creamy round flowers is the variety *sino grande*. With so many varieties in growth, the flowering season extends from January to August, although the main mass of colour, from the common *ponticum*, which has run wild over the north-eastern fringe of the island, is to be seen in June. The castle garden includes also a fine collection of Chilean shrubs, contributed mainly as a result of the botanical explorations of Comber. Perhaps the most memorable of these is the *crinodendron hookerianum*, which is over 20 ft high and covered, in season, with flowers like red chinese lanterns. The garden is now in the possession of the National Trust, and is open to visitors.

ANIMALS

Among the wild animals the most notable is the red deer, which has existed on the island since the dawn of history. Caoilte, a companion of Ossian, the legendary Gaelic poet, was made to utter a panegyric on the island in which he addressed it as 'Arran of the many stags'. Towards the close of the eighteenth century the animal became almost extinct as a result of lawless slaughter by islanders presumably anxious to preserve their crops, but its protection for purposes of sport since the days of Landseer, and the occasional importation of fresh blood, has led to such an increase in its numbers that for some time the population was little short of 2,000, which must have been close to the limit for which grazing was available, for during exceptionally severe winters there could be found, along the inside of the fence marking the southern limit of the forest, the decomposing carcases of many poor creatures which had died of starvation. Although the population is now said to be down to around 1,600, it is still difficult to keep them out of fields and gardens, which have to be protected by a fence some 6 ft high. Weakness in a fence, or carelessness with a gate, can mean that a garden is stripped overnight, or great inroads made on a field crop.

The climax of the year among the red deer is the rut, starting about the end of September, when the stags, having grown new antlers since casting the old in the previous spring, break away from their own herds in the high corries to seek the herds of hinds, which normally lie on the slopes above the moorland. It

37

is at this time that the stags wallow in soft peat bog, to render themselves black and frightening; and roar loudly to intimidate their rivals and work up vigour. The number of hinds gathered by a stag depends on his ability to keep them together, and greed for numbers can be a splendid animal's undoing, for often the need for vigilance on several fronts, and for repeated battle, added to the strain of service, results in exhaustion and consequent defeat. The stags seldom fight to the death, but fierce struggles sometimes do occur before the weaker of the two well-tined animals will accept humiliation, and canter off to become a stinking outcast with a mangy coat.

After the rut the stags run on the lower ground alongside the hinds, feeding near them after dark right down to sea-level, circulating around fields and gardens, and foraging for seaweed on the shore. The stags cast their antlers around April, and later, as the flies of summer start to irritate the new antler growth, so soft that it is called velvet, they move up in their own herds again to the cooler air of the high hills. The hinds remain on the slopes above the moorland, and leave their herds to drop their calves, in hollows among bracken or heather, about the beginning of June. At first they leave the calves hidden, visiting them warily two or three times every day to suckle them. Later the calves follow the hinds into the herd, and the hind herds, with calves of the current and the previous summers grazing alongside the adults, are a delight to see above a glen head in the late summer, if they can be approached carefully, so that they move away slowly and quietly and not in a cantering panic.

Late visitors to the island grow romantic over the roaring of the stags during the rutting period, and indeed the faraway growling sound of the rut in the slopes beyond the moorland has the pleasing evocative quality of a seasonal event. It comes with the brambles and the ling honey. But the sound of a stag groaning in sexual greed, jealousy, and anxiety, in the early hours of the morning, close to an open bedroom window, is a different matter. The maternal bleat of a hind to her calf, or even her warning bark, is much less disturbing.

The other wild animal of the higher ground is the goat, which survives now only on Holy Isle, and has suffered some recent depredation, many having been shot by a shepherd who rented the grazing for the wintering of his hoggs, and grudged the feral animals their sustenance. The goat did at one time inhabit the northern part of the main island, evidently as far back at least as the time of the Norse occupation, if we can judge by the name of the highest peak, Goatfell. It seems to have been eliminated from the main island just after the opening of the nineteenth century.

Rabbits formerly inhabited the lower slopes of the high hills and the hillsides above the raised beach in great numbers, but were almost completely wiped out some years ago in the epidemic of myxomatosis: almost, but not quite, and in spite of surreptitious attempts to revive the epidemic by planting diseased carcases, the rabbit is returning, although in reduced numbers.

There are no mountain hares, or blue hares as they are sometimes called, although an attempt was made to introduce them recently on Dougrie estate; but brown hares exist in considerable numbers, and have increased since the havoc wrought by disease among the rabbits. In the enclosed southern pastures they grow to tremendous size, but are well kept in check. The red squirrel, an import of some thirty years standing, is common in the castle woods at Brodick, and has spread elsewhere, but there are as yet no grey squirrels. Nor are there any moles, weasels, stoats, polecats, or foxes, and hedgehogs, although reported occasionally, are little in evidence. Otters are plentiful, although seen only with difficulty as they slink at dusk among burnside boulders, on their way from pool to pool, fishing for trout. Their burnside haunts are now shared by feral mink, a menace for which blame is placed on an unspecified local farmer. He intended to farm the animals for their fur, but, finding the cost of their food prohibitive, released them. Badgers were said in the *Third Statistical Account*, published in 1962, to be fairly plentiful, but the writer must have been misinformed. Memories of badgers at the Laggan, at North Sannox, above Corrie and no doubt elsewhere, linger among the older people, but keepers and warden alike are agreed that the badger has been extinct for at least 20 years. The common seal, on the other hand, is clearly visible around the rocky promontories, and is especially interesting in late summer, when little herds of females may be seen basking with their young on rounded sea-worn boulders, or swimming

39

and diving playfully just off the shore. Mixed herds of male and female seals are a feature of the Newton shore in winter. A less attractive feature of the shore is the brown rat, which on the approach of winter makes determined efforts to establish itself in farm or domestic buildings. The domestic mouse is not unknown, either, but field mice are much more common, and the most plentiful of the rodents seems to be the short-tailed vole, of which there are periodic plagues.

Arran was formerly reputed to be rather a dangerous place to visit because of adders, but these, although fairly plentiful about 30 years ago, seem to be decreasing, and although one may be seen coiled around the foot of a small birch in Glen Sannox, or lying on a warm rock by the North Sannox burn on a hot summer day, it usually retires speedily when disturbed, and need not be approached too closely. The slow worm is rather more common, and quite harmless, although it, too, seems to excite horror in the uninitiated, being thought by some to be a sinister black variety of adder with an especially virulent venom. The remaining reptile, the common lizard, is harmless also : it is indeed beneficial, and will haunt beehives to prey on the spiders which establish themselves at the junction of wall and roof.

The farm animals of the island will be considered more fully later. Sheep predominate, mostly blackface, with some Cheviots and Border Leicesters on the lower ground. Many crossbred cattle are reared for export to mainland graziers, and dairy cows, mainly Ayrshires, are kept for milk. Although old pigsties in some gardens suggest a tradition of cottage pig-keeping, it must have died out some time ago, as pigs are kept now only in a few piggeries. Poultry, however, are kept both on a commercial scale and in cottage gardens. With so many sheep on the island, the collie is everywhere.

BIRDS

The most spectacular of the island birds is the golden eagle, for some time absent, but now returning and represented by two nesting pairs. They can be seen soaring about their eyries, which they shift from year to year, on the high crags of the north-west. The more recent sightings have been in Glen Catacol opposite the mouth of Glen Diomhan, in Glen Scaftigill, and at Torr Nead an Eoin, a high crag hanging over the strath at Lochranza, between Glen Easan Biorach and Glen Chalmadale. The birds were formerly persecuted by gamekeepers, but their destruction is now forbidden, although the new poisons used in sheep dip may make this change of heart useless, for the birds feed on dead sheep more than on tiny living lambs.

More common birds of prey are the buzzard and the sparrow-hawk, the former the more easily viewed, as it haunts the areas of the String road and the Boguille. It is easily identified by its broad rounded wings, its circling and gliding flight, and its unmistakable mewling cry. The sparrowhawk is seen less often, since it flies low among scrub and old hedgerows, preying on small birds. The hen harrier, extinct for a number of years, has returned, and is now increasing, probably as a result of the fencing in of hill ground for afforestation, which promotes a growth of long grass and so encourages the rats, mice, and voles, which constitute its prey. The kestrel is fairly common, too, a sharp-winged hovering bird of hill scrub and inland cliffs, such as those at Corloch and the Cuithe, in the extreme north of the island; and the peregrine, a fierce bird of the high cliffs of Holy Isle and the less frequented coasts. It preys on seabirds, which it pursues and overtakes in flight. The merlin, a little moorland hawk, which in the Highlands preys mainly on the meadow pipit, is said to nest on the island, but is uncommon.

The meadow pipit is, nevertheless, a common nesting bird of the high ground, and is frequently seen in spring, when it can be identified by its curious dipping flight and its thin, whirring twitter. It inhabits the shorter heather, and even burnt ground. The wheatear inhabits similar ground, and the stonechat and whinchat the longer heather.

By the hill lochs are great colonies of nesting common gulls, with the black-headed, lesser black-backed, and greater black-backed, in smaller numbers. The last named can make a swim in the Urie Loch an almost terrifying experience, sweeping so close that the blast of air from its passing is like a physical blow. The red-throated diver nests in some of the small hill lochs in the vicinity of the Boguille, and at Coirein Lochain.

Ravens nest in the high crags in the north of the island.

Croaking in the corrie below Cioch na h-Oighe when it is dark with mist they add a sinister note to the roar of running water and the rumbling of boulders. Carrion and hooded crows are fairly common also, quartering the moorland after carrion, and are said to inter-breed. But the most numerous bird of the crow family is the jackdaw, which is to be seen everywhere. Large flocks frequent the shores in winter, and birds which have been taught to speak by farm lads have been known to submit amazed visitors to floods of unseemly language.

Among the game birds of the hills and moors the red grouse is still common, although it was formerly much more numerous than today, 13,000 having been shot in 1912. Disease affected the birds in 1944, and from then until 1949 bags were slight. The birds are now increasing, and on some hills, as on the western slopes of Suidhe Fhearghas, are plentiful. The black grouse, although formerly fairly common, is almost extinct. A flock used to feed every spring on the buds of the gean at High Corrie for several years before the severe winter of 1946-7. There was a 'lek' nearby (from the Gaelic *leac*, 'flat place' or 'slab'), where the male birds did mock battle, and the flock frequented the scrub below Coire nan Larach and Cioch na h-Oighe; but since 1947 there has been no sign of them. Peewits disappeared from High Corrie after the same winter, although they returned to other parts of the island, and are said to be recovering their former numbers. Woodcock can be glimpsed among the birches at the glen heads, but are not plentiful; nor are the common snipe, which seem to be decreasing, since their drumming, formerly a common sound on misty evenings in spring, is now seldom heard.

The long dirling call of the whaup, or curlew, and the high pulsating song of the lark, are fortunately still common all over the moorland, and their absence in late summer and throughout the autumn and winter leaves the area strangely silent, since their echo, after even a single hearing, never quite fades from the memory. They are augmented fairly early by the call of the cuckoo, which can be heard in every glen far up into the moorland, and the bird shows itself so frequently and fearlessly as to cause wonder why any poet should ever have asked if it was but a wandering voice. Swallows and house-martins follow, too, to nest around the farm buildings. Sand-martins are said to nest in the south of the island, and swifts rarely. The common nesting birds of the gardens are the blackbird, song-thrush, chaffinch, robin, and wren, and these nest also in the wooded sides of the glens, the wren often quite high up. In the woodlands and orchard gardens the great and blue tits are common, the coaltit fairly so, and the long-tailed tit rare, although seen occasionally in flocks in winter. Of other woodland birds the tiny goldcrest, although rarely seen, is said to be fairly common, as also are the equally decorative goldfinch and bullfinch. All of these, with the wood pigeon and the long-eared owl, should increase as the new forests develop.

The largest bird of the burnsides is the heron, which fishes systematically up and then down water, rising above the burnside trees after exhausting the possibilities of one favourite station, to fly some little distance to the next. The water ousel is common, too, white-breasted and full of curtsies, but is almost outdone in this last respect by the pied and grey wagtails. The kingfisher is said to nest in the Brodick area, and can certainly be seen in Glen Rosa. The moorhen is not common, but can be seen on the level stretch of the Black Water across the fields from Shiskine. From marshy ground in the same area, too, the quiet evening angler may hear the curious explosive groan of the water-rail, a bird very rare on the island. Its close relative, the corncrake, is becoming rare also. It could be heard regularly in the hayfields of Corrie 30 years ago, but is never heard there now.

Of the game birds on the lower ground the pheasant has been fairly common since it was introduced shortly after 1832, but the partridge, introduced some 80 years earlier and once common, is becoming scarcer with the decrease in the amount of ground under the plough, and is hardly ever seen.

Of the birds around the coast it is impossible to do more than give a mere impression. Most numerous of the nesting waders are probably the sea-pyat and the common sandpiper. The lovely sea-pyat, known in England as the oystercatcher, although the great majority never see a single oyster, is the shalder of the Shetlands and the *tjaldur* of the Faroes, where its arrival in great whistling flocks at the end of the long dark winter causes such an uplift of the spirit that it is regarded as sacred and never molested. In Arran it can be seen on the shore all the year round.

The redshank is common also, and the beautiful little ringed plover, but the golden plover and the dunlin nest only sparingly. The nesting gulls have already been noted. Common and Arctic terns nest on Pladda, and the gannet and guillemot on Ailsa Craig, a huge rock rising out of the lower Firth of Clyde about 15 miles to the south. The shag and cormorant are to be seen all round the coast, the former being the more common, but although the shag is said to nest on Holy Isle, there is no evidence that the cormorant breeds either there or on the main island. Of the nesting ducks the mallard is the most common, but is eclipsed in interest by the colourful shelduck, which nests on some parts of the coast fairly close to the road, and can be observed conveniently in a red sandstone inlet little less than halfway between Brodick and Corrie, or on the northern shore of Lamlash Bay. The eider, too, can be seen in summer, with its young, swimming offshore both south and north of Corrie. Teal are said to nest mainly between Machrie and Blackwaterfoot. The shoveler may nest, but it is doubtful. The heron, already mentioned as a bird of the moorland waters, is even more common on some parts of the shore, as below the castle woods at Brodick, where there is a heronry. The rock-dove nests in the King's Cave near Drumadoon, and the stock-dove in the cliffs between Kilpatrick Point and Corriecravie.

Winter visitors are too numerous to list, but include, among the ducks, the wigeon, the pochard, the scoter, the scaup, the goldeneye, and the red-breasted merganser. The grey-lag goose frequents the west of the island, particularly the low ground near Shiskine, in great numbers, and is said to flight to Loch Nuis and, when disturbed, to Loch Tanna. The whooper swan, too, is a regular winter visitor, and may be seen on Loch Tanna and on inlets of the coast. Of the smaller birds the most evident of the winter visitors are the fieldfare and the redwing, the former sometimes in such tremendous flocks that when they are disturbed, and take off from their favourite perch on the island's overhead electric cables, they look exactly like a swarm of honeybees, circling and rising and tumbling in a dense cloud, each bird so tiny against the sky that it hardly has a separate identity. The birds alight on the rowan trees so thickly that in the course of half an hour the berries are stripped completely. The holly, too, suffers, only trees very close to the cottages being allowed to keep any berries for Christmas, and even then only if action is taken at the first sound of the voracious chattering which accompanies a raid. The flocks pass on quickly when the food supply has been cleared. Although flocks of starlings too appear in winter they are seldom large, and since they feed during this period by searching the ground for grubs and insects, are not so unwelcome as they seem to be in some of our cities. One of the rarest, and certainly the most beautifully coloured, of the smaller winter visitors is the waxwing. A number of these were seen on telephone wires at Sannox in the late autumn of 1956, and since that sighting fairly regular visits seem to have occurred to the same area.

INSECTS

Like the bird life of the coasts, the insect life of the island is multifarious, there being butterflies, moths, and beetles, peculiar to every type of vegetation. No more can be done here than to mention the creatures most persistent in compelling attention. The midges are notorious, and in certain seasons can make the enjoyment of a picnic, or of an evening's angling, quite impossible. On the moorland the sheep tick, which unfortunately does not confine its attention to sheep, is rather too common, but grasshoppers are fortunately just as plentiful, and enliven the warm days with their chirping. Dragonflies provide interest, too, during their brief lives about the mossy pools at the heads of burns, emerging, mating, laying, and expiring, in the course of a single day. In the lower woodland of the glens the giant wood-wasp may be seen, a terrifying creature until it is discovered that its ovipositor, which looks like an enormous sting, is innocent of venom. Clegs and blowflies abound, the former greedy for human blood, and of course wasps and bees.

The black honeybee, kept almost universally in cottage gardens until it was ravaged by the acarine mite in 1907, survives in the wild, and in the roofs of dwellings, colonies having maintained themselves for years in the roofs of Lagg Inn, Kildonan Schoolhouse, and Farchan Mor at Sannox, in spite of frequent attempts to dislodge them. It has re-established itself in garden hives, too, in spite of much importation of Dutch and Italian queens in the years following its eclipse. Its queens can maintain a reasonable brood-nest for four years after mating, and its colonies winter on moderate stores of food. The comb it produces is beautifully white, with a space between the honey and the seal, and is most attractive on the table. The island honey, mostly from bell heather and ling, is superb.

<h2 style="text-align:center">FISHES</h2>

The burns of the island which come straight off the granite and flow through peat are acid, and their brown trout, although considerable in number, run to little size. Fish of the angling association limit of 7 in come only one in every five or six which rise or nibble, although quarter and even half-pounders may be taken in the deep pools of the higher reaches, where the burns drop fall by fall, as in the main southern tributary of the Glen Chalmadale burn; or in the deep potholes worn where granite boulders have rested on beds of red sandstone, which are plentiful in such burns as the Glencloy. The waters of the south-west, away from the granite, and flowing through peat only in their upper reaches, offer a richer fish diet, but on the whole angling in Arran for brown trout is a pastime for boys. Sea trout run up the main waters both east and west of the island, and salmon up some of the western waters, certainly the Iorsa and the Machrie, but the distinction between sea trout and salmon, determined by counting the number of scales between the medial line and the dorsal fin, is one which few trouble to make, and the extent of the salmon run is doubtful. Young sea trout, known as finnock or herling, come into the estuaries at high tide in July; and from the end of that month and on into October, and even later, the mature fish run up the waters to spawn. The finnock run from half to three-quarters of a pound, and the sea trout average 4-5 lb. Salmon are said to average 8-9 lb. Slimy fresh water eels sometimes proclaim their existence by fouling the tackle of those who fish mistakenly for game fish in the dark recesses of almost stagnant water.

Cod, haddock, and whiting, are plentiful round the coasts, frequenting certain banks whose marks are known to local sea

46

anglers. The saithe or coal fish, and the lythe or pollack, are common on certain rocky parts of the coast, and there are flukes or flounders in the sandy bays. A curiosity of the rocky coasts, where there is a dense growth of seaweed, is the ballan wrasse, a deep fat bronze-coloured fish with large hard scales and pale green bones, and a toothy, supercilious facial appearance. Boiled or steamed it tastes like wet blanket, but baked it is toothsome. Shoals of mackerel appear off the coasts in July, and herring are sometimes netted close inshore, in late autumn, by boats from Dunure in Ayrshire. Lobsters are plentiful, and conger eels, although not sought after, are encountered occasionally. Porpoises are fairly frequent but irregular in their appearances, but the basking shark can be expected fairly regularly in July, unmistakable as it swims lazily with it large dorsal fin sticking out of the water just like a sail. It is harmless, any damage it does to boats or nets being unintentional. The more vicious thrasher shark is seen very occasionally, or rather heard, for attention is normally directed to it by the loud smack it makes as it shoots out of the water, soars through the air, and comes down flat on its belly. It appears so seldom that for all its reputation it is as little of a menace as the stinging jelly-fish, which very occasionally plagues the sandy beaches so thickly that, although clearly visible and almost inert, it can hardly be avoided, and makes bathing a risk.

Clams are sufficiently plentiful to attract commercial fishermen, and among the baits available for sea anglers are spoutfish, mussel, wilk or whelk, limpet and lugworm. The rock pools contain an infinite variety of marine life, fascinating alike to small children and to the biologist. Unfortunately, for the former, the crabs to be found are inedible, and the shrimps, although edible, so scattered that it takes a day to gather enough for a small sandwich.

3   PREHISTORY

THE changes in climate, and their accompanying changes of sea level, which followed the glacial period, have been noted at the close of the first chapter. Well before the period of the 25 ft beach, 5500-3000 BC, the island would be wooded and inhabited by wild animals. The wild ox, the wild boar, the red deer, the reindeer, the elk, and the brown bear, are known to have existed on the mainland of Scotland, and some of these may well have established themselves in Arran also. There would certainly be fish and coastal marine animals. Conditions were ripe for the arrival of human inhabitants.

MESOLITHIC PERIOD 5000-3000 BC

These were hunter fishermen of a mesolithic or middle stone-age culture, who began to appear on both sides of the North Channel early in the period during which the sea was rising to the level of the 25ft beach. They used weapons and implements of flaked flint, chipped and ground pebbles, ground bone splinters, and ground and perforated deer antler. They lived almost exclusively on the coasts, inhabiting caves, and leaving traces of settlement mainly in the form of middens, composed largely of shells, from which it is concluded that their chief article of diet was shellfish. That limpets bulked largely in their diet is argued not only from the evidence of the shells themselves, but from the belief that long finger-shaped pebbles, ground at one end to a chisel edge, were used for prising the limpets off rocks. That they fished also is proved by their bone fish-hooks and barbed harpoon heads of bone or deer antler, the latter perforated to take a line with possibly a bladder attached. They made spearheads of bone or deer antler also for hunting deer or other animals, and mattocks of deer antler, perforated to take a shaft, which they are said to have used to remove blubber from seals and the carcases of stranded whales, for seal bones have been found among their refuse, and several of their mattocks

48

have been found beside whale skeletons buried in clay deposited during the rising of the sea.

The population of mesolithic settlers in the south-west of Scotland is thought to have been slight. Although some of the shell middens are of considerable size, it has been calculated that the largest of them, a mound of 100 by 60 ft, some 2-3 ft in thickness, could have been amassed by a family group of ten people in less than seven years of continuous occupation. Some caves, too, contain deposits separated by a layer of gravel, showing them to have been abandoned when the sea began to encroach on them, and then reoccupied by people of a similar culture, perhaps centuries later, when the sea had begun to retreat. From this it would appear that the mesolithic population of south-west Scotland was not only slight but, considering the length of the period during which it prevailed, from 5000 to 3000 BC, extremely inconstant.

Until fairly recently there was some doubt as to whether these people had ever visited Arran. Sites of their settlements had been found in northern Ireland, around Luce and Wigtown bays on the Solway shore, near Oban, on the Isle of Oransay, and on the islet of Risa, in Loch Sunart. Traces had also been found on the Ayrshire and Argyll coasts, and on Bute, Kintyre, and Islay. There was, therefore, a probability that they had visited Arran, since they were obviously capable of making the sea passage, although the fact that most of the Arran caves were being created during the period of the 25 ft beach, when they prevailed in the area, meant that much less shelter was available for them than would have been the case much later. That they did visit Arran was established by the discovery on the island, by A. D. Lacaille, author of *The Stone Age in Scotland*, published in 1954, of two groups of characteristic flint implements, one in the Catacol area and the other at Shiskine.

There is thought to have been a link between these coastal mesolithic settlers of the south-west of Scotland and people of a similar culture in the south-west of France who prevailed during a somewhat earlier period, but since much of the evidence for this belief may have been buried beneath the sea, it can be no more than a conjecture. But it does seem plausible that the route followed by these people as they spread northward after the close of the glacial period was from the south-west of France to the south-west of England, and then up the Irish Sea to northern Ireland and south-west Scotland. They are thought to have used dugout canoes, possibly with outriggers.

There is evidence in southern Scotland of another group of mesolithic peoples, inland hunters with minute and delicate flint implements used as barbs or tips for their weapons, who seem to have spread from the north-east of England into Tweeddale and over the Biggar gap into upper Clydesdale, and they may have reached the Ayrshire and Galloway coasts, and even Kilmelfort in Argyll. They are thought to have progressed from an earlier paleolithic or old stone-age culture during their settlement in England, and may have spread there from the Continent some time before the two areas were separated by the sea. No trace of these people has ever been found in Arran, and since they do not seem to have been a seafaring people, it is unlikely that any ever will.

NEOLITHIC PERIOD 3000-1900 BC

With Britain cut off from the Continent by the sea, the route by which the coastal mesolithic people came to Arran seems to have come increasingly into use, and was almost certainly that followed by the next group of people to settle in the island, in this case in much more considerable numbers. They may indeed, by the time they arrived, somewhere around 3000 BC, have found the island very sparsely or perhaps no longer inhabited. They were of a neolithic or new stone-age culture, and used a considerably improved range of implements and weapons, all but the axeheads, which were usually of polished stone, being worked out of flint not only flaked but delicately chipped all over its surface to give a fine finish. The stone and flint used were imported, but in time many of the smaller articles came to be made of Corrygills pitchstone. These people are thought to have worn skins, but although they seem to have known nothing of spinning or weaving, they did have some knowledge of pottery.

They must have lived to some extent by hunting, fishing, and trading, but they were also agriculturalists, who grew grain and kept animals. Whether they brought cattle or pigs to the island,

50

or domesticated wild animals already there, is doubtful, but they are thought to have brought sheep and goats descended from wild animals first domesticated in the Middle East, probably about 2,000 years before. They were, therefore, unlike the nomadic mesolithic peoples, real settlers, enabled and even obliged by their way of life to inhabit a single area over long periods. But they were tied to their area of settlement also by their religious ideas, for the main traces of their settlement are to be found in the remains of their impressive burial chambers.

The first and only comprehensive survey of the chambered cairns of Arran was made by Thomas Bryce for the first volume of *The Book of Arran*, published by the Arran Society of Glasgow in 1910. Of the seventeen examples he examined, the most remote, and consequently least disturbed, was the Carn Ban, situated 950 ft above sea level on a slope by the Allt an t-Sluice, a tributary of the Kilmory Water. This cairn, 100 ft long by 60 broad, with its long axis directed approximately WNW by ENE, rose at the time of its excavation 17 ft above the slope at its lower or western end, but was about level with the ground at the eastern. It was roughly trapezoid in ground plan, but with rounded corners, and curved outward at each side towards its upper or eastern end, which was concave, and contained a level semi-circular forecourt, in the middle of which a portal of two upright stones marked the entrance to the chamber. The chamber, 18 ft 8 in long, and with a breadth of from 2 ft 10 in to 3 ft, was divided into four compartments, roughly equal in length, by transverse slabs. From the floor to the roof of the chamber the height was 9 ft. The headroom above the transverse slab was from 4 to 6 ft. The width of the portal was 3 ft 5 in, but since the stones which formed it widened towards the base, the space was reduced considerably at ground level. The entrance was considerably higher than the floor of the chamber, the first compartment being completed below ground level by slabs set on edge. Indications were that the edge of the forecourt, and the arms of the cairn enclosing it, had been marked originally by upright slabs, but many of these were missing. The position of one upright slab in front of the forecourt suggested that the semi-circle of stones outlining it was continued originally to form a complete circle. Bryce explored the cairn, but the only relics he discovered were a flake of flint and another of pitchstone. The drainage from the hill had escaped through the chamber, so that any bones had long dissolved away.

Sectional plan of the Carn Ban, longitudinal axis

Sectional plan of the Carn Ban,
transverse axis

Among the other chambered cairns he explored enough remained of three to show that in their original state they must have been similar to the Carn Ban in size, structure, and design. These were the Giants' Graves at Whiting Bay and the cairns at East Bennan and Sliddery. Of the others, several had been rifled

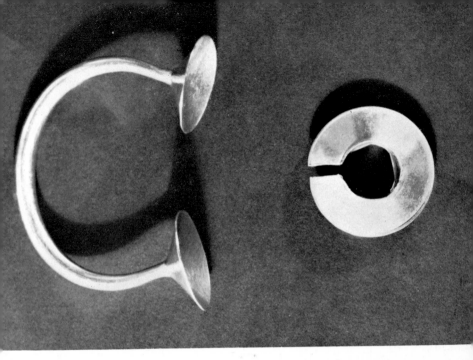

Page 53: (above) Gold ornaments of the late Bronze Age found on Low Whitefarland farm. The cup-ended ornament is possibly an armlet or dress-fastener; the other is a lock-ring through which the hair was drawn, then plaited; *(below)* Drumadoon. The face of a sill of columnar quartz-felspar-porphyry some 80-100 ft thick. On the summit is a fort of the Iron Age

Page 54: (above) The King's Cave, worn from new red sandstone by the sea during the period of the 25-ft beach. On the walls are some faint carvings which may date from the Early Christian and Viking periods; (below) ruined church of St Brigid in Kilbride graveyard. Once the parish church of Kilbride, it was built in the fourteenth century but damaged by fire during the English raid of 1406

of stone to such an extent that their original state was a matter of some doubt, but the likelihood was that they, too, had been similar. Others had been built either before the ideas behind the Carn Ban archetype had matured, or after they had begun to decline.

Human remains were found in at least one of the cairns, which, although greatly denuded of stone by local farmers for dyking, gave every sign of having corresponded to the archetype. This was at Torrylin, in the corner of a field above the shore by the

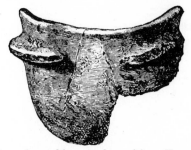

Piece of round-bottomed vessel from Torrylin
cairn, showing lugs below rim

east bank of the Kilmory Water, not far from Lagg. At least three of the compartments had already been disturbed, presumably by raiding farmers, and a story related by MacArthur in *The Antiquities of Arran*, published in 1873, suggests that fear and guilt arising from the disturbance of the dead had brought the raiding to an end. One compartment was still intact, and in it Bryce found the bones of six adults, and those of a child and a baby. They were scattered in great confusion, but mainly in the corners and along the sides. Besides the human remains there were bones of adult ox, pig, fox, dog and otter, and of piglet, lamb and kid. With a flint scraper was a fragment of dark-coloured pottery, coarse in texture and finish. It belonged to a round-bottomed vessel without decoration by any impressed pattern, but had two projections or lugs in the part of the neck still intact. Among the black earth in the compartment some wood charcoal was discovered.

Human remains were found also in a cairn situated close to

a disused limekiln on a terrace above the 25 ft beach, about half a mile north of Kilmory Water, on the farm of Clauchog. This cairn, with only two compartments, and no trace of a frontal fore-court, yet roughly similar in plan to the archetype, Bryce thought to be a later and modified version. The interest to us is that in this cairn the bones of fourteen skeletons discovered were rather better preserved than at Torrylin, and it was found that the skulls lay invariably at the corners, and the bones of the extremities along the sides of the compartments, suggesting that the bodies had been laid on their sides in a crouched position. Again animal bones were discovered, of ox, sheep, and pig, including many of very young animals. In the inner compartment another fragment of dark pottery was found, with a lug in the

Decorated round-bottomed vessel from lime-kiln cairn, Clauchog

small part of the neck still intact, suggesting a vessel similar to that found at Torrylin. Near it was an axe of polished stone. In the compartment closer to the entrance, and, therefore, the later in use, was a further vessel of dark-coloured paste, slightly reddish in tinge, thin and delicately fashioned, rounded from the base to the shoulder, then sloping gently inward to meet a shallow vertical rim. The sloping shoulder surface was decorated by alternating groups of vertical and horizontal lines, impressed on the soft clay by a fine toothed instrument. Round the shoulder was a double row of dots similarly impressed, and the upper part of the rounded bottom had three rows of dashes horizontally arranged, interrupted at intervals by four vertical lines of dots, the latter immediately below the vertical lines above the shoulder.

Bryce's detailed descriptions of all seventeen chambered cairns in Arran and their contents can be found in the first volume of *The Book of Arran*. The detail given above has been selected because from it we can deduce the chief characteristics of the primary neolithic culture of the island; the type of cairn, the method of interment, and the implements and pottery placed with the dead. We have also a clue to the animals kept or hunted, and a vague indication of possible funeral rites.

Archeology has made great progress since Bryce's day, but his deductions as to the origins of the primary neolithic people of Arran are still largely accepted. From the skeletons found he deduced that they were probably dark-complexioned, rather small in stature, with long heads and faces, and of a type which he called, after the ethnologist Sergi, Eurafrican. In thinking that they had come from the south-eastern Mediterranean by way of the Iberian peninsula, however, it is now thought that he may have been mistaken. Cairns of the Carn Ban type are now known, because of the arms enclosing their semicircular forecourts and the lateral segmentation of their chambers, as horned gallery graves, to distinguish them from what are known as passage graves, the latter usually contained in a round cairn with a narrow passage leading from the entrance into a corbelled dome-shaped chamber situated at the centre. It is now thought that it was the passage-grave builders who came from the Iberian peninsula, and that although they followed the south-western England/Irish Sea route to northern Ireland, they virtually by-passed Arran as they made their way up by the west of Scotland and the Great Glen to the north-east and the northern islands. Only one example of a passage grave has been found in Arran, a cairn at Carmahome, near Kilpatrick, excavated in 1924 by Ludovik Mann.

The kind of pottery found in the horned gallery graves of Arran is called by archaeologists Beacharra ware, because it was at Beacharra in Kintyre that it was first discovered. Distribution of this type of pottery has led to the belief that the people who built the horned gallery graves came from the south-eastern Mediterranean by way of southern France, establishing themselves in Britain first in the Severn-Cotswold area, then moving up the Irish Sea to northern Ireland, Galloway, Arran, Bute, and Argyll, including Kintyre and Islay. As for the cairns themselves, there is thought to have been adaptation and development during the slow passage to the north. The people of the Severn-Cotswold area built long barrows of earth, with transepted chambers intended for successive interments, but these contained little of the Beacharra type of pottery. A group of long barrows in north Wiltshire, whose semicircular forecourts most resemble those of the Arran cairns, have so far revealed none of this pottery. The pottery and the tombs may, therefore, characterise two parallel movements of colonisation which became fused as they proceeded northwards. There was further adaptation in the north when stone was used instead of earth for the covering mound. The horned gallery graves of the type found in Arran became known after Bryce's time as Clyde-Carlingford cairns, and then as Clyde-Solway, because those in the south-west of Scotland differ slightly from those associated with Carlingford in the north-east of Ireland. Lately the fashion has been to distinguish them even from the Solway cairns, and call them simply Clyde cairns, and even this fashion may soon be changed by the incidence of fresh discoveries in Argyll. But so far as is yet known they are most densely concentrated in Arran, and Arran lies at the centre of their distribution.

It is interesting to speculate upon the religious ideas behind the building of these cairns. It will be seen from illustrations of typical examples that they are trapezoid in ground plan, and the idea has been advanced, on the basis of a neolithic homestead excavated at Townhead, Rothesay, where faint traces of a timber house, trapezoid in plan, were discovered, that the cairns were built in imitation, and were simply houses for the dead. This corresponds with the view of many Egyptologists that the mastaba tombs built for the pharoahs of the first and second dynasties, 3200-2780 BC, were imitation palaces, in which the pharoahs were supposed to live on after death. But by the time of the third dynasty, 2780-2720 BC, the mastaba tomb had been succeeded by the pyramid, a sort of staircase by which the dead pharoah, after a funeral ritual symbolising the passing of the twelve hours of darkness, could ascend into the heavens like the sun at dawn. Entombment in the pyramid was a prelude to rebirth.

It may be that burial in the horned gallery grave had a similar significance, but for a people to whom the earth was a more congenial deity than the sun. The ground plan of the Arran cairns may have been trapezoid, but there is no evidence to suggest that the mound of stones raised over the chamber was ridged. If rounded, it could hardly have resembled the Townhead house. The mound would have the appearance of a rounded heap, higher and broader towards the end containing the portal. In addition, the chamber was situated, not under the centre of the mound, but at the portal end. The greater part of the mound covered nothing. This, and the fact that the bodies were interred in a crouched position, resembling that of the foetus in the womb, suggest that we should look to the type of symbolism by which Jung, in *The Psychology of the Unconscious*, interpreted the great mythologies, for an explanation of these burials. If it is supposed that the mound symbolised a belly, the portal contained in the forecourt a vulva, and the chamber a womb, the idea that in these horned gallery grave burials the dead were being returned to mother earth for rebirth is at least plausible.

Whatever the underlying symbolism it is certain that the Arran cairns were used for a succession of interments over a long period, and the semicircular forecourt seems to have been a place of ritual and ceremony. Even if we do not accept the view that in the case of the Carn Ban the semicircular forecourt was extended by a series of upright stones to enclose an area completely circular, the shape of the forecourt alone is enough to suggest that the area likely to be occupied by the ritual was circular, and it may be that there is a link here with an element at least in the rituals associated with the stone circles of a later age. That the ritual, whatever it was, was accompanied by some kind of feast, for which animals were killed, and part of the flesh placed in the grave as food for the dead, and part eaten by the participants, is reasonably certain. Part too may have been burnt as a sacrifice, possibly to the earth goddess, and the ashes placed in the grave also.

SECONDARY NEOLITHIC PERIOD 2200-2000 BC

Since Bryce's time a culture known as secondary neolithic has been distinguished in Scotland. This overlapped the later

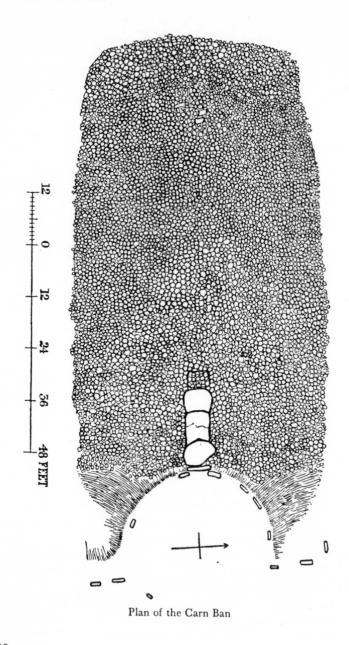

Plan of the Carn Ban

stages of the primary. It had its centre in Buchan, the only major source of flint in the country, and is thought to have resulted from the association of the earlier mesolithic population with the neolithic peoples not only of the passage-grave culture already mentioned, but of the unchambered long barrow culture of south-eastern England; the latter having found its way to the far north-east by way of the east coast, with perhaps a further penetration from an outpost established earlier in northern Ireland. Some of the features of this secondary neolithic culture are, therefore, intrusive, having evolved in England or northern Ireland before their extension to the north-east : others appear to have been indigenous.

Archaeologists determine the distribution of this culture by the finding, in some degree of association, of certain types of pottery and implements, and articles of personal wear or ritual use. Of the pottery, the relevant types, named after the sites with which they were first associated, are Rinyo-Clacton (Rinyo being a site in Orkney), Lyles Hill and Sandhills (both in northern Ireland), and Peterborough. Other clues to the distribution of the culture are long or discoidal flint knives with polished edges, jet sliders and belt fasteners, perforated stone mace-heads and carved stone balls, the last two considered indigenous to Scotland. Cremation burial was a further feature of this culture. That it impinged on Arran from the north-east, probably through trade links, is indicated by the discovery, in the first of the two Tormore cairns excavated by Bryce, of a fragment of Rinyo-Clacton ware, a perforated stone mace-head, and a long flint knife with a polished edge. Another similar flint knife, now in the National Museum of Antiquities, Edinburgh, is said to have been found at Whiting Bay.

Although no carved stone ball has been found in Arran in association with other clues, Martin, in *A Description of the Western Islands of Scotland*, published in 1695, records a globular 'healing stone' as having been in the possession of a Margaret Millar of Ballymeanoch, which besides its power to remove stitches from the sides of sick persons, was thought to have belonged originally to the Lord of the Isles, who could be sure of victory if he cast it into the enemy! Balfour in the first volume of *The Book of Arran* also records a 'healing stone' in the possession of a Crawford family, but this, having been oval and flat on one side and egg-shaped on the other, does not seem to have been a ball of the type under consideration, although it is recorded as having at one time been damaged. But a less doubtful record does exist. At the end of the first volume of *The Book of Arran*, under the heading 'Miscellanea', is an account of a stone ball found in 1891, about 14 in under the surface of the ground, when the road was being widened near Dippen. The photograph of this ball shows it to have been a carved one of the secondary neolithic period, and although there is no proof that it reached Arran during the period of its origin, its discovery on the island, in conjunction with the records of other possible examples, affords a fair possibility that it did so. Final evidence of the impingement of secondary neolithic ideas upon Arran comes from the fact that in riddling the soil from a chamber in the despoiled Giants' Graves near Whiting Bay, Bryce found some fragments which he identified as being of burnt human bone, so establishing the introduction of cremation before the horned gallery graves went out of use.

The introduction of secondary neolithic ideas and implements into Arran probably came through trade contacts, and the fact that Arran traded with the mainland during the period is suggested by the discovery of fragments of Arran pitchstone, in a secondary neolithic context, on several sites in Tweeddale. It may have found its way there through the Biggar Gap. There is no evidence that during this period the original population was displaced, or even dominated by a conquering minority. When we come to the next period in prehistory, the Bronze Age, evidence of conquest by a new element in the population does exist, although it would seem that this element was later absorbed.

THE BRONZE AGE 1900-300 BC

Again the only systematic survey of the monuments of the period is that carried out for the first volume of *The Book of Arran* by Thomas Bryce. In this he considered evidence not only from his own excavations, but from others conducted and recorded by predecessors. In the main his findings are still accepted, although as before they have to be modified in the light of subsequent discoveries. Characteristic of most of the bronze-age burials excavated was individual interment in a short cist, made of stone, covered by a stone slab, and accompanied by a deposit of pottery, weapons or implements, and articles of personal adornment. Some of these short cists he found intruded into cairns of the neolithic period, some were at the hearts of circular mounds of earth or cairns of stone, some were marked by a monolith, some were without any overground structure whatsoever, and some were within the area of stone circles. In some cases the cist contained not a crouched interment but burnt human bones. Since in other parts of Scotland crouched interment in short cists was accompanied mainly by a type of pottery known as the beaker, which from certain other associations was placed early in this period, and cremated burial mainly by a type of pottery known as the food vessel, which came later, he regarded the cremated burials as having followed the crouched. He noted three cases in Arran in which burnt human bones were interred in a further type of coarse pottery known as a cinerary urn. These urns were buried in the ground, normally mouth downwards, without the accompaniment of any grave goods, and with neither stone encasement nor overground structure. These he regarded as generally later than the short cist burials accompanied by food vessels.

Full details of the excavations he considered are recorded in the first volume of *The Book of Arran*. Here we shall consider only such finds as seem specially significant. Many of the short cists opened by Bryce or his predecessors contained no bones, or mere fragments. Only in two cases, that of a short cist at Cnoc a' Choilich farm, found by workmen when they were levelling a hillock, probably a circular earthen mound, and that of a short cist found within the radius of the most westerly of the group of five stone circles on Machrie Moor, were skeletons found, and although they were imperfect they were enough to satisfy Bryce, along with evidence from other short cist interments in nearby Bute, that the short cist builders were probably dark-complexioned like the builders of the horned gallery graves, but rather taller, 5 ft 9 in as against 5 ft 6 in tall, and round rather than long headed. He regarded the type as having dispersed from

Asia into central Europe, where it was still represented, and called it, after Sergi, Eurasian.

It is still generally accepted that the beginning of the Bronze Age in Britain coincided with the arrival from Europe of people who buried beakers with their dead, and that these people landed originally on the east coasts of both England and Scotland, finding their way to the west later, although not in great numbers. The earliest wave of settlers, who brought bell beakers mainly to England, and cord-zoned beakers mainly to the east of Scotland, where they are thinly but evenly distributed, arrived about 1900 BC. These were followed about 1700 BC by settlers who brought short-necked beakers, mainly to the north-east of Scotland, where they are distributed very thickly. Examples of both cord-zoned and short-necked beakers have been found in the west of Scotland, but not in such a quantity as to suggest great penetration. Long-necked beakers followed the short-necked in Britain as an insular variant, but only one has been found in the west of Scotland, at Kilmartin in Argyll, and this has been taken to mean that by the time the long-necked beaker was coming into use in Scotland the west was under another cultural influence.

Although the crouched interment in a short cist was characteristic of the people who brought the beaker to the east of Scotland, Bryce did not find a single instance of a beaker accompanying a short cist burial in Arran. He did find fragments of both cord-zoned and short-necked beakers in chambers intruded into the sides or far ends of neolithic horned gallery graves, suggesting that they had been acquired, possibly through trade, by people who still adhered to neolithic practices. But where in his excavations of short cists he found pottery more or less intact, as in that intruded into the neolithic cairn at Clauchog, or in those found under the round mound at Cnoc a' Choilich farm, in the centre of a round cairn at Brown Head, or within two of the stone circles on Machrie Moor, it was of a type of food vessel which, being divided into three by two mouldings, is known as tripartite. These food vessels, which tapered under the lower moulding to a flat bottom and contracted slightly above the upper to a wide mouth, were decorated with a variety of impressed designs, some of them, like that from one of the Machrie Moor stone circles, very elaborately and beautifully.

Decorated tripartite food vessel from stone circle on
Machrie Moor

Bryce then found no beakers with the short cist burials in
Arran, yet the bones he found were of the round-headed people
from central Europe who brought the beaker culture. The answer
would seem to be that they had been long enough on their way
across the country to have abandoned the beaker before they
arrived, and it may be that they reached Arran, not directly
from the east of Scotland, nor even indirectly from the north-
east down the Great Glen and then by the west coast, but by the
Irish Sea from the south-west of England, descendants perhaps
of the early wave of bell beaker users who had settled there. The
evidence for this latter assumption is based mainly on the one
instance of a bronze weapon found in a short cist on the island.

Pennant in his *Tour of Scotland, and Voyage in the Hebrides*,
published in 1772, had mentioned a 'stupendous cairn, 114 ft
over, and of vast height', at Blackwaterfoot. By the time
MacArthur wrote *The Antiquities of Arran*, in 1873, the cairn
had been despoiled of its stone for building purposes. In 1900
the site was identified, and a short cist uncovered at what was

considered to be the centre. It was a relatively large short cist, indicating a crouched burial rather than a cremated one, but it contained no traces of bone or pottery. It did contain, however, a bronze dagger blade and gold fillet. The rivets which had attached the blade to the handle were still in place, and the blade was decorated by a moulded midrib on which two laterals converged towards the point. The gold fillet was decorated with parallel flutings, and probably served as a mount for the butt end of the handle of the dagger.

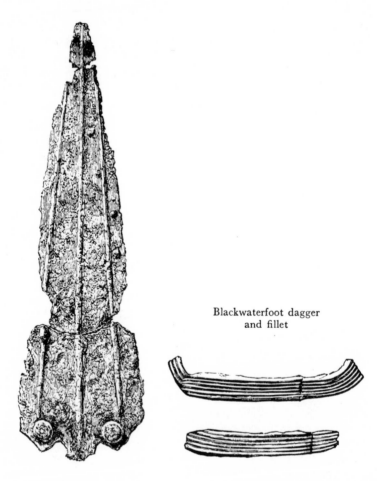

Blackwaterfoot dagger and fillet

Round mounds or cairns over short-cist burials have been found to occur more frequently in the south than in the north of Britain, and the large cairn and dagger are both characteristic of the burial of a chief. The Blackwaterfoot dagger is now considered to show affinity with a type of dagger characteristic of the first phase of the Wessex culture of southern England, dating from 1650-1500 BC, the chief monument of which is the famous circle at Stonehenge.

Further evidence of a link with this phase of the Wessex culture is less direct. The tripartite type of food vessel found in the Arran short cists is considered to belong to a slightly later period, 1500-1000 BC. Associated with it in many short cist burials, although not in Arran, was a type of necklace made of jet or lignite, and named crescentic because it consisted of triangular terminal plates pierced to take several strings of barrel-shaped beads, arranged in curves one above the other, sometimes with intermediate plates and a medial pendant.

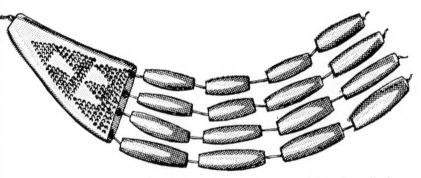

Part of crescentic jet necklace from a chamber incorporated into the wall of the byre at Tormore farm

In Arran fragments of two such necklaces have been found, one with fragments of a beaker in a chamber intruded into the southern end of the neolithic type cairn named Dunan Beag at Blairmore, Lamlash; and the other in a chamber which by the time it was excavated had been incorporated into the wall of the byre at Tormore farm, where it may still be seen. This chamber too was of neolithic type, and is said to have belonged originally to a large white cairn whose stone was used in the building of the steading. The fact that in Arran neither necklace was found in a short cist, or associated with a food vessel, has a significance which will be discussed later. Here we are concerned with its design, which is similar to that of a type of necklace which in Wessex was made of amber. It is considered that the amber necklace of the early phase of the Wessex culture was later copied in jet along the south-western seaboard of Scotland, proving contact and a spread of influence from the south.

Crescentic jet necklaces have been found at Mountstuart in Bute, where one was accompanied by a tripartite food vessel in a short cist containing the skeleton of a young woman, and at Kilmartin in Argyll, where several were accompanied by tripartite food vessels in short cists, and one by a later type of food vessel in the final round cairn of a series forming a linear cemetery. MacArthur suggests that at one time there was such a cemetery in Glencloy, but if so the cairns have been levelled, and we have no visible evidence. But the Kilmartin linear cemetery is still visible, and is a further proof of a link between the coastal area of south-west Scotland and Wessex, for there is a similar cemetery near Stonehenge.

Apart from its crescentic jet necklaces and its linear cemetery, Kilmartin has other echoes of the Wessex culture. The sides of some of its short cists were grooved so that the end pieces could fit neatly into them, a technique derived from carpentry, as was the technique employed in the construction of the Stonehenge circle itself, with its mortise and tenon, and tongued and grooved joints. On the side slab of one of the short cists at Kilmartin was carved a multiple lozenge design, similar to that on a gold-plated ornament from Wessex, found in one of the round barrows of the linear cemetery there. Also at Kilmartin is a complex of standing stones, and this of course is a similarity shared by Arran but without other evidence would be no indication of the area from which the culture spread.

Of great interest, too, is the fact that many of the features which Kilmartin shared with Wessex it shared also with the contemporary Mediterranean of eighteenth-dynasty Egypt, late Minoan Crete, and Mycenae. The shaft graves of Mycenae were surrounded by double circles of upright stones, and the carpentry technique applied to stone, the multiple lozenge design, and the crescentic necklaces, are all parallelled in Mycenae, although the Mycenean necklaces, like the Wessex examples, were made of amber. Cup and ring markings found on the grooved short cists and standing stones at Kilmartin, and, therefore, thought to be contemporary with them, are considered by some to be a version of a concentric circle design common in bronze-age Egypt, Crete, and Mycenae, but this is disputable. In the Mediterranean examples the concentric circles are arranged to form a coherent design. In the great majority of cases in Britain these cup and ring markings are haphazard, and carved, like those on the Stronach ridge in Arran, on the living rock, suggesting that their purpose was ritual and served by the act of carving them rather than by the artistic value of the result. At one time they were thought to have been made to contain the blood of animal or human sacrifices, but since many are carved on perpendicular or sloping rock faces they could not have done so. Their presence is now thought to have coincided with that of metal prospectors, and in fact the clue to the link between Kilmartin and Wessex lies in the fact that the former is situated close to deposits of copper.

Kilmartin lies not only beside copper deposits, but on the main route from the north-east of Scotland by the Great Glen and the west coast to the south-west of England. The beaker people of the north-east of Scotland used copper and then bronze, but could not obtain the necessary ores locally. They did so either from Europe across a great stretch of sea, or from the west of Scotland and from Cornwall, the nearest centre for the supply of tin. It is considered that in the early Bronze Age there was considerable traffic between the north-east of Scotland and the south-west of England along the western seaboard, that the route lay through Crinan and Lochgilphead, and that Kilmartin, close to the copper deposits, was an important centre of the trade.

If Kilmartin was for a time an outpost of the Wessex culture, the route from Lochgilphead to the south of England would pass Arran, and it would be important that the island was under friendly control. We are almost into the period recalled by Homer in the *Iliad* and the *Odyssey*, and we know from the latter that Ulysses sailed in sight of land, and in daylight, whenever possible, drawing up his ships towards nightfall on the first suitable beach. Such being the habit of the period it would be important for the

metal traders of the west of Scotland that beaches should not
be subject to hostile attack. It is likely that the chief buried
under the 'stupendous cairn' at Blackwaterfoot was the ruler of
a band of colonists from Wessex, living on the island to protect
the route from Kilmartin to the south. Although the excavators
did not find his bones, and we cannot be sure that he was round-
headed, we have the evidence of his cairn, his short cist and his
dagger as to his period and status, for the dagger was a badge
of rank, ceremonial rather than utilitarian. The indications are
that towards the close of the early Bronze Age the population
of Arran, still using implements of flint, was under the domination of overlords from Wessex engaged in the copper trade, and
that much of the copper from Kilmartin went south, and some
eventually east, to enrich the armour, weapons and palace
treasuries of men who must have been very like the legendary
Agamemnon of Mycenae and Idomeneus of Crete. But the link
with the homeric world can be stressed too strongly. The poems
attributed to Homer, although they referred back to the Bronze
Age, were not put in writing until at least 800 BC, and many of
the ideas they contain are more appropriate to the early Iron
Age. The Wessex culture, in spite of the evidence of links with
the bronze-age Mediterranean, was unique, and in no respect
more than in its elaboration of the stone circle.

Stonehenge is at present the subject of much controversy as
to the extent of its calendrical sophistication, and much that has
been said about it cannot apply at all closely to the stone circles
of Arran, for these differ greatly not only from Stonehenge but
from each other. Traces of no fewer than ten circles remain on
the island, seven being concentrated in the west in the vicinity
of the Black and Machrie waters, with others at Largybeg Point
and Aucheleffan, and near the head of the Brodick to Lamlash
road. All received the attention of early travellers to the island,
who recorded the local tradition that they were connected with
the legendary Fionn and his warriors. James Bryce, who wrote
also a work on the geology of the island, surveyed them in 1861
and left records used by Thomas Bryce in his own survey for the
first volume of *The Book of Arran*. James Bryce concluded,
because he found short-cist burials within several of the circles,
that their purpose was sepulchral, and Thomas Bryce seems to

Page 71: (above) Clauchan graveyard and the ruin of the old preaching-house re-built in 1805. The site was probably a sacred place from the Early Christian period onward; (below) the Duchess Anne, from the portrait by David Scougal now in the boudoir of Brodick castle

Page 72: (above) Ruins of an outlying blackhouse of the runrig farm of North Glen Sannox, from which emigrants left in 1829 for Canada; (below) Sannox kirk and manse, built in 1822 by the Independent congregation established as a result of the Haldane brothers' mission to Arran in 1800

have agreed. More recent investigation has been directed almost exclusively towards accurate measurement and an assessment of the mathematical and calendrical ideas they contain, but so far no conclusions have been published except that the measurements of MacArthur and James Bryce are 'grossly inaccurate', that two of the circles are irregular in a similar and possibly significant way, and that one is not a circle but a true ellipse.

Until more research has been done little can be said about the ideas of the people who raised them that is not highly conjectural. Only a minority would accept today that their purpose was primarily sepulchral. The existence of tombs inside a church does not imply that the latter was a monument raised in honour of the dead, but rather that its interior was regarded as sacred. Many circles have contained no interments, and many have contemporary burials in their vicinity, as in the case of the linear cemetery near Stonehenge. It seems likely that the circle was primarily a place of worship, and that its structure was dictated by the ritual it was built to contain.

The calendrical significance of some of the stone circles is obvious. Two of the smaller circles in Arran—one of them on Machrie Moor and the other at Aucheleffan—have their stones orientated to the cardinal points of the compass. That such a significance has not yet been discerned in others is no guarantee that it does not exist, for people concerned with a particular animal, either through husbandry or a totem association, might have a special interest in some movement of the heavenly bodies coincident with its period of gestation. At any rate the probability that the circles had a calendrical significance is considerable.

They almost certainly provided a setting for ritual dances, although here we have to rely on evidence from anthropology and folklore rather than from any of the more exact sciences. That some at least of the dances celebrated occasions important to people engaged in agriculture and animal husbandry, such as the vernal and autumnal equinoxes, and the summer and winter solstices, is equally likely. That the concern of the dancers was to ensure fertility in their fields and animals, by simulating such movements of the heavenly bodies as they wished to encourage, is likely also. So, too, is the idea that the general fertility aimed at was held to be encouraged by a sexual element in the dances,

73

discernible in the circular intermingling of the sexes which is characteristic of the eightsome reel and other dances of today, whose movements are an obvious refinement of ritual originals. In dances where one couple clasps hands and holds them high, to let the others pass under in procession, there is a link with a superstitious belief, common throughout stone circle areas, that by passing under the capstone of a trilith a couple can ensure that their union will not be fruitless. This is considered by anthropologists a miming of the act of birth, and so in terms of sympathetic magic an encouragement.

It does not seem that Arran remained long under the domination of its Wessex overlords, although it absorbed many of their ideas. There was, not long after their establishment, some penetration into the area of warriors from Ireland who used halberds, since these have been found near Kilmartin, and on Islay and Bute, and although none have been found in Arran the discovery of a few food vessels of a contemporary Irish type suggests that the halberd-users may have reached Arran also. There was some penetration, too, into southern Scotland, during the second phase of the Wessex culture, dating from 1500-1400 BC, of warriors who used shaftholed battleaxes of polished stone, and buried a small pottery vessel, known as a pigmy cup, with their dead; but neither this type of battleaxe nor the pigmy cups have been found in Arran, or to any extent in Bute or Argyll. Either the battleaxe-users were not interested in the area, or the halberd-users were strong enough to fend them off.

Mention was made earlier of a short cist at Mountstuart in Bute, in which a crescentic jet necklace and tripartite food vessel were found in association with the skeleton of a young woman. Such an association was not uncommon. Most archaeologists accept the view that the necklace was a female adornment. Some are even inclined to the view that originally at least the food vessel itself was the mark of a woman's grave. A crescentic jet necklace was found with a food vessel of an Irish type dated as late as 1300 BC in the final round cairn of the Kilmartin linear cemetery. The cairn is therefore thought to mark a woman's grave, and since the cairn was the mark of a chief, or in this case a chieftainess, it is argued that after the passing of the Wessex overlords, and the absorption of the Irish newcomers,

74

society in the Kilmartin area became matriarchal, possibly as a result of the re-emergence of the neolithic veneration of the earth goddess and the preoccupation with fecundity. That this happened in Arran could be similarly argued, from the evidence of a jet necklace found in a short cist in the centre of a round cairn at Brown Head, which can still be seen in a depleted state near the twenty-third milestone. The necklace, found with a tripartite food vessel, was not in this instance crescentic, but made of pierced jet discs, graduated in size and so strung together that those of greatest diameter occupied the middle and those of least diameter the ends of the string. The type is considered to have been roughly contemporary with the crescentic, and like it an article of female adornment.

The deposition of crescentic jet necklaces of the early middle Bronze Age in neolithic type chambers, mentioned earlier as having occurred at the Dunan Beag cairn at Blairmore, and at Tormore farm, is proof of the persistence into the later period not only of neolithic religious ideas, but of neolithic tomb architecture. It would seem that side by side with the short cist and round cairn building of the early bronze-age incomers the descendants of the original neolithic population, or some of them at least, continued to intrude their own type of segmented burial chamber into the sides and far ends of the old horned gallery graves of their ancestors. But of course their grave goods had changed, and no doubt they had moved their rituals from the old semicircular forecourts to the new stone circles.

Since fairly early in the middle Bronze Age, which lasted from 1500-1000 BC, cremated burials in cinerary urns gradually began to take the place of burials in short cists or in neolithic type chambers, and since no grave goods were deposited, evidence of occupation during the remainder of the Bronze Age is confined to articles discovered where they had been abandoned at a time of crisis, or hidden and never recovered. The discovery at Bally-meanoch of a shaft-flanged bronze axehead, at Cloined of bronze spearheads, and at Corriecravie of palstaves, all characteristic of the later middle Bronze Age, suggests continued occupation and the adaptation of weapons in response to new ideas introduced in the course of trade contacts. That much of this contact may have been with Ireland is indicated by the discovery of such articles in gold as a lunula found at Kiscadale, a lock-ring and cup-ended ornament found together under a boulder at White-farland, and further cup-ended ornaments found in Ormidale and at Whiting Bay. In the late Bronze Age, 1000-300 BC, Ireland was the centre of a gold industry, and these articles were probably an Irish export, although there is a slight possibility that they may have come from Leadhills, which during the same period was the centre of a gold industry in southern Scotland. Whatever their place of origin, and they closely resemble a multitude of Irish examples, suggest at least that from the early middle to the end of the Bronze Age women in Arran continued to be, if not dominant, at least important enough to possess beautiful and valuable articles of personal adornment.

4 CELTIC AND VIKING INVASIONS

THE people who inhabited Arran have so far been identified by their tombs and monuments, their weapons, implements, and ornaments. In the Iron Age evidence comes mainly from forts. These were surveyed for the first volume of *The Book of Arran* by J. A. Balfour, and although he drew plans and gave measurements, and did some desultory digging, the conclusions he drew are disappointingly general, and he was able to make few strictly scientific deductions of the kind provided by Thomas Bryce.

The Arran forts are scattered fairly evenly around the island, and it will be convenient to classify them initially in terms of their size, which may be considered to have had a bearing on their function. First there are forts which vary from circular to oval in plan, and have an average size through their longest axis of about 110 ft. These include Torr an t-Sean Chaisteil at North Sannox, An Cnap at Mid Sannox, Dun Fionn at the east end of the Clauchland hills, and the forts at Glenashdale, Dippen, Kildonan, and Bennan Head. In this size group Balfour saw two exceptions in Torr an t-Sean Chaisteil, above Coillemore at Lochranza, which he described as 'oblong', and 'a doubtful structure'; and Cnoc a' Chlochair, at the junction of Gleann Easbuig and Gleann an t-Suidhe, which he described as 'the only example of a rectilinear fort in Arran', although in his own plan its southern wall is curved and there is a wall running across it which divides it into two segments unequal in size. Balfour gave the measurements of the Lochranza fort as 231 by 117 ft, and Cnoc a' Chlochair as 144 by 103 ft.

Examination of what is visible of the two forts today suggests that Balfour may have misinterpreted the evidence. Without skilled excavation it is impossible to be certain, but the Lochranza fort seems to have been originally a broad crescentic wall built around the vulnerable side of the summit it defends. Although the other side is not perpendicular it is sufficiently precipitous to have afforded as much protection as the wall itself. Towards the western end of the crescentic wall, which is composed of large blocks of stone lying in confusion, a narrow wall runs straight out along the flat bog lying to the SSE. This is obviously not part of the original structure, and would seem to have been of much later date, perhaps forming part of an enclosure for cattle. Towards the eastern end of the crescentic wall are the ruins of a small rectangular building, which may have been a summer shieling. Until excavation proves otherwise, this fort should be regarded as an oval one in the same size range as those already listed, as the length of the crescentic wall is about 107 paces.

So too with Cnoc a' Chlochair, which on examination seems to consist of two overlapping forts of differing wall structure, one of them circular, and the other of an irregular shape dictated by the lie of the ground. The measurements given by Balfour embrace the area covered by both structures, and it would seem that, in point of size, they, too, belong to the first group. The forts of this group, since they differ from each other in wall structure, are obviously not all the work of one people or one period, but the social unit they sheltered was probably the household and dependants of a single chief, with his stock.

Forts of the second class are represented in Arran firstly by Drumadoon, where a fairly level hilltop area of about 12 acres is defended on the west or seaward side by perpendicular cliffs, and on the east or landward side, and at its northern and southern ends, by a crescentic wall of stone, possibly originally about 10 ft thick but so depleted that its original height cannot be estimated. The other example of a fort covering a big acreage is at Cnoc Ballygowan, where an area comparable to that at Drumadoon is enclosed by faint traces of an earthen wall and ditch, evidently never quite completed. Neither Drumadoon nor Ballygowan is likely to have been the stronghold of a single chief and his dependants. They are too large. The social unit they were intended to shelter was probably tribal.

The third class of fort is represented by examples at Kilpatrick, Corriecravie, King's Cross Point, and possibly Glencloy. Little more than the foundations of these are visible, but they are all circular, with walls formed of two courses of dry stone filled with rubble. The average diameter of the circular courtyard is about 45 ft, so these forts are small compared with those of the other two classes, although they are likely to have been higher, and in view of their position may well have been built as strong points on lines of marine communication. They probably housed garrisons of fighting men rather than the household and dependants of a chief. Certainly they are too small to have provided a refuge for stock.

When we come to place the forts in their chronological order we obtain little help from Balfour, except in the case of the third class of small round forts, which we shall consider later. Headrick, a mineralogist, although certainly an amateur, considered that Dun Fionn was a vitrified fort, but he seems to have given no concrete reason for thinking so. Balfour's dismissal of this idea, although probably sound, is weakened by his statement that 'no Arran fort has shown any sign of even the least trace of vitrification'. His statement may have been true when it was made, but he had not been told about, or visited, An Cnap at Mid Sannox, which was excavated by V. A. Noel Paton in 1927, and evidence of its vitrification definitely established.

It was for a long time a matter of doubt as to whether these vitrified forts, in which the stones forming the wall have been fused into a solid mass by firing, were fired deliberately by the builders to create a more solid wall, or by attackers with a view to their destruction. There was even a theory, enthusiastically supported by MacArthur as he considered the possibilities of Dun Fionn as a signal station, that the vitrification was due to the heat of beacon fires. It seems now to be accepted that the heat came from the enemy. These forts were built of unworked stone interlaced with timber, and against the inside of the wall there was a platform providing not only a walk for the guards but a passage connecting the first floors of a series of timber houses surrounding the courtyard. This type of fort was obviously open to fire danger, and J. R. C. Hamilton, in an essary on *Forts, Brochs and Wheel-Houses*, has suggested that it went out of use as a result of the introduction into iron-age warfare of fire spears and slings.

Objects found during excavations of timber-laced forts vitrified by fire, particularly that at Rahoy in Argyll, have enabled archaeologists to determine building dates of about 200 BC, and from the distribution of the forts the builders are thought to

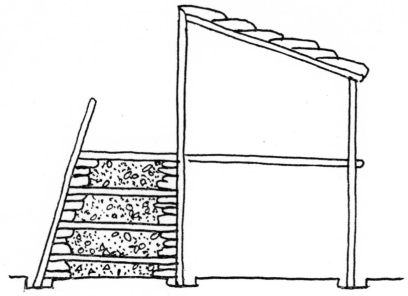

Timber-laced fort. Section of wall and peripheral range

have been a Celtic people who made their way from the Continent first of all to southern England, and then by the old route of the mesolithic and neolithic peoples up through the Irish Sea to the south-western coast of Scotland, from which they continued, by the upper Clyde and the Great Glen, into east central Scotland, where they eventually settled. Since there are vitrified forts at Dippen in Kintyre, and at Dunagoil in the south-west of Bute, just opposite An Cnap, it would seem that An Cnap marked a stage in the route north-eastward.

It has been suggested that the first Celtic peoples to arrive in Britain during the great wave of migration which took place at the close of the Bronze Age, in the period between 500 and 200 BC, built the size of fort appropriate to the household of a chief and his dependants, but as subsequent invaders attempted to gain a foothold in their territory, banded together into more powerful tribal communities and built larger strongholds, of the kind which the Romans found when they arrived in Britain and named *oppida*. It may be that this process occurred twice in Arran, for one of the forts of intermediate size, at Bennan Head, shows faint traces of an earthen wall and ditch similar to that embracing the much greater area on Cnoc Ballygowan. If the latter was never finished, as would seem to be so, it is likely that the first wave of settlers, who built Bennan Head fort and possibly others later superseded, was surprised and overcome by the second, who, when they in turn were threatened by the timber-laced fort builders, built Drumadoon as their tribal stronghold.

The subject is one on which the scope for conjecture is limitless, but it can be said that the sites of some of the forts of intermediate size are likely to have been occupied more than once, and certainly at Cnoc a' Chlochair this seems to have been so. It is possible also that An Cnap is not the only timber-laced fort on Arran or even the only vitrified one. And it is plausible to assume that fairly elaborate stone structures are likely to be later than simple ones in either stone or earth.

A few of the other forts of intermediate size, such as those at North Sannox, Glenashdale, Dippen, and Kildonan, seem to have been faced on both sides with dry stone and filled with rubble core. Traces of what seems to have been a mural chamber have been discerned at North Sannox, although its apparent adaptation into a small sheep pen has confused the evidence. This suggests the type of fort now classified by archaeologists as a dun, which Hamilton considers a stage in the process by which a dry-stone, rubble-cored, ring-walled type of fort developed in the west into the galleried dun, a higher structure, and in the far north into the compact and lofty broch, built in great numbers in the early centuries of the present era.

The duns would, therefore, seem to have followed the timber-laced forts, which vitrified when destroyed by fire. Excavations at Dunagoil, the vitrified fort directly across the Sound of Bute from An Cnap, show that after being vitrified it was rebuilt, for pieces of vitrified rock were incorporated into a later cross-wall, not timber-laced, which reduced its size. Finds suggested that the later and smaller fort was occupied until as late as AD 100. This gives only a general indication of the date of the firing of the original timber-laced fort, but it was certainly before AD 100, and may have been considerably earlier, possibly close to the beginning of the century. We know that fire weapons were being used in Gaul in the latter half of the first century BC, for they were sufficiently novel to be mentioned by Caesar. They would not take long to spread to Britain. Since An Cnap was vitrified, it, too, must have been attacked by fire weapons, possibly about the same time as Dunagoil, and there is no evidence that it was re-occupied. The dun on Torr an t-Sean Chaisteil at North Sannox is hardly any distance away, and may well have been built after An Cnap was destroyed, by the people who destroyed it.

We have seen that the distribution of the timber-laced forts suggests that the people who built them around 200 BC had come from the Continent, by way of southern England and the Irish Sea, to bypass southern Scotland and settle in east central Scotland south of the Great Glen. Distribution suggests similarly that the people who built the dry-stone, rubble-cored forts, which were later developed into galleried duns and finally into brochs, came from the Continent by way of south-western England and Ireland into the west of Scotland, and passed on to settle in the far north, including the Orkneys and Shetlands. They are thought to have gone north because they could settle there without having to dislodge the earlier Celtic immigrants.

We come now to consider the third class of fort in Arran, the small round fort with dry-stone, rubble-cored walls about 12 ft thick, enclosing a courtyard about 45 ft in diameter. It was in connection with these forts, probably high enough to be called towers, that Balfour made some of his more positive deductions. On excavating the fort at King's Cross Point he discovered that it was built of a type of sandstone not obtainable close at hand, and considered that it had been ferried across from Holy Isle, the nearest source of supply. On excavating the nearby Viking burial, which will be considered later, he found rubble of a similar red sandstone in the mound. This led him to reflect on the improbability of the fort having been built after the mound, which blocked its access from the landward side, or of the mound having been raised while the fort was still in use, so he concluded that the mound had been raised after the fort was destroyed, and some of the material of the fort incorporated into it. Although he did not say so specifically, the small round type of fort obviously predated the Viking invasions of the ninth

82

century. Further, he found that the small round fort at Kilpatrick was incorporated into a cashel, or wall of turf and stone, which enclosed an area of about two acres running down to a hollow beside a burn, which was overlooked at its far extreme by rising ground. Reflecting that in AD 545 St Brendan, during his voyage to the western isles, had founded a monastery of the Celtic church which had never been satisfactorily identified, that the name Kilbrannan Sound suggested a link with St Brendan, that the early Celtic monasteries were not infrequently set up around a fort relinquished by the chief of the territory about to be evangelised, and noting that the cashel wall was useless as a fortification, Balfour concluded that the cashel at Kilpatrick was one of the earliest outposts of the Celtic church in Scotland, predating Iona itself.

PICTS

We shall return to St Brendan later. Meanwhile we have a tentative chronology for the Arran forts which preceded the feudal castles, and some idea of the number of separate Celtic peoples who built them. Two early waves of settlers would seem to have preceded the arrival of the timber-laced fort builders. The first wave were in all probability overwhelmed even before they had time to finish their tribal stronghold on Cnoc Ballygowan, but the second wave must have built Drumadoon in time to hold out against the third arrivals, who nevertheless succeeded in obtaining a foothold, and maintained An Cnap as a stage on their route to east central Scotland between 200 BC and sometime around the beginning of the first century AD. An Cnap was destroyed by a further wave of Celtic invaders, probably those who built the nearby dun in North Glen Sannox. The people who built An Cnap, and who finally settled in east central Scotland, probably contributed an element to the population which was later to become the Southern Picts of early historic times. The people who built the dun at North Sannox, and probably others at Glenashdale, Dippen, and Kildonan, spread northwards as far as the Orkneys and Shetlands, and probably contributed an element to the population which was later to become the Northern Picts. Since in the fourth century AD the

Picts were in the south-western area, joining Scots from Dalriada in northern Ireland in raids on the western end of the Antonine Wall at Bowling, it is likely that the Arran dun-builders established overlordship over the Celtic immigrants who built Drumadoon, and later became amalgamated with them into the wider Pictish unit.

When sometime towards the end of the fifth century AD a body of Scots came over from Dalriada in northern Ireland to found a sister kingdom in the south-west of Scotland, it seems they were replacing Picts, whether by right of conquest or by arrangement is not clear. Certainly when St Columba followed his countrymen to become abbot of Iona in AD 563 it was partly by arrangement with the Pictish King Brude Mac Maelchon, who was king of the Northern Picts, not of the Southern, which is what we should expect if the link between the duns and the Northern Picts was as has been suggested. Incidentally, Martin in 1695 visited a village in the Drumadoon area which he called Druimcruney, obviously from *druim*, 'ridge', and *Cruithni*, 'Picts', proving at least an old tradition that the Scots had followed the Picts on the island. That the Scots who founded the Scottish Dalriada built the small round forts fits also into place. These forts were a more specialised type of building than the dun, though related to it in wall structure. They seem indeed a sort of cousin to the broch, and were probably a parallel development originating in Ireland. And we have Balfour's evidence for thinking that they predated the Viking invasions.

It is unlikely that the earlier Celtic invaders of Arran, or even the pre-Celtic inhabitants, were completely replaced either by the builders of the timber-laced fort at An Cnap, or of the duns such as those at North Sannox or Glenashdale. Unless excavation establishes that there were other timber-laced forts on the island, it is likely that the builders of An Cnap maintained an uneasy existence in the north of the island, while the earlier Celtic inhabitants dominated the rest. But it is likely that the subsequent dun-builders originally dominated the rest of the population, before becoming integrated and possibly absorbed. It is difficult even to guess whether the dun-builders or the earlier Celtic invaders were the Epidii of the map prepared by the Alexandrian geographer Ptolemy in the second century, and indeed there is no guarantee that the Epidii did inhabit Arran, as is generally assumed. The Epidii of Ptolemy's map clearly inhabited Kintyre and Islay, but that they inhabited Arran, too, is no more than a probability. It is certainly more likely than that the Arran people were of the Damnonii whom Ptolemy places across the Firth of Clyde on the mainland. These were subject to Roman rule, and in the post-Roman period emerged as the Britons of Strathclyde. The Roman rule never reached Arran, so the possibility that the island and the mainland were linked at the time by a common population, with established lines of communication, is slight.

If the Epidii did inhabit Arran it would seem that the first Celtic language spoken on the island was Brythonic, as was the Celtic spoken in early historic times by the Britons of Strathclyde, and represented today by Welsh, Cornish, and Breton; rather than Goidelic, as was that spoken in early historic times by the Dalriadic Scots, and represented today by Irish, Manx, and Scots Gaelic. Epidii means 'the horse people', the fragment *ep* being Brythonic for 'horse'; the Goidelic equivalent being *ech* and the modern Scots Gaelic *each*. Since the use of horses was common to all the Celtic tribes it is hardly likely that a tribe would be given such a name unless it held the horse in veneration as a totem animal, and there are certainly traditions of mare worship in Irish, although not in Arran, folklore, and there are records of inscriptions on shrines, in both Roman Gaul and Roman Britain, to a goddess Epona.

That the Celtic spoken in Arran in the days of Ptolemy's map was Brythonic, of a variety to arrive fairly late in Britain, and likely to retain fresh Gaulish developments, would match the view that the dun-builders, the latest arrivals before the Scots who founded Dalriada, were an element in the population who were later to become the Northern Picts. The lost language of the Picts is thought to have been a blend of some non-Indo-European language of the bronze-age peoples, and a language Gallo-Brythonic rather than simply Brythonic. Pictish elements in place-names survive today, however, mainly in the area of the Southern Picts, because the Picts were replaced in Dalriada by the Scots, and in the north-west and north of Scotland, and in the northern isles, by the Vikings. Pressure on the Picts seems

85

not only to have united them, but to have driven them into a more compact territory.

SCOTS

Certainly the earliest language extant in the Arran place-names of today is the Gaelic introduced by the Scots who founded the kingdom of Dalriada, comprising a territory corresponding roughly to the present Argyll, stretching from the south-western end of the Great Glen southward to the Mull of Kintyre, and from Drumalban westward to Islay and Jura. With their arrival we are on the threshold of history, having various king lists, annals, and chronicles, to add to the evidence of archaeology and place-names, although for some time yet evidence is slight, and much of it recorded some time after events, and later copied and re-copied, and the originals lost.

The story told is that the Scottish kingdom of Dalriada was founded by three sons of Erc, king of Dalriada in northern Ireland, originally as a subject kingdom. The three brothers were Angus, Loarn, and Fergus. Fergus, although the youngest, was the first king, and from him were descended Kenneth MacAlpin, who in 844 became king of both Picts and Scots, and Malcolm II, who defeated the Angles of the south-east of Scotland at Carham in 1018, and in the same year, on the death of the British king, and as a result of intermarriage between earlier members of his own and the British dynasty, took control of Strathclyde on behalf of his grandson Duncan, the heir to the kingdom. Malcolm is, therefore, considered to have been the first king of Scotland as we know it today, but we must remember that shortly after the time of Kenneth MacAlpin the Scots' ruling family had shifted its headquarters into Pictland, and the Vikings were arriving on the scene, and were to establish the kingdom of Man and the Sudreyjar, which included all the western isles of Scotland; so Arran did not become part of the united kingdom of Scotland until after the battle of Largs in 1263.

Yet until the Vikings arrived Arran was not only ruled by the descendants of Fergus, the first king of the Scottish Dalriada, but owned by them, not as individuals, but as a kindred. The kindred of Angus occupied Islay and Jura, the kindred of Loarn the northern part of present day Argyll, and the kindred of Gabran, a grandson of Fergus, Knapdale, Kintyre, Bute and Arran. The kindreds of Loarn and Gabran played the chief part in Dalriadic politics, and for a long time were rivals for power, but in the end the kindred of Gabran prevailed. Few of the events of this rivalry affected Arran. The most notable of the Dalriadic kings, Aedan, a son of Gabran, seems to have spent most of his time fighting battles on the mainland, some of them in the north-east against the Picts, and others in the Firth of Forth area against both the Picts to the north and the Angles to the south, apparently to protect the petty British kingdom of Manau Guotodin, which had emerged after the Roman withdrawal in the area occupied in Ptolemy's map by the Votadini. It is said that he had some claim to this kingdom through his British mother. His son Artur was killed in one of these battles, and Nora Chadwick suggests in *Celtic Britain* that he may have been the historical Arthur of the Arthurian legends of Welsh and Cornish tradition, for of course the British of Manau Guotodin were eventually displaced by the Angles, and their traditions followed them south-westward to survive in Wales and Cornwall.

Succession to the kingship in Dalriadic times was not patrilineal, as in later feudal times, or matrilineal, as with the Picts, but according to the law of tanistry, by which the kindred of the ruling dynasty chose their head. Aedan is said to have succeeded his cousin Conall against the claims of an elder brother through the influence of St Columba, who may, therefore, have been of the kindred, as indeed he is said to have been. But he is known more certainly to have been a grandson of Conall Gulban, the founder of the Ui Neill, the so-called high kings of Ireland, and may have owed much of his influence in Dalriadic politics to that connection. It is thought to have been through his influence that in AD 575, at the Council of Druim Cett, which both he and Aedan attended, an agreement was reached with the high king that the Scottish Dalriada should no longer be a subject kingdom.

In this consolidation of the Scottish kingdom of Dalriada, and its ultimate extension into the kingdom of Scotland, we see three influences at work : the first, and possibly the least effective, that of conquest, the second that of intermarriage, and the third that of the Celtic church. Aedan seems to have lost more battles than he won, but his son Eachadh Buidhe was described as *rex Pictorum* before the union of the Scots and Picts under Kenneth MacAlpin, and this must have been through marriage with a Pictish princess. This, and the fact that even before the union of the two peoples Pictish names began to appear in the Dalriadic king lists, suggests that the Scots system of succession gradually replaced the matrilineal in Pictland itself, allowing the kingship to pass to the Dalriadic dynasty, by now of mixed Scottish and Pictish descent. But this alone cannot account for the ultimate spread of the Gaelic language of the Scots throughout the greater part of what is now Scotland. Only the influence of the Celtic church can explain that.

By AD 563, when in the reign of Conall, Gabran's nephew and successor, St Columba founded his monastery on Iona, it is likely that Christianity had already been introduced to the area of Scottish Dalriada lying nearest to Ireland. St Brendan had visited the western isles of Scotland in a voyage said to have begun in AD 545 during the reign of Gabran. The places he visited can only be guessed, and while place-names are an uncertain guide, it is fairly generally agreed that Kilbrannan Sound, lying immediately below the cashel at Kilpatrick, incorporates St Brendan's name. The 'kil' in Kilbrannan may be derived from *caol*, a 'sound' or 'narrow', and not from *cill*, a 'cell' : that is no matter. There is the further fact that by tradition the people of Bute are known as Brandanes, allegedly from association with the saint. There is only one Brendan place-name in Bute itself, however, and the earliest monastic foundation on that island appears to have been that of St Blane, in some way related to Aedan, Conall's cousin and successor. A curious fact is that on the site of St Blane's monastery is the ruin of a round fort similar to that at Kilpatrick. It seems likely that in the early days of the Dalriadic kingdom monasteries were established both at Kilpatrick and on Bute on the sites of round forts relinquished for the purpose as soon as sufficient stability was achieved to allow the missionaries to follow the original settlers.

When St Blane founded his monastery on Bute we do not know, but he was an established figure there by AD 574, when Aedan succeeded his cousin Conall. This is only eleven years after St Columba's foundation of Iona, and although the possi-

88

Page 89: (above) The String Road, the first of three roads to cross the roof of the island, was planned by Thomas Telford and built in 1817; *(below)* the late Mrs John Sillars of West Mayish. In 1886, when she was maid to Mrs Adams-Acton, she pushed a perambulator containing baggage and a year-old child all the way from London to the Broomielaw

Page 90: (above) PS *Glen Sannox*, first of three vessels to bear the name, she burned so much coal that the LMS scrapped her at the end of the 1924 season; (below) TS *Glen Sannox*, said to have been the fastest steamboat ever to sail on the Clyde, was capable of $22\frac{1}{2}$ knots in normal service with ease

bility that St Blane's was the result of a mission from Iona cannot be ruled out, it is more likely to have been founded direct from Ireland, following the voyage of St Brendan. It should be remembered that the Scottish Dalriada was a subject kingdom until AD 575, the second year of Aedan's reign. It is not likely that the development of the Columban, as opposed to the wider Celtic church, could take place before the Scottish Dalriada achieved political independence, and from its situation Iona was obviously established in the first place as the centre of a mission to the Picts.

Much ridicule has been poured on Balfour's rendering of Torr an Daimh, the name of the hill above the cashel at Kilpatrick, as 'the hill of the church', since in modern usage the name means 'the hill of the bullock', and indeed the use of place-names to add weight to an argument is dangerous, because they can be manipulated almost at will. Mackenzie MacBride, the author of a highly romantic volume on the island, *Arran of the Bens, the Glens and the Brave*, rejects Balfour's view of the Kilpatrick cashel as a monastery, yet in doing so indulges in such etymological juggling as puts Balfour in the shade. It is more significant that W. M. Mackenzie, the sardonic author of the second volume of *The Book or Arran*, published four years after Balfour's first volume appeared, completely ignores the latter's view, which probably means that he did not accept it, and yet could find no safe ground on which to contradict it. That he would have contradicted Balfour if he could cannot be questioned. He did not hesitate on other occasions. Perhaps expert excavation will settle the matter, but that there was an early monastic establishment on Arran seems likely, and no other site has appeared to compete with Kilpatrick as a possible alternative.

That Arran, closer to Ireland than Bute, was Christianised about the same time is probable, and the method of the Celtic church was invariable. An outstanding personality of religious force would leave the Irish monastery in which he had been trained and set out with a few followers to an area hitherto unconverted, to establish a monastery of his own. The abbot was responsible not only for the rule of the monks within the monastery itself, but of those who set up *cillean*, or 'cells', in the surrounding area, and presumably preached to the people. The bishop in the Celtic church had purely ritual functions, and held no authority over a diocese. The abbot alone ruled his area, and although he had an obvious link with his parent monastery, and no doubt kept in touch with other abbots in neighbouring areas, he was independent.

That such a monastery was established at Kilpatrick, possibly after a visit from St Brendan, gains added support from the Celtic character of the dedications of many of the early Arran chapels. Among the ecclesiastical sites in Arran are Kilpatrick, Kilmory, Kilbride Bennan, Kildonan, Kilbride at Lamlash, Kilmichael at Brodick, and Clauchan near Shiskine. With the exception of Clauchan, an archaic form of *clachan*, used frequently to denote an early ecclesiastical site, all these names contain the prefix 'kil', from *cill*, 'cell'. Other sites, without the prefix 'kil' in the place-name, are of St Michael's chapel at Sannox, St James's at Lochranza, St Mary's at Sliddery, and that of the chapel of St Blaise on Pladda. The sites without 'kil' in the place-name date almost certainly to the later period of the Roman church. Some of the ruins on the other sites, like that at the Lamlash Kilbride, date also from a period later than that of the Dalriadic kingdom, but probably replaced earlier buildings. It is a reasonable probability that the dedications to Patrick, Bride, Donan and Maelrubha, are linked with the first *cillean* of Dalriadic times.

Apart from St Brendan, whose association with the island depends on a single place-name and the doubtful identification of a lost monastery, only one other holy man of the period can be personally linked with the island. It is said that when in AD 557 Gabran was killed in a battle, in which the Picts drove the Scots south into Kintyre, his son Aedan fled to Ireland with his daughter Mathgemm, who there married a chief called Cairil or Cuinid, and gave birth, in AD 566, to a son Las. Sometime before AD 574, when Aedan succeeded his cousin Conall, he returned to Dalriada in Scotland, bringing Mathgemm and Las with him. Where Las stayed in Dalriada is doubtful, but it was probably at Monadh, near Loch Crinan, for his mother is named 'Mathgemm of Monadh' in a chronicle. There he was visited by St Blane of Bute, said to have been his uncle, who was impressed by his piety. He was destined for the church, and at fourteen was sent to Ireland to be educated by St Findan, a former pupil of St. Columba, and later, presumably after his academic education had been completed, he came to a cave on what is now Holy Isle to spend, like the young Christ, and in the fashion of his time, a period in the wilderness. He later made two visits to Rome, and was ordained successively priest and bishop, becoming a champion of Roman usages against those of the Celtic church. He died in AD 639, abbot of Leithglinn in Leinster.

Las had the prefix *mo*, meaning 'my', attached to his name, as was common with holy men, and became known as Molas. Dean Monro, writing after a visit to Arran in 1549, referred to Holy Isle as the 'yle of Molass'. Its Gaelic name was *Eilean Molaise*, from *eilean*, 'island', and *Molaise*, 'of Molas', and this has been corrupted through Elmolaise and Lemolash to Lamlash, which was the name of Holy Isle before 1830, after which it became attached to the village then developing on the shore of the bay opposite. The saint's name is usually written Molaise, which is an archaic genitive, but sometimes Moloise, the modern genitive, and even Molios, which is the result of a confusion. Molios derives from *maol*, 'bald', and *Iosa*, Jesus, and denotes a ton-sured man of Christ, or simply a monk. The name Molios, applied to a tonsured figure carved on a stone formerly in Clauchan graveyard but now built into the wall of a church at Shiskine, has given rise in that district to the belief that the stone is an effigy of St Molas, but the vestments portrayed are, according to a learned essay in the second volume of *The Book of Arran*, more appropriate to an abbot of the thirteenth century, and the person commemorated was possibly an abbot of Saddell, just across Kilbrannan Sound in Kintyre.

Since St Molas was born in AD 566 and returned to Ireland when he was fourteen years of age, he must have arrived for his sojourn on Holy Isle some considerable time after AD 580. This was some thirty-five years after the voyage of St Brendan, so it it likely that by that time the monastery at Kilpatrick, if there was a monastery, was well established, and various *cillean* active throughout the island. The extent to which St Molas figures in island tradition may be due to the position of his cave, close to a bay providing one of the best natural harbours in the west of Scotland, and in the age of sail constantly thronged with sheltering ships, but is more likely to have resulted from the fact that he championed the usages of the Roman against those of the Celtic church, so that his memory was held in reverence by the Roman churchmen of later times, and that of his predecessors neglected or even spurned. That he introduced Christianity to Arran, as many assume, is very unlikely. It is even a matter of doubt as to whether his cave on Holy Isle is the only cave on the island to have been distinguished in Dalriadic times by a holy inmate.

A carving on the central pillar of the cave at Drumadoon, now

On left, figure with axes from Pictish cross at Glamis; on right, figure with bow from King's Cave

known as the King's Cave, after Robert Bruce, but associated by both Martin and Pennant with Fionn, has been thought by some earlier writers to represent a two-handed sword. It is plainly a cross, rising out of stylised foliage, and to the right of its head there is a carving of the upper half of a human figure with both arms raised, and in the hands what appears to be a bow, held in such a way as to form an arc over the head. This bears in outline some stylistic resemblance to the human part of a centaur carved on the upper right-hand corner of a Pictish cross slab situated in the manse garden at Glamis, except that in the latter two axes are held aloft instead of a bow. Norah Chadwick has discerned a further similarity in style between one of the horse carvings in the King's Cave and others in Inverurie and Burg-head. The carvings suggest not only early use of the cave as a chapel, but some traffic in Dalriadic times between the Scots and the Picts, not only in missionaries, but in stone-carvers.

VIKINGS

It is significant that in Lamlash, a name commemorating the sojourn of an anchorite, the island has its single link with a member of the kindred of Gabran, its Dalriadic owners. The island seems at this period to have been away from the centre of warfare and politics, a sanctuary for holy men rather than a battleground for heroes. It may not always have been peaceful, though we have no record to the contrary. Then, less than 300 years after Dalriada was founded, the Viking raids began. There was a descent on Iona in AD 795, and another on Kintyre in 797. These early raids were carried out by lesser chiefs, not by kings or earls. They were not attempts at colonisation, or at conquest to establish political supremacy : they were crude acts of piracy. The raiders were heathen, and the monasteries attracted them because of their treasures. Lindisfarne, a daughter monas-tery of Iona, was raided as early as AD 793, and Iona again in 802 and 806. Ireland received attention during the same period, and many of its monasteries, too, were ravaged, by men who would tear the gold mountings from a beautifully illuminated manuscript gospel and throw the book away. Yet they may not have been worse than the pre-Christian Celts, or even than some of those who claimed to have been converted, and indeed many of the most ruthless of them were subdued in the end, not by the sword, but by the cross, and some of them died as monks.

That Arran suffered in the early raids is almost certain. The evidence of the Viking impact on the island comes partly from archaeology, partly from place-names, and partly from chronicles and sagas. Balfour, in the first volume of *The Book of Arran*, discusses two grave mounds. The first, situated by the right bank of the Blairmore burn, about 170 ft above high-water mark, was levelled in 1896 to provide a site for the house now named Douglas Villa. This was four years before Balfour made his survey, but the fragments discovered were given to him for examination. These were an *umbo*, or shield boss, and a *sax*, or single-edged sword, which had been doubled when placed above the shield in the grave. The *umbo* was exactly of the type found in Norway in grave mounds of the late eighth or the early ninth century, so the Lamlash mound was considered to have covered one of the earliest Viking burials in Scotland. If the dating is sound, it seems probable that the Viking who met his end at Lamlash was from the fleet which raided Kintyre in AD 797, and if there really was a monastery at Kilpatrick it may well have been that fleet which closed its history.

The second of the Viking burials, under a boat-shaped mound, has already been mentioned. It lies landward of the small round fort on King's Cross Point. Under it Balfour found, among other things, some calcined human bones, the rivets of a ship, and a small coin, the latter a *styca* of Wygmund, Archbishop of York, which may have been minted at any time between AD 837 and 854. The mound must, therefore, have been raised either towards the end of this period or some time later, how much later we can only guess.

In AD 851 the Irish were fighting with Danes against Norwegians in Ireland, where they gained a victory, but in the same year the Norwegian Olaf the White appeared there and achieved supremacy, and for about twenty years was king of Dublin. Mackenzie links the grave mound on King's Cross Point with an expedition in 870 by Olaf the White to Alcluyd, the stronghold of the Strathclyde British at Dumbarton, which he besieged for three weeks. Mackenzie suggests that the burial at King's Cross Point may have been that of a Viking, perhaps of Arran, who belonged to the Norwegian company and met his death during the siege; and to explain the passage of the coin from York he claims that Olaf the White was accompanied on the Dumbarton raid by Ivar the Boneless, a Dane who, with two brothers, Halfdan and Ubbi, had captured York in AD 866, and fought in the north for several years before marching south to winter in London in 871-2. This is a neat theory, but attempts to substantiate it reveal disturbing differences of opinion between authorities as to the identity of the Ivar who was active with Olaf the White in AD 870. Earlier writers on the Vikings agree with Mackenzie, but the author of a volume published as recently as 1960,

Johannes Brøndsted, maintains that the Ivar who was active with Olaf the White in AD 870, and who followed him as king of Dublin when he had to return to Norway later in the same year, was his own brother. It was this Norwegian Ivar, according to Brøndsted, and not the Danish Ivar the Boneless, who founded the dynasty which was to be engaged in warfare from that date to the end of the century, first with the Irish, who in AD 901 temporarily drove the Norwegians into the north of England, and then with the Danes under Halfdan, who by that time was back in York colonising Northumbria. If Brøndsted is right, the passage of the coin from York to the ship burial on King's Cross Point is likely to have belonged to this later period.

A grandson of Ivar of Dublin, Olaf Cuaran, was king of York for a short time in the 940s. He became converted to Christianity while in the north of England and subsequently married a daughter of Constantine, king of the united Picts and Scots. He returned to Dublin to rule until near the end of the century, when Brian Boroimhe, the first king to secure the sovereignty of all Ireland, defeated him at Tara. After his defeat Olaf Cuaran retired to Iona to spend his remaining years in the by now Roman monastery there. In the light of his travels, the possibilities for the passage of a coin from York to Arran are endless. Yet Brøndsted is not infallible. He states, for instance, that a cremated ship burial in the Ile de Groise off southern Brittany, opposite Lorient, is the only known Viking cremation grave in western Europe; but if Balfour found calcined human bones in the ship burial at King's Cross Point, as he says he did, at least two have been known for some time.

It is now denied that in the last quarter of the ninth century Harald Finehair, king of Norway, brought Man and the Sudreyjar even nominally under his sovereignty, but Magnus Barefoot certainly exerted a compelling sovereignty at the end of the tenth century. Yet the kingdom was far from the centre of Norwegian authority, and for much of the Viking period was probably very loosely knit. That Arran was occupied throughout the early Viking period is almost certain, but it would appear from the evidence of place-names that the earlier population was not to any extent supplanted, and this is probably true of most of the former Dalriadic area, although not of the Outer Hebrides,

Lewis in particular. Some prominent Arran place-names the Vikings adapted to their own Norse, as *Eilean Molaise*, which became Mallasey or Melansay, the suffix 'sey' or 'say' being Norse for 'island'. Arran itself, in modern Gaelic *Arainn*, they called Herrey or Hersey, and this, too, has been interpreted as an adaptation, Mackenzie regarding it as Norse for 'lofty island' and Firsoff, the author of *Arran with Camera and Sketch-Book*, as Norse for 'stag island', these being the meanings respectively attributed to the Gaelic original. The manipulation of place-names is a pleasant pursuit, but until some meaning can be suggested which fits Arran equally with the Island of Aran off the coast of Donegal, and the Aran Islands off Galway, it would be wise to regard the derivation as unsolved. The Irish islands are neither noticeably lofty nor populated by red deer, and are not likely ever to have been so.

The Vikings gave their own names to the more prominent features of the landscape, as the highest hill, *Geita-fjall*, 'goat mountain'; and some of the main bays, as *Sandvik*, 'sand bay', in Gaelic *Sannaig*, now Sannox, and *Breidavik*, 'broad bay', now Brodick. Such general place-names would indicate no more than a fairly short-lived settlement, and it has been argued by Mackenzie MacBride that the Vikings never conquered the west of the island, but simply maintained a harbour or two in the east. But a study of Appendix D to the second volume of *The Book of Arran*, in which Robert L. Bremner lists the Norse place-names, shows not only that they are spread fairly generally throughout the island, but prove a fairly prolonged domination. It is true that there are no farm or village names in Norse, no 'bosts', as in Lewis, which where plentiful indicate a thorough colonisation. But many of the glens have obviously been long enough settled by Vikings to retain the memory in their 'dale' endings, and several such as Glen Chalmadale, Glen Scorrodale, and Ormidale, may even commemorate the name of the settler. But the most certain indication of the nature of the occupation comes from a group of place-names which are not Norse but Gaelic.

These are the farm or field names which indicate that a Gaelic-speaking population paid rent to Viking overlords. In Dalriadic times, at least in Ireland, the unit on which dues were paid to the chief was a standard *baile* or village of twenty houses, each house having land for twenty-one cows and their followers, and paying the value equivalent of three cows in rent. Modified forms of this system were introduced into Dalriada in Scotland, and traces of it survive in the place-names of other Dalriadic areas, so it almost certainly applied in Arran also. Now in Arran, where the more fertile land is scattered in limited pockets, larger communities would be comparatively rare, and we should expect to find place-names with the prefix 'kerry' or 'auchter', from *cearadh*, 'quarter' and *ochda*, 'eighth', denoting a quarter or an eighth of a standard *baile*. We can deduce little from the fact that there are several place-names prefixed by 'bal' or 'bally', as Balnacoole, Ballygowan, Ballymeanoch, and Ballygonachie, for the word *baile* came to denote simply a village, standard or not. What is significant is that there are no place-names with the prefix 'kerry' or 'auchter', examples of which survive in Bute and even in Kintyre. The reason would seem to be that Arran was occupied by the Vikings long enough for its Dalriadic rent place-names to fall into disuse. The pre-feudal rent place-names of Arran are such as Dippen, Pien, Penrioch, Penalister or Benlister, Aucheleffan, Levencorroch, and Feorline, which indicate that the farms or fields in question paid rent valued in multiples or fractions of a penny: the Gaelic for twopence being *da pheighinn*, for a penny *peighinn*, for a halfpenny *leath-pheighinn*, and for a farthing *feoirlinn*. The penny in question was of silver, containing a twentieth of an ounce. It was first introduced into Scotland by the Vikings.

The number of these Viking rent place-names is not large, but rent place-names in general are never plentiful, because they cannot without qualification distinguish between one farm and another paying the same rent, and they lack the ability to describe, and so to identify. The majority of the old Arran place-names carry the prefix *achadh*, 'field', and this too is interesting. The *achadh* was not the enclosed piece of land which we know as a field today, but the old open field, in Dalriadic times, and probably even earlier, cultivated communally. The communal system was Celtic, and was called by the Dalriadic Scots the 'running share' system, from *raoin*, 'share', and *ruith*, 'running', later adapted into 'runrig', 'rig' being the Scots for 'ridge'. We

99

shall discuss the system more fully later. Meanwhile it is enough to say that it not only preceded the Viking occupation, but continued until the agrarian revolution of the early nineteenth century. The Vikings themselves did not enclose their fields, but where they settled in farming communities they held their strips of arable ground in individual ownership. They would not permit such ownership to a subject people. The fact that the language of the field names in Viking times was Gaelic, as Aucheleffan (*achadh leath-pheighinn*) proves, while showing that the Dalriadic population was not supplanted, suggests also that the Scots were left, so long as they paid their rent, to cultivate their fields according to their own traditional system.

The Vikings had come at first as mere plunderers, with few or no womenfolk, and when they settled many of them selected mates from among their female captives. The result was to undermine their hold on their conquest, for in the former Dalriadic area of the Sudreyjar there arose a mixed population deriving its language and traditions from its Gaelic-speaking mothers. By the twelfth century the name Scot was being applied to the people of the new united kindom of Picts, Scots, British, and Angles, and the term Gael to the original Scot of the former Dalriada. The term applied to the Vikings was *gaill*, 'strangers', and the new mixed race of the Sudreyjar became known as *gaill-Gaidheil*, 'stranger Gaels', in English rendered Gall-Gael. They began their struggle for independence not only against the Viking rulers of Man and the Sudreyjar, but against the new feudal kingdom of Scotland, which was anxious to wrest the western isles from the overlordship of Norway.

The first leader to emerge as a virtually independent ruler of the old Dalriadic territory, and soon to style himself king of the Isles, was Somerled, a man of mixed Norwegian and Scottish descent, who had married Raghnildis, a daughter of Olaf Bitling, king of Man and the Sudreyjar. When Olaf's son and successor, Godrod the Black, proved unpopular with the Gall-Gael, Somerled did not hesitate to set up his son Dugall in opposition to his brother-in-law, in an insurrection possibly constitutional in terms of the old Celtic law of tanistry. The issue was fought out at sea in 1156, and the galleys of Somerled, some of them almost certainly from Arran, gained the victory. The old Dalriadic area was ceded to him, Godrod retaining Man and the Hebrides north of Ardnamurchan. From that date until Norway sold the western isles to Scotland Somerled's kingdom was virtually independent, although nominally he and his successors were under the overlordship of Norway for their island, and of Scotland for their mainland territories.

Somerled's struggle for independence, and possibly for the acquisition of a more extensive kingdom, brought him into conflict with the Scottish king, Malcolm II, and in an expedition into the upper Clyde he was killed at Renfrew. After his death his son Dugall, chief in Argyll, was king of the Isles, and then Dugall's brother Ragnvaldr, more commonly known as Reginald or Ranald, chief in Kintyre and Islay, followed him. Ranald and a younger brother, Angus, chief in Bute, both seem to have claimed Arran, and in the dispute Angus and his sons were wiped out. From Dugall are descended the MacDougalls of Lorne and the Campbells of Argyll; from Ranald, whose descendants maintained their grip on Kintyre and the Dalriadic islands, the MacDonalds of the Isles. Later feuds between Campbells and MacDonalds were probably due to the growth of feudal as opposed to Celtic ideas of succession. The Campbells, descended from Dugall, king of the Isles after Somerled, could in terms of feudal ideas claim plausibly to be heirs to the kingdom. Ranald had followed Dugall, however, under the law of tanistry. The MacDonalds took their name from his oldest son, Donald, who succeeded him as king of the Isles. Until this time permanent surnames had been unknown. Ranald was Ranald MacSomerled, and his son Donald MacRanald, but after Donald's son Angus, who was of course Angus MacDonald, all direct descendants were surnamed MacDonald.

Another permanent surname originating at this time, which was to dominate Scottish and British history for several centuries, and to figure with that of MacDonald in the history of Arran, was Stewart. For a granddaughter of the slaughtered Angus MacSomerled, known in folk poetry as Angus of Arran, married Alexander the *Hie Steuart* or High Steward of Scotland, a

Norman who on the strength of his marriage claimed Bute and Arran, and invaded them to enforce his claim. He was not unopposed. Ruari MacRanald, a brother of Donald, king of the Isles, claimed Bute and Arran also, and probably under the law of tanistry had a better right than Alexander. Alexander had of course the backing of the Scottish king, and in the end the Stewarts prevailed, to gain not only Bute and Arran but Scotland, and eventually Great Britain itself, but for a long time the struggle between the MacDonalds and the Stewarts in the southwest of Scotland was a source of disruption, and in standard histories the MacDonalds have come to be treated as lawless rebels. It should be remembered that they probably held Celtic, as opposed to Norman, ideas of political right, and if they had some of the piratical blood of the Vikings in their veins, so, too, had those who brought the feudal system to England, by way of Normandy, in 1066, and to Scotland, by invitation of David I, less than 100 years later.

Although the Stewarts ultimately prevailed, Ranald MacSomerled did not fail to leave his mark on Arran, and it was a mark of his piety rather than of his prowess in war. After the death of his father he founded in his memory the monastery of Saddell in Kintyre, and among the lands with which he endowed it were twenty merklands in the fertile strath of Shiskine. Since this grant precedes the incorporation of Arran into the Scottish kingdom, which took place three years after the battle of Largs in 1263, it has a bearing on whether the establishment of the ancient monastery on Holy Isle was the work of Ranald, or of his descendant, the 'good John of Islay', Lord of the Isles under the Scottish king, who died in 1380. Balfour accepts the former view, and Mackenzie the latter.

Now while Arran was in the Sudreyjar it was in the episcopal see of Sudreyjar and Man, and the archiepiscopal see first of Hamburg, and then of Trondhjem; although the archiepiscopal link must have been nominal only. The old Celtic chapels in Arran may have fallen into disuse, for their link with Man, after the defeat of Godrod by Somerled in 1156, would be seriously weakened. It is, therefore, almost certain that with the grant of the Shiskine lands to Saddell would go responsibility for any Arran chapels. If Holy Isle had by this time become a place of

102

pilgrimage, as is suggested by the names cut in the walls of the cave of St Molas, some of them stylistically earlier than the date of the battle of Largs, it is likely that a small hospice would be established for the accommodation of pilgrims, and the collection of their offerings. On the other hand, the 'good John of Islay' was indeed granted Kintyre in 1377, and would, therefore, acquire an interest in Saddell Abbey. But although the Shiskine lands were retained by Saddell Abbey until it fell into disuse about 1467, the rest of Arran was by 1377 in the possession of the Stewarts, and it is unlikely that John of Islay would have the right to establish a monastery on Holy Isle, in spite of his interest in Saddell Abbey.

As early as 1357 the Stewart lord of Knapdale and Arran had granted the 'churches of St Mary and St Brigid in the island of Arran' to the monastery of Kilwinning, in Ayrshire. That the chapels and offerings of the two churches were stipulated as part of the grant proves that by this time Arran had been divided into two parishes. Both were thus linked with the eastern mainland, and probably remained so until they were attached to the presbytery of Kintyre in 1638. The church of St Mary was probably that just traceable on the left bank of the Sliddery Water, opposite the point where it is joined by the Allt Duilleachry, on the farm of Bennecarrigan. The church of St Brigid was almost certainly that whose ruin stands in the graveyard at Blairmore, Lamlash, and which Balfour judged from its style to belong to the fourteenth century. It seems likely that by the time this church was built Holy Isle had lost its link with Saddell Abbey, and that the little Gothic chapel there, whose ruins are mentioned as having been seen by Robertson, who toured the western isles shortly before 1768, was built while the two parish churches of Arran were under the jurisdiction of Kilwinning, or shortly after they were granted with most of the island to James, Lord Hamilton, in 1503. This small chapel would, until it fell into ruin, serve those who crossed to Holy Isle for burials, which continued there until about 1790. The great probability is that the original monastery, and the old pilgrim way which led to it from Shiskine by the Clauchan and Benlister glens, passing on the summit the *Cnoc na Croise*, or 'hillock of the cross', belong to the days of Ranald.

103

CELTIC AND VIKING INVASIONS

The last of the Viking names carved on the walls of the cave of St Molas on Holy Isle are Arran's only visible link with an event which practically settled the conflict between the Stewarts and the MacDonalds of the Isles as far as Arran was concerned. This was the battle of Largs. On a wider scale it settled the conflict between Norway and Scotland over the former's claim to all the western isles of Scotland.

When Alexander II succeeded William the Lion in 1214 he inherited a kingdom consolidated by the subjection of the mainland territories most resistant to feudal rule: Galloway in the south-west, a nest of Gall-Gael, and the far north, for a long time under the Vikings. He turned his attention now to the mainland holdings of the descendants of Somerled, and brought these under the superiority of the Scottish crown. This was too much for one Ospak, a son of Dugall MacSomerled, who preferred to be loyal to Norway rather than Scotland, probably because it was further away. He went to Norway and was despatched by king Hakon with a fleet to restore Norwegian supremacy. Although he gained some support and succeeded in capturing Rothesay castle after three days of hard fighting, he had to retreat, died of sickness, and his fleet of about eighty ships, after wintering at Man and raiding Kintyre, which was being encroached upon by the Stewarts, returned to Norway. Alexander II offered to buy the western isles from king Hakon, but the offer was refused, and Alexander collected a fleet to take them by force. He died, however, in Oban Bay in 1249.

Alexander III determined to finish the work his father had begun, and so alarmed Hakon that the latter levied all Norway for men, and took to sea with a fleet which by the time it reached Kintyre had more than 120 ships. With Hakon were Magnus of Man, Angus of Islay, nominally king of the Isles but losing his grip on Kintyre and Arran, and other leading descendants of Somerled. The only exception was Ewan, now chief of the kindred of Dugall MacSomerled, who had once refused to break with Hakon to satisfy Alexander II. He now refused to break with Alexander III to satisfy Hakon. He either naïvely believed that having made a promise, even under duress, he ought to keep it, or he was trimming his sails to the wind.

If the latter he was shrewd. After harrying Kintyre, Hakon

104

brought his fleet round the Mull and anchored in Lamlash bay. Here he began to parley with messengers from Alexander III, who was willing to compound for the possession of Arran, Bute, and the Cumbraes, but Hakon would make no concessions. The fleet moved up to the Cumbraes, and negotiations dragged on. It was late in September, with the weather likely to break, and it became clear to Hakon that Alexander was playing for time. The truce was abandoned, and Hakon sent some ships up Loch Long to harry into the Lennox. Then on Monday, 1 October, with the main fleet lying at the Cumbraes, a storm began. By morning, four of the ships, one of them laden with supplies, were stranded at Largs. Scots there started to loot the supply ship, but the wind slackened, Hakon was able to send reinforcements, and the Scots were forced to retire. On Wednesday the looting was renewed, Hakon himself landed with a force, and the supplies were being transferred into smaller ships when a Scottish army was sighted. There are said by Mackenzie, whose excellent account of the battle is based on the *Saga of Hakon*, to have been 8-900 Norwegians on the beach, while the Scots were ten times as many, 500 of them mounted. There may have been some bias in the saga estimate, but it is likely that the Norwegians were outnumbered. They seem to have put up an excellent fight, and after a battle which raged all day succeeded in getting into their ships and sailing away. On the Thursday they landed, presumably under truce, to take away their dead, and on Friday, the storm having slackened, they returned to Lamlash, and for several days lay anchored there, wondering whether to winter in Ireland as they were invited to do, or return to Norway. Hakon was for remaining, but his men were against it, so he sailed for home.

Before doing so he made a distribution of the islands. Bute was given to one Ruari, not Ruari MacRanald, but one who seems to have claimed descent from Angus MacSomerled, and so was a rival to the claims of Alexander the High Steward. Arran was given to one Murchard or Margad, whose descent is uncertain, but whose name would appear to be derived from *murcadh*, 'sea warrior', in which case he may well have been an ancestor of the Murchies, who survive on Arran, and in Kintyre, to this day.

These grants were made by Hakon when his power to support them was slipping away. He fell ill at Kirkwall in Orkney while on his way home, and died there on the thirteenth of December. Three years later, in 1266, his successor agred to sell the western isles to Scotland for 4,000 marks down and 100 yearly, the Norway Annual. So the Norwegian occupation of Arran, whose opening had its record in the grave-mound at the mouth of the Blairmore burn, associated with the raid of AD 797, was brought to its close when the great fleet of Hakon, which first anchored in Lamlash bay in September of 1263, sailed out of it in October, having been defeated more by skilful strategy and bad weather than from lack of valour.

It was probably in September that certain of Hakon's men, whiling away time at Lamlash awaiting the outcome of nego- tiations, cut their names on the wall of the cave of St Molas. A few of the runes belong to an earlier date, but that others were cut in 1263 is clear from that which reads *Vigleikr stallari reist*, 'Vigleikr the king's marshal cut this'. Whether the runes were a piece of vandalism, or the record of a pious pilgrimage, can only be guessed, but if the latter, Vigleikr's piety must have been rather a matter of superstitious awe than of genuine devo- tion. The saint's self-abnegation was surely beyond his compre- hension, for he was one of the leaders of the savage raids into the Lennox.

Page 107: (above) Brodick castle before the building of the Victorian wing of 1844. The drawing shows the castle as it was left by the Cromwellian garrison, with entrance through the battery; *(below)* the drawing-room of Brodick castle, in the Victorian wing. Among the portraits visible are those of Princess Marie of Baden and of Mary Louise, Duchess of Montrose

Page 108: (above) Lamlash in 1895. The large white building is the old parish church. The larger vessel on the beach is the revenue cutter *Wickham*; the smaller is the factor's yacht; *(below)* Hamilton Terrace, built by the 12th Duke of Hamilton, replaced the row of white-washed cottages shown on the right of the picture above

5   FEUDAL OVERLORDS

IT is known that sometime in the thirteenth century, before the battle of Largs, Angus MacDonald, king of the Isles, and his uncle Ruari MacRanald, ancestor of the MacGrories of Bute, had garrisoned the castles of Rothesay, Lamlash (probably on Holy Isle), and Brodick (possibly in Glencloy), against Alexander the High Steward, who claimed Bute and Arran through his marriage with a granddaughter of Angus MacSomerled. After the cession of the western isles of Scotland to Alexander III Bute and Arran were brought formally into the kingdom of Scotland, and no doubt the Stewart claim to the island had from this time the authority of a feudal right.

It is necessary to understand that with the introduction of the feudal system into Scotland, which followed the accession of David I, two considerable changes took place in regard to the Scottish monarchy. The first was that succession became patrilineal instead of by tanistry. The second was that the king became the owner of the land of the kingdom, part of which he retained for his own use, and parts of which he granted to his earls, who held them as his vassals. The earls in turn could grant land to barons, who in turn could grant land to knights, all of whom had to have their grants approved by the king, and were vassals of the king as well as of their more immediate superiors. Under the ancient Celtic system the king was elected by the chiefs, and the chiefs by their kindred, the kindred for this purpose being the descendants of a common great-grandfather. Land too was owned by the kindred. The king was not, therefore, the owner of any land but that shared with his kindred. He was leader of the people. That this attitude to the kingship persisted among the Scots even late into feudal times is apparent from the fact that in Scotland the king was known as king of Scots, rather than of Scotland.

A common criticism of the Celtic law of tanistry is that conflicts between contending branches of a dynasty arose with great frequency, and of the system of land ownership that it weakened the power of the king to deal with rebellious chiefs. With the introduction of the feudal system the right to the succession was thought to be put beyond doubt, and where a vassal rebelled he could be deprived of his lands and another, whose interest it would be to subdue him, appointed in his place. But the claim for the feudal system that it did indeed knit the kingdom more closely under the royal authority carries little conviction. A great drawback was that its introduction in the early stages was entrusted to men alien in race and speech to the people on the land. Unaccustomed to the new system, the latter saw no right by which the king could send a stranger into their territory to claim it from the kindred of their chief, and they resented it all the more because the stranger was a Norman, speaking French, and ruthless into the bargain. It is doubtful if Scotland could ever have been moulded into a nation had it not been that so many of the Normans insinuated themselves into their new territories, like Alexander the High Steward, by marrying native women, so that in time, as an effect of the maternal influence, their descendants came to acquire a degree of national feeling which they could use, when the claims of the English king to the overlordship of Scotland conflicted with their personal advantage, as an excuse for putting that advantage first.

THE WAR OF INDEPENDENCE

There is little evidence that the heroes of the Scottish war of independence, save the comparatively humble William Wallace, were motivated primarily by national feeling. But although the Normans in Scotland put their own advantage first, they were able to do so with an appearance of patriotism because they were sufficiently in touch with national feeling to understand its force, and since it became stronger as the war continued and the English became more oppressive, they were the more readily accepted as leaders in a great struggle for freedom. What really welded the people of Scotland into a nation was the need to resist English aggression, a need created by the thirst for domination inseparable from the feudal system, no doubt, but deriving its real force from the old system of land ownership by kindred,

110

which gave the people as a whole a deep conviction of their right to live freely on their own land.

The English claim to overlordship came with the death of Alexander III, when in spite of the alleged superiority of feudal to Celtic ideas, the succession became a matter of dispute. On the death of Alexander's granddaughter, the Maid of Norway, his only surviving descendant, there were three main claimants to the throne, Balliol, Bruce, and Hastings. Balliol was descended from the eldest of the three daughters of David of Huntingdon, a brother of William the Lion, and Bruce and Hastings from the younger two respectively. If Balliol seems the man with the obvious right, it should be remembered that the matter was more complicated than it appears. Balliol was a grandson of the eldest daughter, and Bruce a son of the second. Bruce was, therefore, closer in male succession. The Scottish lords could not agree, and sought a verdict from Edward I of England, who was already the superior of many of them for lands they held in England. He chose Balliol, on condition that he became his vassal. Bruce would have accepted the same condition. Balliol soon found his position impossible, eventually defied Edward, and was dethroned. As the other rival claimants manœuvred for position Edward tightened his grip on the country, ostensibly to keep the peace, but obviously with a view to its complete subjection. Insurrection broke out under William Wallace, a Strathclyde Briton by origin, who at first gained grudging support from some of the lords. In the end he was deserted by them, went into hiding, was betrayed by a Stewart, and ultimately condemned in Westminster Hall, hanged, beheaded, drawn and quartered.

During this period, when Edward was carving up Scotland among men he could trust, we have him first granting Arran to Thomas Bysset. This was a descendant of Walter Bysset of Aboyne, who in 1242, in the reign of Alexander II, had been beaten by the Earl of Atholl in a tournament held at Haddington. By what seemed more than a coincidence, the earl was that night burnt to death in his house. The Scottish lords laid the blame on Walter Bysset and his brother John, and the king having banished them they took service with Henry III, who gave them estates, Walter in England, and John in Ulster. Walter is said to have died in Arran in 1251, well before the battle of Largs, and it may be that he was helping his Ulster brother to establish a foothold there. His property went to his nephew Thomas, possibly a son of John of Ulster. At least it was from Ulster that shortly after the defeat of Wallace at Falkirk, a Thomas Bysset turned up at Ayr, where Edward had gone after the battle, and although it seems that Bysset had come to Scotland to help the Scots, on hearing of the defeat of Wallace he offered himself to Edward. He maintained that the people of Arran had submitted to him, and asked that the island should be granted by Edward to himself and his heirs. To this Edward agreed, and soon a Hugh Bysset was operating a fleet in the Clyde on Edward's behalf. In 1306 Robert Bruce, grandson of the Bruce already mentioned and of the native Marjorie of Carrick, defied Edward and was crowned at Scone, only to have to go into hiding, and by January 1307 Hugh Bysset and John of Mentieth, the Stewart betrayer of Wallace, were occupied together in the isles 'putting down' Bruce and his accomplices.

Bruce had a supporter in Angus MacDonald of the Isles and naturally, when he had to flee the mainland through lack of support there, he went with his followers to the west. Even there he does not seem to have been safe, and he took refuge, in the winter of 1306-7, in Rathlin, a little island off the north coast of Ireland. The story of his adventures at this time we have from a verse chronicle of John Barbour, Archdeacon of Aberdeen, entitled *The Bruce*. Barbour lived from 1316 to 1395 and was not, therefore, an eyewitness, but he wrote when people who had participated in the events were still alive, and he had met and talked to some of them. His aim was to tell the truth as far as he knew it, and although his work has a natural bias in favour of his hero, and has been proved inaccurate in some unimportant details, it is not a romance like Scott's *Lord of the Isles*, a later poem covering the same events, in which poetic licence is taken without scruple. Nor is it a frankly chauvinistic work like Blind Harry's poem on Wallace. It is a reasonably sober verse chronicle, conflicting with other available evidence in no important essential.

This is stressed because the chronicle provides the only nearly contemporary account of Bruce's adventures in Arran, and in view of the extent to which these have been embroidered by

112

tradition, it is important to note exactly what it says. When Bruce had wintered in Rathlin Douglas and Sir Robert Boyd approached him for permission to take a party and visit Arran, in the hope that they might be able to strike a blow against the English governor there. This was no other than Hastings, already mentioned as one of the main claimants to the Scottish throne. What had happened to the grant of Arran to Thomas Bysset we do not know, nor how John of Mentieth, the betrayer of Wallace, stood with Edward now, but the latter had granted to Hastings the earldom of Mentieth and the Isles, once held by John of Mentieth's elder brother, the son of a High Steward. Hastings was now in Brodick castle holding the island for England.

Douglas and Boyd left Rathlin with a small party of men in a single galley, crossed to Kintyre, and 'rowit all-wayis by the land' until night was near, when they crossed over to Arran

> And under ane bra thair galay dreuch,
> And syne it helit weill ineuch;
> Thair takill, ayris, and thair stere,
> Thai hyde all on the samyn maner .
> And held thair way rycht in the nycht,
> Sa that, or day wes dawyn lycht,
> Thai war enbuschit the castell neir,
> Arrayit on the best maneir.

It would seem from this that they landed somewhere in the west of the island and drew their galley up under a brae, or hillside. They 'helit' or covered it, and hid their tackle, oars, and rudder in the same way, and then immediately made their way across the island by night, to arrive in the vicinity of Brodick castle just before dawn.

It happened by chance that the under-warden of the castle had the previous evening brought to the shore below it three boats containing provisions, clothing, and arms, and these a party of over thirty men now began to unload. Douglas and his men attacked and overcame them. The sound of the fighting was heard in the castle, and more men were sent to attempt a rescue. Douglas saw them coming and immediately went to meet them.

> And quhen thai of the castell saw
> Hym cum on thaim forouten aw,
> Thai fled forouten mair debate;
> And thai thame followed to the yhate,
> And slew of thame, as thai in past;
> Bot thai thair yhet barrit so fast,
> At thai mycht do at thame no mair;
> Tharfor thai left thame ilkane thair,
> And turnit to the see againe.

In other words, Douglas chased the castle party back to the gate, which was shut against him so fast that he could do no more, so he turned to the sea again.

Back on the shore Douglas found that the three unloaded boats had put to sea, but the wind was so strong that the crews could hardly row against it, and two were wrecked. The arms, clothing, provisions, 'wyne and othir thing' which had been unloaded were seized by Douglas and his men, who 'held thair way, rycht glad and joyfull of thair pray'. Where they went we cannot be quite certain, but it was 'till a strenth', that is, to some sort of stronghold. A later reference describes it as having been in a 'woddy glen'. The only strength near Brodick castle, and in a woody glen, would be the old fort near the head of Glencloy. It would of course be in ruins, even if it were not a Dalriadic round fort but a later structure raised after the Viking occupation by the kings of the Isles, but there might be just enough of it left to afford some protection, and in any case the site would be a defence in itself.

Ten days later, to continue the story told by the chronicle, Bruce himself arrived in Arran with thirty small galleys. Where he landed we can only guess. The chronicle says

> The King arrivit in Arane;
> And syne to the land is gane,
> And in a toune tuk his herbery:

By 'toune' is meant a *baile*, a clachan or small village composed of the dwellings and outbuildings of a runrig farm community. Which 'toune' in Arran is indicated again we can only guess, but since there is no mention later in the chronicle of Bruce having moved his fleet before he left the island, it seems likely that he landed on the east coast, possibly at Whiting Bay, or in the bay opposite Holy Isle, then still Lamlash. Exchequer rolls of 1449, some 140 years later, list farm communities in the area at 'Knokanelze, Achinarn, Ardlavenys, Monymor, Penycroce, Latternaguanach, Blarebeg, Blaremore, Dowbrowach, Marcynegles and Clachlan', represented today in all but two cases by the names Knockankelly, Auchencairn, Monamore, King's Cross, Letter, Blairbeg, Blairmore, Margnaheglish and Clauchlands. The change of the name Penycroce to King's Cross is the result of a tradition linking that place with Bruce's visit, and if he did take shelter in the 'toune' at King's Cross it is likely that his fleet was drawn up on the shore at Whiting Bay during the period of his stay on the island.

When Bruce had taken up his quarters in the 'toune' he

> . . . sperit syne full specialy,
> Giff ony man couth tell tithand,
> Of ony strangers in that land.

A woman told him that their governor had recently been discomfited by a party of strangers, who were now encamped in a 'stalward place heirby'. He told her that the men were his and asked her to show him the place. This is curious, for even if his fleet had been in Lamlash bay the walk to the old fort in Glencloy would have been long enough to justify his asking for a man to guide him. Later in the story we learn that his 'hostes', who may or may not have been the same woman, had two sons who joined Bruce's company. The fact that a man was not asked to guide Bruce to the camp of Douglas suggests that on the arrival of Bruce's fleet the men of the island had taken to the hills until they learned that it was safe to return. On being shown the 'sted' in the 'woddy glen' where Douglas had camped, Bruce blew his horn three times in a way recognised by Douglas and Boyd, who joined him, and returned with him to his 'herbery', or quarters in the 'toune'.

Then follows the story of how Bruce decided to send Cuthbert, a native of Carrick, over the firth to that district to find if it was held by friends or enemies, and if the former to light a fire on an arranged date at Turnberry Point, as a signal that it was safe for Bruce to cross with his fleet and make a landing. The story of how the blaze was seen towards evening on the date arranged, and how it turned out to be the glow from a fire made by farmers who were burning pease straw, is not relevant here. What is important is that every detail of the story after the reunion of Bruce and Douglas suggests that the fleet lay throughout on the east of the island, and more probably at Whiting Bay than elsewhere, since from King's Cross Turnberry would be clearly visible, whereas from any 'toune' near Lamlash bay the view would have been impeded.

How long Bruce remained on the island before crossing to Carrick is not clear from the chronicle, but it must have been for some days, and during that time no doubt Bruce's party kept an eye on Brodick castle to ensure that there was no attack from it, nor any escape of messengers to the mainland. If Bruce had captured Brodick castle, defeating Hastings, the event would have been sufficiently noteworthy to be remembered, and Barbour would surely have recorded it, but there is no hint of any such thing. Nor is there any mention of any stay by Bruce in the King's Cave at Drumadoon, nor is such a stay likely, since it is explicitly stated that he had quarters in the 'toune' near which he landed. Some men of Douglas's advance party, however, must surely have gone back to the west coast to retrieve the galley they had hidden there, and these may have spent some days in the cave at Drumadoon. The association of the cave with Bruce may have that justification.

The woman who sent her two sons to Carrick with Bruce is described as his 'hostes'. She claimed to have second sight, and told him that he would ultimately succeed and free his kingdom, sending her sons with him to show her faith in her own prophecy, and hinting that she expected them to be well rewarded. Bruce was somewhat comforted by what she said,

> The-quhethir he trowit nocht full weill
> Hir spek, for he had gret ferly
> How scho suld wit it sekirly

In other words, he did not altogether believe her, for he wondered how she could be so certain. The sending of the two sons and the hint at the reward expected is all that is to be found

116

in Barbour in support of the local tradition, not recorded by Martin in 1695, but repeated regularly since the visit of Pennant in 1772, that several of the oldest Arran families, in particular the Fullartons of Kilmichael in Glencloy, were granted lands in Arran by Bruce in recognition of the loyal service they gave him during this particular visit to the island. Who his 'hostes' was we do not know, nor if her two sons lived to be rewarded. But we do know that there is no record of any grant by Bruce of land on the island to any Arran man. Fullartons were granted land in Arran later, as we shall see, but that they were indigenous and lived there before Bruce's visit, or that their original name was MacLouy or McClowy, meaning 'son of Lewis', survives scrutiny no better than the tradition that they were granted their Kilmichael estate by Bruce. Mackenzie has suggested feasibly that *Macluaidh*, 'son of the fuller', is an attempt to translate into Gaelic the original surname, which was derived from the name of a place. There is a record of a grant of land at 'Foulerton', in Ayrshire, by James the High Steward, sometime between 1281 and 1292, to 'Adam, son of the late Alan de Foulerton'. The family was most probably Norman, and continued to be closely associated with the Stewarts, as we shall see.

That Glencloy takes its name from McClowy, the bogus Gaelic surname of the Fullartons, as Mackenzie suggests, is challenged by the rendering of the name by Nils M. Holmer, author of *The Gaelic of Arran*, as *Gleann na Cloiche*, 'glen of the stone'. Holmer, who made a close study of Arran Gaelic speech, gives the local pronunciation in international phonetic symbols as 'glaN ə kłoç', which would clinch the matter if the stone concerned could be identified. There is one very tempting probability. Martin, recording the monoliths of Arran in 1695, says 'The highest of these stones that fell under my observation was on the south side of the Kirkmichael river, and is above fifteen feet high'. The Kirkmichael river is the burn running past Kilmichael house, and known now as the Glencloy burn. What has happened to the great stone is doubtful. In Martin's time the cist near the foot of it was beginning to be disturbed by the burn, which seems to have been shifting its bed. The stone may have collapsed and may now be in the bed of the burn. But the probability is that it was removed and possibly fragmented for building

117

purposes sometime after the Revolution in 1689, when it became pious on the island to pillage not only the graven images of popery, but the megalithic evidences of heathendom.

The matter of the independence of Scotland having been settled at Bannockburn in 1314, for the time being at least, the island became once again the property of the Stewarts. Walter the High Steward, who as a young lad had fought at Bannockburn under the watchful eye of Douglas, married Bruce's daughter Marjory, and it was probably through this connection that the Mentieth branch of the Stewart family won itself back into favour. The Mentieth branch was descended from a younger brother of a former High Steward, who as his vassal held the earldom of Mentieth and the Isles, and a younger brother of the earl held as his vassal, in turn, the lands of Knapdale and Arran. Whether John of Mentieth, the betrayer of Wallace, won himself back into favour in time to acquire Knapdale and Arran before his death we do not know, but his son, of the same name, certainly was lord of Knapdale and Arran, as was his grandson, also named John of Mentieth, who granted the churches of St Mary and St Brigid in the island of Arran to the monastery at Kilwinning. Since he made the grant for the salvation of the souls of his ancestors, as well as of his own, he may have felt some of the burden of his notorious grandfather's guilt.

This younger branch of the Stewart family having failed to produce a male heir, Robert the High Steward, son of Walter, the young warrior of Bannockburn and husband of Bruce's daughter Marjory, took the lands of Knapdale and Arran back into his own possession, compensating the heiress of the last John of Mentieth with a payment of 100 pounds annually from the burgh rents and fishings of Aberdeen. This grant was made by Robert in 1387, by which time he had, as grandson of Bruce, become Robert II of Scotland. He must have acquired Knapdale and Arran before making this grant, however, for he was still High Steward when, sometime before 1371, he made a grant of Knightsland in Arran to Sir Adam de Foulartoun, son of Reginald of that Ilk in Ayrshire. Knightsland, variously described in later transactions as 'Drumruden', 'Drumrudyr or Knightslands', and 'Knychtisland alias Tonreddyr', was known to a south-end man who corresponded with Mackenzie at the begin-

ning of the present century as 'Tonereacher', which very
accurately conveys the sound of the Gaelic *tonn ridire*, from
tonn, 'wave' or 'crest', in this case a terrace of land, and *ridir*,
'knight'. The land lay between Kildonan and Levencorroch, and
was held by the Fullartons until resigned by John Fullarton of
that Ilk, lord of Corsby, in Ayrshire, in favour of James Stewart,
sheriff of Bute, and his heirs. That did not happen until 1541,
and meanwhile, in 1391, Robert III had granted to 'Fergus of
Foulartoune of Arran', presumably a younger son of the Knightsland Fullartons, the land of 'Erqwhonne', now Strathwhillan, in
Arran, and in 1400 the same king granted 'Killemechel', now
Kilmichael, to the son of this Fergus, with his father's office of
crowner of the Arran baillary. The last two grants were presumably connected with the office of crowner, which was hereditary, and remained linked with the name of Fullarton, and
the estate of Kilmichael, until it fell into disuse.

We have seen that the Fullartons were granted their Ayrshire
lands by the High Stewards, and they held their Arran lands,
in the first instance, from the same source. Before they were
granted the office of crowner in Arran the new hereditary
sheriffdom of Bute was in the hands of 'Black John Stewart', a
bastard son of Robert II, and among the perquisites of the
sheriffdom were the lands of Corrygills in Arran, close to Strathwhillan. In the Bute sheriffdom Arran was a baillary, and the
bailie the sheriff's deputy. He may have occupied Brodick castle,
and he seems usually to have been a Stewart, like the sheriff.
Quite what the duties of the crowner were is not quite clear,
but they seem to have borne some resemblance to those of the
modern coroner, which is an English but not a Scottish office.
A suggestion has been made that the office of crowner was made
necessary by the tendency of the native peoples to murder the
new Norman intruders, and that the crowner's duty was to
investigate any case of the sudden or mysterious death of a
Norman, and bring the culprit to light. Feudal justice was largely
a matter of enforcing the acceptance of the new system, and it is
obvious that the Fullartons were henchmen of the Stewarts in
this activity. The relationship would begin to alter in 1609 when
a commission of justiciary over the whole island was conferred
on the first Marquis of Hamilton, to be confirmed in 1622 to

the second Marquis, and made hereditary in the Hamilton family in 1633. They held it until after the Rising of 1745, when all such private hereditary jurisdictions were restored to the crown, and by 1772, at the time of Pennant's visit, the function of the crowner seems to have been modified into that of providing a show of force when the island rents were being collected.

'Black John' Stewart, the first of the hereditary sheriffs of Bute, and the founder of the family now represented by the Marquis of Bute, was not the only royal by-blow to receive lands in Arran. Robert III also had a bastard son John, to whom he granted the lands of Ardgowan in Renfrewshire. In 1406, the year of his death, the king added to Ardgowan's possessions 'Kildonan, with the castle, Two furlongs, Duppeny lands, the three Largies, two Keskedelis, Glenascadale and Clachan'. Mackenzie thinks the 'Two furlongs' are the two Feorlines, and that 'Clachan' is Clauchan, all in the Shiskine district. It is more likely that all the lands specified are in the south-east of the island between Kildonan and Clauchlands. 'Clachlan' for Clauchlands we have already seen, and from that to 'Clachan' is a likely slip. The Shiskine lands granted to the monastery at Saddell in the thirteenth century by Ranald MacSomerled, and subsequently confirmed to it by kings Alexander III, Robert I, David II, and Robert II, were to be confirmed by James IV in 1507, after the monastery of Saddell had been deserted, in favour of the bishop of Lismore, and remained church lands until the period of the Reformation. They may in 1406 have been temporarily filched from the church, but Mackenzie's interpretation of these two doubtful place-names is the only evidence.

We have now two bastard offshoots of the royal Stewarts holding lands in Arran, and two branches of the Fullartons. The rest of the island is royal, and while it remained so it suffered the attention of the king's enemies, the chief of which was England, still intriguing hopefully for the overlordship of Scotland. Robert III made the grant of the Arran lands to his bastard son Ardgowan in the closing months of his reign, when he was old and feeble and his brother the Earl of Albany was usurping his position. The king's elder legitimate son, the Duke of Rothesay, had been murdered by Albany, and anxious for the safety of his younger son, Prince James, Earl of Carrick, then a boy of

120

fourteen, he decided to send him to France. The prince embarked at North Berwick, but his ship was captured by the English off Flamborough Head, and although the two kingdoms were in truce he was taken prisoner. During the conflct which followed an English fleet entered the Clyde, destroying the king's castle at Brodick and burning his chapel, presumably that of St Brigid, built before 1351. Brodick castle was to suffer again in the same struggle, but not before receiving unwelcome attention from royal enemies much closer at hand. These were the descendants of Somerled, who seized every opportunity offered by the weakness at the centre of feudal authority to regain their ancient possessions.

After Bannockburn, Bruce, in spite of the help he had received from Angus Oig, grandson of the first Donald of the Isles, regranted Knapdale and Kintyre to the Stewarts, letting Angus have other lands hitherto held by those of his kindred who had joined the side of Edward I. But Angus's son John, already mentioned as the 'good John of Islay', married as his second wife Lady Margaret Stewart, a daughter of Robert the High Steward, on whose accession to the throne as Robert II John of Islay was given the new title of Lord of the Isles, a proviso being that the sons of his second and not of his first marriage were to succeed to the lordship. The king's hope in making this arrangement was no doubt that a loyal Lord of the Isles would help to consolidate his kingdom, and no doubt this might have been so, but the Lords of the Isles were not always to be loyal to their feudal sovereign. It may have been due to the Viking blood in their veins, but it arose just as surely from the inability of the feudal system of patrilineal succession to provide the country consistently with a strong king.

ROYAL MINORITIES

This becomes apparent when we consider the position of the island during the minority of James II. James was six when he succeeded, and as usual when the king was unable to rule, the nobles of the country banded into factions and manœuvred for power. One of these was headed by the Earl of Douglas, who later came into conflict with the king himself. To the Douglas

121

faction belonged the Lord of the Isles, now also Earl of Ross through the marriage of John of Islay's successor to Mary, Countess of Ross. This powerful descendant of Somerled encouraged his kinsmen, the MacDonalds of Kintyre and the MacAlisters of south-west Knapdale, to harry the king's property in Arran, and they were so vindictive towards one of their own race, Ranald MacAlister, who was loyal to the king and tenant of the royal farms in the north-west of the island, that he had to be excused payment of rent on various occasions because his farms had been laid waste.

The position was so unsatisfactory that in 1452, when the king was twenty-one, he decided to plant yet another Norman in Arran, this time in Lochranza castle, and granted to Alexander Montgomery, Lord Skelmorlie, ancestor of the Earls of Eglinton, the lands of 'Kendloch of Ransay, Cathaydill, the two Turreguys, Alltgoulach, Auchegallane, Tymoquhare, Dougarre and Penreoch', the farms, in fact, which had formerly been rented to Ranald MacAlister. If the Montgomery grant was intended to make the north-west of the island immune from attack, it did not at first succeed. Ranald MacAlister became an enemy and tried to hold on to his farms, and when in 1455, after being defeated at Arkingholme, the Earl of Douglas fled to the Lord of the Isles for shelter, the latter sent out a great fleet under his kinsman Donald Balloch, who wrought great havoc in Arran, 'storming and levelling to the ground' the remaining royal castle on the island, that of Brodick, presumably rebuilt since its destruction by the king's English enemies in 1406.

Three further transactions deserve notice before we come to the establishment on Arran of a family which was ultimately to own the whole island except for the small estate of the Fullartons. In 1452, the same year as he installed the Montgomeries in the north-west of the island, James II, in order to pay back a loan from the funds of Glasgow Cathedral, assigned to bishop William Turnbull, and in the event of his death to the dean and chapter of the diocese, the rents of Bute, Arran, and Cowal, from which 100 pounds was to be retained, and the balance paid to the royal exchequer. The bishop secured a payment in the first year, but the next year, probably in despair, he leased the royal property remaining on the island to none other than Ranald MacAlister,

122

just recently replaced by the Montgomeries in the north-west. The raids from Knapdale and Kintyre continued, and Ranald paid no rent for the four years in which he lived to be lessee. This link between Arran and Glasgow Cathedral has been held by J. Kennedy Cameron, author of *The Church in Arran*, to be responsible for two place-names, Gleann an Easbuig, 'glen of the bishop', and Lettir na Ganach, 'slope of the canons', but we have already seen that the latter at least was in use in 1449, three years before the royal lands were mortgaged. The second transaction to be noted came in 1467, just twelve years after the devastating raid of Donald Balloch, with Brodick castle possibly still in ruins. This was the grant of the royal lands in Arran by James III to Sir Thomas Boyd, who was created Earl of Arran on his marriage to the king's sister. The third transaction was the resignation to Ninian Stewart, sheriff of Bute, and a descendant of the bastard 'Black John', of the Ardgowan lands in the south-east of the island, in return for certain lands held by Ninian at Abernethy. The Bute hereditary sheriff was consolidating his position in Arran. He had added the lands between Kildonan and Clauchlands to his holding at Corrygills.

Sir Thomas Boyd, a descendant of the Boyd who had figured with Douglas in the Arran visit of 1307, was Earl of Arran for only two years. His family had risen to power during the minority of James III by the habitual device of abducting the young king's person. For a time they thrived, and won the young king over, but when the Earl of Arran was absent in Denmark helping to negotiate the marriage of the king with Princess Margaret of that country, his enemies were able to convince the king that the Boyd power was dangerous. The Countess of Arran, the king's sister, knowing of the feeling growing against her husband, went on board his ship to warn him while the returning fleet was coming into Leith, and they fled together to Denmark. Immediately after his marriage, while he was still only eighteen, James III brought the earl's father Lord Boyd, his brother Sir Alexander Boyd, and the absent Earl of Arran himself, to trial for the abduction. Lord Boyd fled to Norway, but Sir Alexander was sick, and was compelled to be present at the trial. All three were condemned to death, and Sir Alexander was executed. The lands and titles of the Earl of Arran, who later rose to high office with

123

Charles the Bold in Burgundy, were forfeited to the crown, and his countess ordered home by the king her brother. A divorce was arranged and her hand given to the elderly James, first Lord Hamilton, whose previous wife had been the widow of the fifth Earl of Douglas. It was over thirty years, however, before Lord Hamilton's son, another James, was made Earl of Arran. This happened in 1503, in the reign of James IV, on the occasion of that king's marriage to Princess Margaret, daughter of Henry VII of England. Lord Hamilton attended the ceremonies with such a splendid retinue, and tilted so nobly with the illustrious foreigner Anthony D'Arsie de la Bastie, that the king was delighted, and conferred on his aunt's son by her second husband the earldom which had been held by her first.

Thus another Norman family was established on the island, for the Hamiltons were descended from Walter Fitz Gilbert, who was granted the estate of Cadzow when he surrendered Bothwell castle, and the English lords who had taken refuge there after Bannockburn, into the hands of Bruce. He had been placed in command by the English king. Mackenzie speaks of this as a betrayal. If so, the reward was as reprehensible as the deed. Yet Mackenzie's condemnatory attitude is justified, for members of the family displayed a consistent indifference to political and even religious loyalties when these conflicted with their thirst for possessions, and for a period when they were almost within reach of the succession to the crown they did not shrink from murder.

As each succeeding royal Stewart infant followed his father, treacherously assassinated or killed in battle, the succession of leaderless gaps in the country's history plunged the nobility more and more into sordid intrigues for power, best to be obtained by securing possession of the infant himself. While James V was a lad in the grip of the Douglases, led by the Earl of Angus, the Stewart Earl of Lennox made a second bid to free him. The Earl of Arran opposed Lennox in this enterprise, and was so successful that Lennox was forced to surrender, only to be treacherously killed by Sir James Hamilton of Finnart, a man known for both literal and metaphorical reasons as the Bastard of Arran. It is said that Arran himself was appalled by this breach of faith, and for a time fell into a deep decline. His conscience was to become less tender later. The assassination of

Page 125: (above) Brodick today: beyond the bay is Glen Rosa, and above it, from left to right, Beinn Nuis, Beinn Tarsuinn, and A' Chir; *(below)* holiday cottages at Corrie which Asquith thought one of the prettiest villages in Europe

Page 126: (above) Members of Arran Mountain Rescue team on North Goatfell, with Cir Mhor beyond; (left) South Sannox burn. The hill above is Cioch na h-Oighe (from cioch, 'breast', and oigh, 'virgin')

Lennox opened a feud between the Stewarts and the Hamiltons which two years later, in 1528, led to a raid by two sons of Ninian Stewart, sheriff of Bute, on Arran's island castle of Brodick, which was again 'destroyed', although the extent to which it suffered is not clear.

As has been mentioned, the Knightsland estate of the Fullartons of Corsby was finally resigned into the hands of James Stewart, sheriff of Bute in 1541. This James was the elder of the brothers who raided Brodick castle. On the death of his father Ninian he had inherited the lands between Kildonan and Clauchlands, and the Corrygills lands pertaining to the sheriffdom, so by 1541 he was a more considerable Arran landowner than his father, and much more so than the Lochranza Montgomeries or the Kilmichael Fullartons. He is referred to by Dean Monro, who is thought to have visited the island in 1549, as holding Kildonan castle, and it is said by the dean that 'he and his bluid are the best men in that country'. This in spite of the illegitimacy of his ancestor 'Black John', and the unblemished descent of the Hamilton Earl of Arran.

James Stewart was to lose all his Arran possessions, except the Corrygills lands inalienable from the sheriffdom, in the very year of Dean Monro's visit, because of an event which had occurred some five years earlier. It was during the minority of Mary, and the Earl of Arran, through his descent from the sister of James III, had achieved the regency. His rival for this position had been the new Earl of Lennox. Arran, judging the change of wind at this time with considerable skill, changed from Catholic to Protestant and so stole a march on Lennox, who remained Catholic. Arran was later to be won over by Cardinal Beaton to the cause of the Catholic Queen Mother, Mary of Lorraine, and the French alliance, upon which Lennox turned Protestant, and gave his support to the cause of Henry VIII of England, who followed his predecessors in striving for the mastery of Scotland. Henry, knowing that Lennox could rely on the Bute Stewarts for support against the Hamilton regent, entrusted him with an invasion of the Clyde, the aim being to capture Dumbarton castle. This he failed to do, but he did great execution in the regent's lands in Arran, 'utterly destroying' Brodick castle.

This happened in 1544, and we begin to see why Dean Monro,

writing in 1549 of the Arran castles, and after mentioning Brodick, refers to Lochranza as 'ane uther auld house'. It looks as if between raids on Brodick by the English, supported by the Bute Stewarts, and on Lochranza by the MacDonalds and MacAlisters, who believed they had ancient rights on the island, the two castles had been rendered less noteworthy than Kildonan, now by far the least visible of the three. Yet in 1549 the regent was powerful enough to compel James Stewart to resign all his lands in Arran, except Corrygills, for the sum of 4,000 merks, plus certain lands in the Cumbrae and a promise of help in reconciling Stewart with the Earl of Argyll. Argyll had been defeated at Dunoon during the English raid on the Clyde, and had instigated a summons against Stewart to answer for his treason in supporting Lennox. It was alleged later that the regent was behind Argyll in the matter, and that in return for his help against Stewart had promised the latter's Arran lands to James MacDonald of Dunyveg, who had married Argyll's daughter. The promise evidently had been made, and MacDonald had to be bought off later with the grant of certain church lands in Kintyre.

The minority of Mary continued. Arran resigned the regency to Mary of Lorraine, for which he was comforted by the grant of the French dukedom of Chastelherault. The alliance with France grew closer, and was sealed in April, 1558, by the marriage of the young queen to the dauphin. English hostility intensified, and in September of the same year the Earl of Sussex made a raid into Kintyre, Arran and the Cumbraes, but not, significantly, Bute. The whole island was burned and devastated, including no doubt the old church lands of Shiskine, which had just been transferred by James Hamilton, bishop of Argyll and the Isles, to his kinsman Chastelherault, for a yearly duty of forty-two merks. The Sussex raid seems hardly to have slackened the Hamilton grasp. By 1563, Alan 'MacKloy' or Fullarton was induced to resign his lands in Arran, by now Kilmichael and Whitefarland, to Chastelherault's son, who granted them anew. There is a local tradition to the effect that to bring this about Alan Fullarton was plied with liquor.

The tragic Mary reigned and left, after her defeat at Langside, for England and the hospitality of her 'dear sister' Elizabeth, and Scotland was left once more with an infant king. Chastelherault, who had been regent during Mary's minority, thought he should be regent again. After her infant son he was next in succession to the crown. The regent chosen was in fact Mary's bastard half-brother, James Stewart, Earl of Moray. In 1570, when he was leaving Linlithgow on a journey, he was shot from a window by Hamilton of Bothwellhaugh, who fled first to Hamilton Palace and then 'to the duke's house in Arran'. To have been able to shelter this distinguished murderer Brodick castle must have been rebuilt by Chastelherault some time between this date and the Sussex raid of twelve years earlier.

The Hamilton murder of the regent Moray did their cause no good. The next to be appointed was not Chastelherault but the Earl of Lennox, father of Henry, Lord Darnley, Mary's second husband and father of the infant James VI. This earl had already won a victory over Chastelherault in the matter of his son's marriage. Darnley, through his mother, a daughter of the Earl of Angus, who had married Margaret Tudor, the widow of James IV, had at the time been next after Mary in succession to the English crown. The marriage was a shattering blow to Chastelherault's dearest hopes, for he, too, had sons, the eldest of whom was, himself apart, next after Mary in succession to the Scottish crown. Had this son succeeded in marrying Mary he might have fathered not only a Scottish dynasty but an English one. The loss of the regency to Lennox now was salt in this earlier wound. Before long there was another murder, at Stirling, this time of the regent Lennox.

This served Chastelherault no better. Two other regents followed, the first of whom, the Earl of Mar, created almost a record by dying a natural death. Even before he died the power of the Hamiltons, even in Arran, seems to have been on the decline, for in 1572 the charter of Robert III in favour of the Fullartons was confirmed in the name of James VI, and Kilmichael resumed the character of a royal holding. Mar was succeeded as regent by the Earl of Morton, whose ruthless self-interest alienated not only the Catholic party of the exiled queen, but the Protestant party also, to such an extent that he was deposed from the office; but before being executed for the murder of the syphilitic Darnley, a crime which became the excuse for more than one judicial murder, he regained a temporary control of affairs by seizing the young king. It was at this time that he broke the Hamiltons. Chastelherault was dead, and the family was represented by Mary's unsuccessful suitor, the Earl of Arran, and his younger brothers, Lord Arbroath and Lord Claude Hamilton. Charged with being implicated in the murders of Moray and Lennox, they were stripped of their lands and titles. Arran, by this time an imbecile, was made prisoner, Arbroath fled to Flanders, and Lord Claude crossed the Border and 'threw himself upon the compassion of Elizabeth'. Their eclipse continued for a little even after James VI grew old enough to free himself from the bondage of Morton, which he contrived through the agency of two favourites from France: Esme Stewart or Monsieur d'Aubigny, who became Earl and later Duke of Lennox; and James Stewart, a son of Lord Ochiltree and brother-in-law of John Knox, who persuaded the imbecile Earl of Arran to resign his lands and titles to him and James VI to confirm the resignation.

These two young men, whose handsome appearance endeared them to the homosexual king, professed to favour his Episcopalian beliefs, but were alleged to have come from France to further the interests of the imprisoned Mary, and establish her on the throne of England. They were, therefore, considered dangerous both to the Protestant party in Scotland and to Elizabeth herself. The latter consequently did all in her power to engineer their downfall. Lennox fled to France after the king had been 'rescued' from his influence by the Raid of Ruthven. Arran had to escape to the west after the Protestant revolution in 1585, when the Hamiltons exiled by Morton, and the other Scots lords exiled for their part in the Ruthven affair, returned to Scotland secretly, burst in on the king, and asked for his pardon. They virtually dictated their terms, which included an English alliance and a guarantee of Protestantism. Among those pardoned were the two surviving sons of Chastelherault, Lord Arbroath and Lord Claude Hamilton. Arbroath was to win the king's favour and regain his father's lands and titles. By 1599, on the occasion of the baptism of the king's daughter Margaret, he had become such a favourite that he was created the 1st Marquis of Hamilton.

THE WARS OF THE COVENANTS

The two kingdoms were united when James VI succeeded Elizabeth in 1603, and Episcopacy was established in 1606. In 1615 there was a charter of the church lands of Shiskine to James, 2nd Marquis of Hamilton, by his kinsman Andrew, the Protestant bishop of Argyll. This time there was no burden of annual duty. What there may have been of church land in Sannox, which is thought to have been granted at one time to the monastery of Kilwinning, may similarly have fallen at this time into the hands of the Montgomeries. The Reformation had enabled the nobility, in Arran as in other parts of Scotland, to deprive the new church of the lands which were the main source of the old church's revenue. The supply of clergymen on the island throughout the period of the Covenants, when the mainland Presbyterians felt obliged to resist the forcible imposition of Episcopacy, was irregular to say the least, but this may have been due as much to the unsettled state of the island as to lack of funds.

Unsettled the island certainly was, although it is difficult to discover in its history at this time any evidence of consistent adherence by its people to any particular sectarian principle. The truth is that they were obliged to resist their landlords' enemies, whatever beliefs they may have nourished in the privacy of their own minds. The Hamiltons, although vacillating, were predominantly Royalist, while their neighbours across the water to the north, the Campbells, were Covenanters. In 1639, when the 2nd Marquis of Hamilton was representing Charles I in the latter's dealings with the Covenanters, a party of Campbells, on the order of Argyll, invaded the island and seized Brodick castle. If they left a garrison behind it may have been withdrawn during the devastating campaign of the Royalist Marquis of Montrose, who had MacDonalds of Dunyveg in his army. One of these, Alister or Young Colkitto, was a special terror to his enemies, and when on the defeat of Montrose at Philliphaugh the survivors of his army returned to their own territories, there was consternation among the Montgomery dependants in Lochranza castle. The Countess of Eglinton, writing from Ayrshire to her Covenanter husband, absent on parliamentary business, said, in a graphic letter quoted by Mackenzie, 'I assure you they ar looking everi night for him in Arrane, for man, wyf and bairne is coming ower to this syd, and all ther goods that they can gett transportit, both out of Arrane and Bute, for he is veri strong, as I feir we find er it be long'. Mackenzie believes this to suggest that the Arran people as a whole were foes to the cause of Montrose, and, therefore, friends of the Covenant.

If they were Covenanters they were soon again to be strangely at odds with their fellows in the cause, for in 1646 a Campbell garrison was again in Brodick castle, being besieged by islanders loyal to the Hamiltons, when a party was sent to relieve it under the lairds of 'Orinsarey' and 'Strawhur'. The savagery of this raid is completely inconsistent with any but the cynical belief that religious ideals played no part in it. In a complaint made after the Restoration, also quoted by Mackenzie, it is said that the Campbells 'entered imediatly upon the saids inhabitants thair cattel, nolt sheip & bestiall and put them aboard thair saids vessells and transported tham as many of them therein as they could carry over and killed and destroyed the rest they could not transport; and did flay those whilk they killed and tooke away thair hyds and skins amounting in all the killed destroyed & transported bestiall to the number of two thousand kyne or thereabout besides their pillageing of what other pettie goods moveable the bounds did afford, and rivined the houses & cottages'. According to the same account the lands of Arran lay waste after this foray for a space of six years. The suffering must have been appalling.

The year following this the Scottish Covenanting army under General Leslie was in Kintyre, and here we have the foundation for the tradition that Arran was visited by the plague, a tradition which Mackenzie tries to link with the London plague of 1665, and so dismisses. There had been bubonic plague in London in 1625, from which 40,000 people perished. It must have lingered and spread to the north, for the Scottish Covenanting army brought it to Edinburgh after the storming of Newcastle in 1644, and from Dunblane to Dunaverty in 1647. It was at Dunaverty that a massacre of MacDonalds took place hardly less brutal or treacherous than the later one of Glencoe. The men who perished were those who had shut themselves up in the castle. Many others had escaped, some to northern Ireland, and no doubt some across the shorter stretch of water to Arran, where kinsmen had been settled in the south-east on the Stewart resignation of the Kildonan lands to Chastelherault. The tradition is that as a result of the plague many surnames vanished from the island, and this seems to be true of MacBrayne, Macrae, Blue, and Hutton.

Charles I was executed in 1649 and the 1st Duke of Hamilton shared his fate. The 2nd Duke, brother of the first, came over from The Hague to Scotland with Charles II in 1650, but from his arrival until the king's coronation at Scone early in 1651 he was obliged as a Malignant, or anti-Covenanting Royalist, to take refuge in Brodick castle. The crown was placed on the king's head by the Marquess of Argyll, a Resolutioner, or Covenanter who believed that the king, in his own interest, would not try to restore Episcopacy. Later in the year of his coronation Charles II was defeated at Worcester, where the 2nd Duke of Hamilton suffered a gunshot wound in his knee, from which he soon died. At this time Brodick castle was one of four in Scotland holding out for the king, and early in the year following the battle, which sent Charles II into exile, Major-General Deane, holding the Scottish command for Cromwell, sent a detachment from Ayr to take it. This was commanded by a Captain Goldsmith, who left Ayr at 4 AM, landed at Lamlash, approached the castle about 3 PM, and, having drawn up his men, summoned it. The garrison surrendered 'because they were not in a capacity to avoide itt' and shortly afterwards the chief tenants of the island came and 'were very civill to the Captaine and the souldiers'. The writer of the newsletter quoted adds that 'the inhabitants expresse much disaffection to Argile'. So much for the view, expressed both by Mackenzie and by J. Kennedy Cameron, that their sympathies were with the Covenanters.

During the Cromwellian occupation the castle garrison added a battery to the east end, and a wing to the west, augmenting the building as it had stood from the time of its rebuilding after the Sussex raid of 1558. A drawing of the castle as it was immediately before 1844, when the Victorian wing was added, shows it much as the Cromwellian troops must have left it, with the old entrance leading in through the battery (plate p 107). It does not seem that the islanders were disposed to be civil to the soldiers for long. There is a tradition of an attack by islanders on a Cromwellian foraging party some halfway between Sannox and Corrie, in which all the party were killed. The site of the skirmish is said to be identified by the Cat Stone, derived from *clach a' chatha*, 'stone of the battle', although it is now translated back into the Gaelic by some geological and mountaineering writers as *clach a' chait*, 'stone of the cat'. A stone of battle it most certainly is, whatever the etymology, as a recent unauthorised attempt by an employee of the county roads committee to blast a piece off it, in the interests of faster motoring, led to an astonishingly virulent public controversy. The huge stone, a granite erratic of considerable geological interest, bears the scars of the latest conflict in the form of three holes, bored by a pneumatic drill. They will no doubt acquire their own folklore. The burn beside the Cat Stone is identified by Mackenzie as the *Allt a' Chlaidheimh*, or 'burn of the sword', although other and lesser authorities say the name belongs properly to the burn beside Corrie school. *Creag an Stobaidh*, 'rock of the stabbing', in the Merkland wood beside the public road, is said to commemorate another Cromwellian clash, from which the castle governor and his men escaped in a small boat, save one who was found behind this rock and stabbed. These traditions, along with another recounted by James C. Inglis in *Brodick, Old and New*, of a skirmish on the shore near Strabane, are our only record of conflict between the islanders and the Cromwellian troops.

The 2nd Duke of Hamilton was followed by his niece Anne, daughter of the 1st Duke, who on the failure of a male heir became Duchess of Hamilton in her own right. Her estates were heavily burdened with debt, the family having been fined by the Commonwealth government and some of their lands forfeited. By 1657 she had paid the whole fine and redeemed the forfeited property. She married William Douglas, second son of the Marquess of Douglas, who took the name of Hamilton, and on the Restoration of Charles II in 1660 he was, at his wife's request, invested with the titles which were hers by right. She also persuaded the restored king to repay a loan raised on the Hamilton property by her father in favour of Charles I, and she brought before parliament the matter of the Campbell raid of 1646. The guilty individuals were ordered to make good the loss, both from the destruction of 'bestiall & goods' and from the six years' devastation of the island, estimated at 'three score thousand merks Scots money'.

The year after Charles II was restored Episcopacy was restored also. Even now, with the island under the ownership of the Duchess Anne, there is little indication of antipathy to it. It is true that John Cunison, MA, minister of Kilbride parish from 1655, was in 1662 deprived of his charge for refusal to recognise the prelatic government, and he went elsewhere until granted indulgence in the reign of James VII. Although he then returned to the parish he was not restored until 1690, when Presbyterianism was established under William and Mary. In the interval the parish was served by curates, one of whom, Archibald Beith, had the distinction of being condemned for murder. He had thought it part of his duties to seize a vessel illegally importing meal into Scotland from Ireland, which had put into Lamlash bay. When it refused to surrender he fired on it, with the result that two men, a member of the crew and an Irvine merchant, were killed. He was tried in Edinburgh for their murder, found guilty, and sentenced to be hanged. The sentence was remitted by the king, and he was set free, to appear at Rothesay begging for help from the town council. He was refused a licence to beg, but given some money, and disappeared from history. The history of Kilmory parish during this period was less eventful. In 1651 it had a minister, Alexander MacLaine, MA, who went to Kilbride in the same year and in the year following to Strachur. Like Cunison, who followed him at Kilbride, he was deposed for refusing to recognise the prelatic government, but this was some ten years after he had left Arran. Whether he left the island because it was unsympathetic to his views, or because it was still lying waste after the raid of his fellow Presbyterians, the Campbells, is a matter for conjecture. Kilmory parish lay vacant after 1651 until a curate was installed in 1688, only to be deprived of his living shortly afterwards with the establishment of Presbyterianism.

There is thus little evidence in Arran of martyrdom for the Presbyterian cause. There is no record of hill conventicles, defiance of dragoons, or the rabbling of curates, which is not surprising in view of the Episcopalian loyalties of the 1st and 2nd Dukes of Hamilton or the brutality of the Presbyterian Campbells, but surprising perhaps a little in view of the later reputation of the Good Duchess Anne. This description she owed to her support of the Presbyterian church. When it began to appear is uncertain. We have seen that she was a very competent manager of her affairs, and it would seem that she was willing enough to tolerate Episcopacy, although perhaps under silent protest, until she had redeemed the family fortunes. But she is said to have saved the lives of many Covenanters after the battle of Bothwell Brig by requesting the Duke of Monmouth not to allow his soldiers to pass through the woods of Hamilton Palace, where many had taken refuge. She is even said to have helped some of the refugees to escape to Arran, and the Davidsons of Glenrosa claim descent from one of these. Certainly her husband eventually led the opposition to the government of Charles II in Scotland, and was president of the Scottish convention which, on the deposition of James VII, conferred the crown upon William and Mary.

Duke William died in 1694, but the Good Duchess survived until 1716. Between her husband's death and her own she was active on the island as a patron of the now Presbyterian church. In 1705 she presented two communion cups for the use of the island which were preserved at Kilmory until the manse containing them was burned down. In 1708 a preaching house was built at Clauchan, probably replacing a chapel of an earlier date, and in 1712 another at Lochranza, some distance from the old chapel of St James, on the site occupied by the present church. The Clauchan building, like its successor of 1805, whose ruin can be seen beside the graveyard today, was served by the Kilmory parish minister. That at Lochranza was for the use of his assistant, 'catechist and preacher of the Gospel', to whom the duchess granted by way of glebe the tack of Coillemore, a little runrig farm on the hill above the modern village, where not so long after, in the early 1760s, Burns' Highland Mary served for a spell as servant to her uncle, the catechist Daniel Campbell. The buildings at Clauchan and Lochranza were additional to the statutory parish church, and therefore acts of benevolence. Mackenzie would withhold credit here, in view of the church lands misappropriated after the Reformation, but the fact remains

136

that the acts were voluntary. He might on similar grounds have modified his praise for her expenditure of £2,913 on a small pier and basin at Lamlash, well known as the Duchess Anne's Quay until it was robbed, shortly after the beginning of the nineteenth century, to provide stone for the building of the new village. The sum expended, although sterling, was rather less than the amount of compensation awarded for the Campbell raid of 1646, which is unlikely to have been passed on directly to the more immediate sufferers. The portrait of the duchess by the Scottish painter David Scougall, which can be seen today in the boudoir of Brodick castle, shows a lady more shrewd than saintly. It is probably a good likeness (plate p 71). In 1705, the year of the gift of the communion cups, the Lochranza lands of the Montgomeries had fallen to her through their failure to redeem a £3,600 mortgage. The Good Duchess not only established Presbyterianism on the island as soon as it was politic to do so. She ended by passing on more of the island to her family than it had ever held before. Not until 1800 did it add to what she left it. In that year, either by purchase or in exchange for certain Bute lands held by the Hamiltons after the transactions of 1549, the 9th Duke of Hamilton obtained possession of the Corrygills lands held by the Bute Stewarts originally in their capacity as hereditary sheriffs.

THE CLEARANCES

IN 1689 the Duchess Anne had surrendered her titles to her son James, who became fourth Duke of Hamilton, and three years later was created Duke of Brandon in England. Unlike his father Duke William, he was Jacobite in his sympathies, and a leading opponent of the union of the two parliaments. He failed his party at the last minute, and the union took place in 1707. It was not popular in Scotland, and indeed for a long time the benefits often attributed to it were not apparent, nor is it universally agreed today that it has been beneficial to the northern partner. It certainly did not at once end civil war or bring prosperity. In the united kingdom there were causes of dissension, not coincident with national differences, still to be resolved. Presbyterianism had been established in Scotland under William and Mary, but under Queen Anne patronage was restored, by which the ministers were not called by their congregations, but appointed by landlords, and this, coming from a parliament predominantly English, caused dissatisfaction with the union even among the Presbyterians. The Catholics of both countries saw their only hope in a restoration of the Stewarts, or Stuarts, as they had become after some years of exile in France, and the same was true of the Scottish Episcopalians. The adherents of both sects saw more hope of re-establishment for their respective churches under a Stuart king in an independent Scotland than under the Hanoverians in Britain. On the death of Queen Anne, and later, after that of her successor George I, Jacobite risings took place, that of 1715 an abortive affair supported largely by Episcopalians in the north-east of Scotland, but that of 1745 a wider expression of Scottish unrest, incorporating the varied religious dissatisfactions already mentioned, some economic considerations relating to trading disadvantages, and what were considered inequalities in taxation, and a further element rather more racial than national. The rising of 1745 was the last fling of the Gaels against the forces threatening their language, costume, customs, and economy. It is one of the ironies of history that a people whose first effective enemy was a Stewart protagonist of feudalism should have followed a lineal descendant to save a feudalised version of their ancient clan system from the protagonists of a new kind of landlordism being brought about by the growth of a competitive capitalist economy.

The story of the rising hardly touches Arran. James, sixth Duke of Hamilton, was in Paris at the time, and no more than six of the inhabitants, evidently men motivated by personal conviction, were implicated in it. One at least, James Bain Fullarton, described as a 'merchant in Glencloy', is known to have survived to play a part in the later life of the island. Indeed he is the one person recorded as having openly criticised estate policy during the period of drastic change about to be discussed. Other attainted men took refuge on the island, notably Charles Boyd, a brother of the Earl of Erroll, and son of Lord Kilmarnock, who was beheaded on Tower Hill. According to local tradition his place of refuge was the farm of Aucheleffan.

Although the island was not involved in the rising itself, it was involved in one of the consequences of the Jacobite defeat, a phenomenon known to the Highland people as the Clearances, to the landlord class as the Improvements, and to the 'objective' historian as the Agrarian Revolution. In the attitude of the first there is an element of bitterness, in that of the second some self-justification, and in that of the third a detachment divorcing it from the reality with which it professes to deal. The fact is that a situation arose in which it became possible for a few people to submit many to the indignity of being treated as if they were less important than sheep. Let us not forget that after the defeat of the rising of 1745 the Highland people were, naturally enough, very unpopular. They had given the Lowlanders, and the English, a fright. After Culloden they were hunted down with a vindictiveness which they may be said to have earned, and it became possible to treat them brutally without arousing protest. It was in this climate of opinion that the Clearances became possible, although they affected many communities not involved in the rising itself, or involved on the Hanoverian side, and were carried out for what were considered sound economic and agricultural

139

reasons. They were not, like the brutalities committed immediately after Culloden, a deliberate reprisal for the rising, but the inhumanity they involved would have caused greater uneasiness if the people they helped to destroy had not come to be regarded, in the Lowlands and in England, as a nuisance to be eliminated.

The Gaels who had participated in the rising had largely been led into it by feudal overlords who were also their clan chiefs. The people of Arran, on the other hand, had not since the days of Angus and Ruari, grandsons of Somerled, been subject to overlords who were either kinsmen or even fellow Gaels. Their Culloden had taken place earlier, in unrecorded struggles with the High Stewards, and on the beach at Largs. But although they had been subject to alien landlords they had been left, as they were left by the Vikings, to live in their own ancient way, provided they paid the rent demanded of them and suffered the onslaughts of their landlord's enemies. Their tenancies had at one time been hereditary, and the rent demanded of them, calculated on the ability of the land they farmed to support stock, had been fixed. The people were in practice, although not latterly in law, tied to the land, and they farmed it to produce almost everything they required for their subsistence, with a surplus to cover rent and a few imports.

Mention has already been made of the communal system by which they cultivated their open fields. In areas of Scotland which had been farmed by the Angles, the ancient Celtic runrig system had been replaced by open field systems under which the tenants held the same plots of arable ground year after year. Thus when the system of fixed rents was abandoned, and farms were held for the period of a lease at a rent determined by the capacity of a tenant to outbid his competitors, there was nothing to prevent the enclosure of the arable ground by hedges or dykes, and only the cottars could resent the division among the tenants, and the enclosure, of the common pastures. The change to the system of enclosed farming could thus take place without spectacular disturbances, although it did give rise to a wretchedly depressed class of agricultural labourers. In the Highlands and Islands of Scotland, and in Galloway, the runrig system was an obstacle to such change, and attempts to enclose in Galloway after the rising of 1715 had been resented by members of the farm communities deprived of land to such an extent that bands of angry men, who became known as Levellers, actually gathered at night to throw down the new dykes, until troops were called in to quell them. After the Jacobite defeat at Culloden the spirit to conduct this sort of resistance was broken, and the way was open for the Clearances in other areas of Gaeldom.

The obstacle to change created by runrig will become evident if we regard the situation in Arran around 1766, when Douglas, the 7th Duke of Hamilton, was a minor, and his tutors and trustees commissioned John Burrel and Boyd Anderson to come to the island and make plans for the introduction of the new style of farming. At this time the great bulk of the population lived

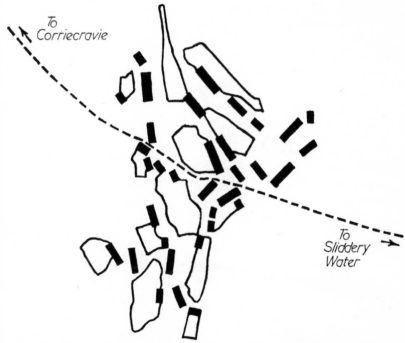

Plan of Sliddery farm before the abolition of runrig, after Bauchop, 1807. The modern road coincides with the old track indicated by the dotted line. Today Sliddery post office stands at the heart of the site of the old clachan, close to the track bend. The longer buildings are blackhouses, the others either cots or farm outbuildings such as stables, barns or kilns. The plan illustrates the compact character of the old communal farm clachans.

141

in clachans situated around the coast, and in the glens, convenient to the open fields. The modern villages of Lochranza, Corrie, Brodick, Lamlash, Whiting Bay, Kildonan, Kilmory, Blackwaterfoot and Pirnmill did not then exist. The largest of the clachans were along the south-west coast, at East Bennan, West Bennan, Shannochie, Torrylin, Clauchog, Bennecarrigan, and Sliddery, in the Shiskine glen at Ballygowan and Shedog, at Tormore, and at North Sannox. There were fairly large clachans also in Glen Rosa and Glen Shurig, at Mossend, between the Knockan and the Rosa burns, at Mayish, Strathwhillan, Clauchlands, Glenkill, Monamore, Auchencairn, King's Cross, the three Kiscadales, Dippen, Kildonan, Ballymeanoch, Auchenhew, Levencorroch, Corriecravie, Kilpatrick, Torbeg, Machrie, Dougrie, Balliekine, Whitefarland, Alltgobhlach, Catacol, Newton, South Sannox, and Corrie. Smaller clachans, some of whose names have disappeared from the map, lay far up the glens and on the now deserted northern coast of the island, as Ballygonachie and Strathgail, near the head of the Kilmory water; Corriehiam and Gargadale, fairly high up on the Sliddery; and the Cuithe and the Laggantuine, above the northern coast.

These clachans were compact clusters of long blackhouses and their outbuildings, the latter mainly cots, stables, and barns. The long blackhouses were built of double courses of dry stone, rubble-cored, and plastered on the inside with clay. They were thatched with heather, or less frequently straw, laid over turfs resting on brushwood. This in turn rested on horizontal poles fastened to the roof couplings, all the timber being undressed. The blackhouses were divided into three compartments: an inner room, a kitchen, and a byre for cattle. The kitchen had two windows, unglazed but shuttered, which faced back and front, so that one or other could be opened, according to the direction of the weather, to provide light. The kitchen hearth was on the floor, usually near the middle. From a rafter above this hung a swee or crane to hold cooking pots, and into the roof directly above was built a plastered wicker chimney, hooded against the prevailing wind. The kitchen was divided from the inner room by two box beds, one usually facing into the kitchen itself, and the other into the inner room. The doorway into the inner room occupied the space between them. The inner room had some-

142

Page 143: (left) Thatching cornstacks at Sannox Home Farm; (below) unloading coal at Brodick Pier

Page 144: *(above)* Sawing timber at Brodick sawmill; *(below)* MV *Glen Sannox* in Brodick Bay. This all-purpose vessel came into service in 1957 and can carry 1,100 passengers and 40 motor vehicles. Her normal speed is 15 knots

times a wooden floor, and the rafters above it were usually covered with boarding, to form a garret above. The window of the inner room was sometimes glazed, and there might be a fireplace and chimney built into the gable. The rafters above the kitchen were not boarded over, but a ladder from the kitchen gave access to the garret above the inner room, which was usually a sleeping place for children. The kitchen floor was composed of a mixture of ashes, clay and lime, beaten until compact. Between the kitchen and the byre there was a wicker partition, hardly high enough to reach to the rafters. The doorway to the kitchen from the open air was usually close to this partition, and was itself protected by a wicker screen. There was of course a doorway through the partition into the byre, and at the far end of the latter, in the gable, there was a second doorway, for the cattle.

In some cases both cattle and horses, the latter small garrons, occupied the byre end of the house, but the horses seem usually to have been housed separately, in small stables sometimes built on to the outside of the inner room gable but more often detached. Grain was thrashed by hand in little barns, which had doors opposite each other so that they could provide a draught, when opened, to clear the grain of shillings. The grain was dried in the clachan kilns, over straw placed on slats above a hearth, and ground in the five estate mills to which the farms were thirled, although small quantities were sometimes ground by hand in the husking-stones still to be seen by the doorways of the older cottages. In each clachan were a few enclosed yards where animals could be penned, and from these a track led out to the hill pastures.

The arable ground closest to the clachans, or infield, was cultivated year after year, being regularly manured with animal dung, seaweed, and shell sand. The outlying arable ground, or outfield, was cultivated originally on a three-plot system, cropping one year, lying fallow the next, and on the third being grazed, and of course dunged, by the farm animals. The crops grown were oats, barley, peas, and beans. Potatoes were coming into use, and were soon to bulk next to oats in the cropping, and flax was being grown. The animals kept were mainly little black milk cows and their followers, with fine-wooled native sheep to

145

about half the number of the cattle, and horses to about a third. There were some goats, but few if any pigs. Cattle and horses were the chief exports. Sheep and goats were killed at Michaelmas, dried for winter provision, and sold at Greenock. Some salt butter was sold on the mainland also, as were herring nets and thread made from the island flax, and there was a herring fishery.

The diet of the people was meal, potatoes, butter, cheese, and eggs, with dried mutton and goat, and salt herrings, in the winter. Little beef seems to have been eaten. The cattle were probably much too precious to be killed for home consumption, by the poorer people at least. The men spent the spring labouring on the land, the summer cutting peat and doing building repairs, the period before and after harvest fishing and burning kelp, and the winter making herring nets. The women set the potatoes, made butter and cheese, helped at the harvest and the gathering of the weed for kelp, and dressed and spun the flax and wool to be made into clothing for their families by the handloom weavers in the larger clachans, and the travelling tailors. Much of the butter, salted for sale on the mainland, was made by the younger women at the *bothan airidh*, or sheiling bothies, up in the hills, where the cattle were shifted in summer to take advantage of the seasonal flush of grass, and incidentally to let the meadows grow to hay, and rest the pastures on the plots of outfield lying fallow.

RUNRIG

The feature of the island life we have to discuss in approaching the subject of the Clearances is that of the runrig, or running share method of allocating the land from which each family's proportion of the farm crop was to be taken. The people of each clachan worked as a community, and the work was allocated among its members by the *fear a bhaile*, or 'man of the village', usually also the tacksman, who collected an annual rent from each family, and himself paid an annual rent to the estate. The rent paid by each family to the tacksman was at first determined by its wealth in cattle, although latterly it seems to have been the other way round, and the stock allowed determined by the rent paid. The hill pasture, held in common by the members of the clachan community, was soumed, each family having so many soums, the soum being the grazing sufficient for a cow or six sheep, or half the grazing for a horse. Each family's allocation of arable ground, and of the meadows, corresponded in turn to its share in the souming, but these shares were spread over the ground in a manner determined annually by lot. It is a simplification to suggest, as Pennant does, that 'each man had his ridge, to which he put his mark'. Each family did have its share of land, but the shares differed in extent, nor were they held, either in the arable ground or in the meadows, in a single piece.

The ground to be cultivated in any one year was in several plots, of varying sizes, determined largely by the lie of the ground, each separated from the other by the fallow of previous years, or by a rocky outcrop, a steep slope, a stretch of bog, or a burn. In each of these plots there would be so many rigs, and it seems to have been in terms of rigs and their constituent furrows that each plot was divided among the sub-tenants.

In setting up a rig the plough turned a furrow and then, on its return journey, turned another against it from the opposite side. The plough then continued up and down the rig, 'gathering' furrows in towards the middle from each side, until the distance it had to cover, at the head and foot of the rig, was so great as to make the setting up of another rig desirable. This was done so as to leave a space between the two rigs, when the gathering process was completed on the second, equal to the amount ploughed on each. The plough then tackled the space between, 'casting' furrows instead of gathering them, or in other words turning them out towards the middle of each rig in turn, away from the space left between until, when the middle of the space was reached, a bauk or depression was left, from which the final two furrows had been turned outward. The rigs were the strips of ground between the bauks, and each sloped gently from the middle, where the furrows had been turned inward against each other, to the bauk, which acted as a surface drain.

It has been necessary to describe a rig in some detail owing to the confusion caused by some writers who suggest that the annual allocation of the land in the plots was made in terms of the plough-gang. This is variously defined as the amount of ground the four-horse wooden plough of the period could turn in a single day, or as the size of farm which could be worked conveniently by a community possessing a single four-horse plough. The second of these meanings would seem to have been applicable in Kintyre, and with either meaning the term could have been used as a unit of farm measurement. But for the purposes of plot division in Arran at least the unit seems to have been the rig, which might vary in length from one plot to another but was constant in width, and so could provide a convenient unit for the division of each separate plot.

In a sixteen-rig plot a family with a quarter share would have four rigs, a family with an eighth share two rigs, and so on. Families who kept no horse and supplied labour only might have as little as a single rig. The carpenter and smith who maintained the plough would be excused much of the field labour. Cottars not contributing to the rent, but who gave labour at planting and harvest, might have a rig divided between them, or in the case of the potato crop, be allocated a single drill. There is ground for believing that a widow, or wife with an invalid husband and no grown sons, would have an allocation also. To ensure that everyone had his chance of the better soils and exposures, and of the better weather at planting and harvest, which of course affected the crop, the *fear a bhaile* cut a number of straws, one for each partner, to unequal lengths. Holding the straws with the exposed ends even, he let each man draw one in turn, and he who drew the longest took his share from the nearest end of the plot, he who drew the next longest followed, and so on until the plot had been allocated among all the members of the community. This process was repeated for each plot in turn.

It is important to remember that in true runrig this allocation was made annually, and the labour of the community applied to the farm as a whole. The different shares in each plot were neither sown nor harvested separately by the different partners, although if the farm community was a very large one the *fear a bhaile* might divide it into teams or squads for working several plots simultaneously. Of course the different partners each provided seed and manure sufficient for their own shares, but they worked together over each plot as a whole, working now on one neighbour's share, then on another's, and in the course of the

148

day, with the help of their neighbours, completing the work on their own. It was only later, when runrig was being undermined by estate pressure, that each tenant worked his own shares for himself, and that allocations were made for periods of two or three years; and only much later, and only in neglected parts of the island, where runrig had ceased without enclosure, as at Balliekine, that tenants held permanently to the shares last allocated under runrig to their fathers or grandfathers. The disadvantages of this scattered distribution of ground being worked by individual tenants, in competition with their neighbours instead of in harmony, are obvious, and much of the ridicule poured on the ancient system, in the period preceding the worst of the Clearances, was based on observations made at this degenerate stage. It has to be said that much of this ridicule came from clergymen with an academic interest in agriculture and a desire to ingratiate themselves with potential patrons. For these were the days of patronage in the church, and livings were in the hands of landlords.

It is of course true that with the end of civil war in Britain the aristocracy were able to turn their attention for the first time almost exclusively to peaceful means of adding to their wealth, and the desire for agricultural and industrial improvement led to experiment and discovery on a scale hitherto unprecedented. Agricultural knowledge grew rapidly from the middle of the eighteenth to the middle of the nineteenth centuries, and there were many useful discoveries in respect of drainage, liming and crop rotation, and in the introduction of new crops, the improvement of implements, and the selective breeding of animals. But many of the new ideas, some of them brought from England by landlords travelling to and fro between their estates and parliament, and tried out first in the Lothians, were in Burrel's time still in their infancy. Some were to prove unsuitable to the Scottish climate. Others were miscalculated in their long-term effects. And even those which were to prove effective were introduced to the runrig areas in such a way that technical progress was achieved at the expense of social justice.

Burrel has received the attention of local historians because he left behind him two journals, one covering the period from May 1766 to January 1773, and the other from July 1776 to Septem-

THE CLEARANCES

ber 1782, which survive in manuscript at Strabane, in the possession of the Lady Jean Fforde. Early in the first of these journals
Burrel provided, under the heading 'Observations', an outline of
the policy he intended to pursue in the resetting of the Arran
farms, whose nineteen-year leases were due to terminate from
1773 onwards. Out of fourteen of these observations four are
concerned with conditions to be laid down for the enforcement
of new ideas for the improvement of the island husbandry. They
relate to the restriction of grain crops to a third of the arable
in any one year, with a compulsion to sow the other two-thirds
with clover and rye-grass; to a restriction on the ploughing of
lea ground without providing a sufficient quantity of 'dung, of
lime, of shells, of coral, of sea-ware or sea-weed'; to the opening
of lime quarries in the island and the obligation of tenants to
cart the lime at their own expense and 'to pay the Duke ten per
cent of the cost of manufacturing from the time of delivery to
the end of the lease', the contemplated leases being from nineteen to thirteen years; and finally to a restriction on the growing
of potatoes on any ground which had grown them before, any
new crops having to be taken from new ground laboured with
plough or spade, and 'no more than two crops from the same
ground under penalty of confiscation of the whole crop'. Little
fault can be found with any of these conditions on grounds of
sound husbandry, but they did not in themselves involve the
doom of runrig.

THE DIVISION OF THE COMMUNAL FARMS

Where Burrel's observations did attack runrig they were concerned with enclosure and the withdrawal of the right of common
pasture. In outline, his proposals, incorporated in seven of his
observations, amount to this: that the farms were to be divided,
and no more ground leased to any man than he himself could
stock, labour and improve. The tenant was to be obliged by
the terms of his lease to enclose such ground as 'might be
improved thereby', including not only the arable but the pasture,
and the formerly common pasture in the hills was to be appor-
tioned to the 'most contiguous' farms below, so that by the time
the last of the old leases had expired, there would not be a
150

'single inch of commonty left in the whole island'. A further observation stipulated that no tenant at any time during his lease should have the liberty to 'assign his tack, or subset the whole or part thereof, without a particular licence in writing agreed and obtained for that effect, under penalty of voiding the tack'. A final observation ruled that the tradition which reserved certain stretches of shore to particular farms for the purpose of collecting seaweed would be refused further sanction, and no seaweed collected without the authority of the Duke of Hamilton, obtained through his agent.

In the course of his many visits to the island Burrel surveyed the land and drew up a scheme for the division of each of the communal farms into a number of individual holdings. These were such as could be worked by a single tacksman with the help of his family and some casual labour, and included a proportion of arable, meadow, and hill pasture, suitable for balanced farming. To arrive at the rent to be charged for each holding he compromised between the old system, which was to value its expected yield in stock and grain, and the new, which was to value its land in terms of acreage. The expected yield was of course based on hopes of increase from the new practices to be enforced, and the value per acre was influenced by the rents obtaining in the already enclosed farms of the mainland. These were rising for reasons other than increasing agricultural productivity. It should be remembered that company banking began to replace private in 1695 with the establishment of the Bank of Scotland. The Royal Bank of Scotland followed in 1727, and other banks later; the Ayr bank of Douglas, Heron and Company in 1769. The landlords of unentailed estates were able to borrow on the security of their land for purposes of agricultural improvement. It is possible that the trustees of the entailed Hamilton estates, in sending Burrel to Arran to prepare the changes to be made when the old leases began to expire in 1773, anticipated the Montgomery Act of 1770, which enabled landlords of entailed estates also to burden their land. The trustees were among the law-makers. But the main point here is that with the increase in wealth from the development of overseas trade there was a growing body of merchants on the lookout for country estates, partly to give them the status of landowners, and partly to enable them to indulge in the craze for improvement. The crash of the Ayr bank in 1772, which deprived the majority of Ayrshire landowners of their ancient estates, threw land on the open market to a degree never known before, and the competition for it raised its price, and so the rents it had to earn to make it profitable.

Burrel's proposals for the division of the communal farms are shown in a map prepared by Christine Elkins for Margaret Storrie's valuable paper on *Landholdings and Population in Arran from the late Eighteenth Century*, published in 1967. The divisions as shown in this map agree fairly closely with those actually attempted by Burrel in 1773 and listed in Appendix B to the second volume of *The Book of Arran*. When this list of holdings is compared with the list of communal farms in 1766, given in the same appendix, it is seen that the great majority of the latter have been divided, some of them, as Benlister and Glenkill, into two or three holdings, and others, as Cloined and Clauchog, into as many as six or seven; and whereas in the 1766 list there is a single tacksman for each of the original communal holdings, in the later list there is a separate tacksman for each of the holdings into which these farms have been divided. That many of the new holdings have no tacksman's name attached may have been due to Burrel's inability to find men with sufficient capital to work them under the conditions imposed for their enclosure, or able to take them at the higher rents demanded. It was certainly a defect in his scheme for competitive individual enterprise that to carry it out required from the tacksman of each new holding more capital than had been required from the tacksman of an undivided communal farm, for the runrig system had enabled a community to pool its resources of implements, horses, and labour. But there were further reasons why Burrel's efforts failed to achieve enclosure at that time, while undermining runrig and leaving the island worse off than he had found it.

In a memorial drawn up by Burrel before he listed the divisions of 1773 he stated that the ninety-nine farms of the estate maintained no fewer than 1,110 families, an average of about ten families to each farm. The head of one of these ten families

D Drimlabarra
G Glenshant
HL High Letter
K Knockan
KB Kilbride Bennan
M Margieniesh
Ma Margarioch
Mg Margnahegliesh
T Torbeg
LL Laigh Letter

Map of original runrig farm boundaries

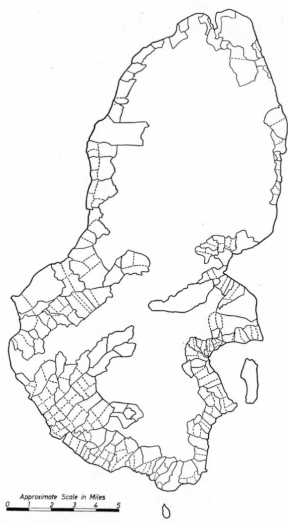

Approximate Scale in Miles
0   1   2   3   4   5

Map of divisions planned by Burrel, 1773

would be tacksman, the heads of the others his sub-tenants. In the list of 1773 the ninety or so communal farms have been divided into just over 250 holdings, each allocated to a tacksman originally forbidden to subset. Had the scheme been carried out as intended the number of heads of families with access to land would have been reduced by three-quarters, from roughly 1,000, the number of tacksmen and sub-tenants originally farming runrig, to 250, the number of tacksmen, or tenants paying rent direct to the estate, to whom the new holdings were to be leased. So some 750 heads of families would have been deprived of access to land, and consequently at that time almost inevitably of the possibility of providing for themselves and their children, except as casual labourers employed by those more fortunate than themselves in obtaining leases.

The scheme could have been carried out as Burrel intended only if there had been a possibility of alternative employment on the island, or of emigration either to the mainland or overseas, for the families deprived of land. The kelp industry was itself seasonal and incorporated by the runrig communities into the year's round of tasks. In any case the quality of the Arran kelp was not high, from lack of suitable weed, and at that time prices were poor, even for kelp of high quality. A bounty system to encourage fishing was not extended to inshore fishermen until 1787, and the industry was crippled by a salt tax. Burrel did make a few sporadic efforts to establish industry, and for a time coal was worked at the Cock and used in connection with the manufacture of salt there. He made trial borings for coal on the shore at Clauchlands, too, where it is now known not to exist. At Glen farm in the Lochranza area he explored the possibilities of the local slate, and for a time slate was indeed quarried there. We know too from the *Statistical Account*, published in 1793, a few years after the end of the Burrel period, that limestone was being quarried at Corrie, and that there were three licensed stills on the island. These few enterprises together fell far short of being able to offer alternative employment for the huge numbers of people he wanted off the land.

As far as emigration to the mainland was concerned, the industrial revolution had begun, but it was to be some years yet before it got into its stride. The first spinning mill for cotton was not established in Scotland until 1778, or for linen until 1789; and the first power loom for cotton until 1793, or for linen until 1810. It was to be some time yet before the growth of manufacturing towns offered employment for those being driven off the land. Similarly with emigration overseas. It had started in Burrel's time, for he records in 1770 'many people intending for America', and he is concerned lest any of the runrig sub-tenants should slip away without meeting their obligations to their tacksmen and so indirectly to the estate. In 1772, however, he records 'to his sorrow' that his hopes for emigration 'are like to vanish'. Emigration westward would certainly be difficult during the war with America, which lasted from 1775 to 1783, and in 1772 the war was threatening.

Pennant, writing in 1775, speaks of the people of the island as having a 'look of deep dejection', which he attributes to their having to slave without remission to pay the high rents demanded. It was probably due also to the threat of exile hanging over many of them. He criticises the system of competitive leases, too, pointing out that a man who expended capital on improving the fertility of his holding not only made it more attractive to those who might bid against him for it on the expiry of his lease, but diminished his own capacity to bid successfully. Curiously, this recalls an argument later used against runrig, whereby it was said that no man was likely to manure a piece of ground liberally, when he knew it would pass the next year to a neighbour. This argument clearly applied to runrig in its degenerate stage, when each man worked his own ground for himself, and this must have been the stage reached when the mineralogist and agricultural 'expert' Headrick reached the island in 1807, for he reported that the ground was then being divided every two or three years, instead of annually as reported earlier by Pennant. Three years is the time it takes before the residues from a single application of manure are exhausted by cropping. Clearly by Headrick's time co-operation, on some of the farms at least, had given way to competition.

An idea of the state to which Burrel's efforts had reduced some of the farms can be obtained if we consider the case of Bennecarrigan. In 1772 Burrel indicated that as a communal farm it had had a tacksman and ten sub-tenants. In his 1766 list the tacksman was Robert McCook, and in 1773, although he had planned to divide it into seven or eight holdings, he had to let the whole farm to the same tacksman. The factor of 1784, J. H. Cochrane, reported that in 1776 the farm was let to a John McCook, possibly Robert's son, and that in three years he went bankrupt. The farm was, therefore, let in 1779 to twelve tacksmen, none of whom had the resources to farm even a twelfth adequately, so each was allowed to subset half of his holding to a sub-tenant. So in the end, instead of a tacksman and ten sub-tenants working together and pooling their resources, there were twelve tacksmen and twelve sub-tenants, each of the twelve pairs working independently, although still periodically redividing the ground. Cochrane reported, not surprisingly, that since the twelve tacksmen had come to the farm they had spent their time wrangling.

The same fate overtook other farms. The factor of 1800, William Stevenson, stated that Burrel's plan for the management of the estate caused the tenants to run into great arrears, of no less than three years rent, and they soon went bankrupt, and that a subsequent crop of arrears in 1792, of one and a half years rent, was liquidated by the tenants as a result of 'perseverance, care and exertion' on the part of the new factor, none other than William Stevenson himself. And as the people became poorer the size of the holding they had the means to work and improve grew smaller, and the same subdivisions of the holdings as at Bennecarrigan, far beyond the original intentions of Burrel, occurred over the greater part of the estate. Not only so, but the hope of one day attracting substantial farmers from the mainland, skilled in the enclosed style of farming, led Stevenson in 1792 to reduce the period of the leases offered to native tenants to five, eight, eleven, or thirteen years. So the pressure to exploit instead of to maintain the fertility of the soil increased. No wonder that in 1807 Headrick was unimpressed by the condition of many of the farms, although he attributed it, as did William Aiton, another 'expert' who followed him in 1810 and 1813, to the 'barbarous system of management the island has been under for two centuries back'.

It is remarkable that Burrel should have been so singleminded in his devotion to the new type of husbandry being evolved in the lowland areas of the mainland, and to his duty of bringing the rents paid per acre into some sort of relation to the rents which had proved possible there, that he was untroubled by the tremendous problem he was creating for the great bulk of the island people, and never considered that there might be an obligation on the part of the landlord to make some provision for the people who were to be deprived of land, before proceeding to carry out his plans. Yet he did realise that his policy involved displacement, and only regretted that speedier emigration was not possible. In the case of Headrick, whose ideas for agricultural improvement were in the main those of Burrel, it might be argued that since his schemes for the island included several mainly impracticable industrial enterprises which might have employed thousands, he can be excused for disregarding the fact that his agricultural ideas involved displacement. Yet he specifically said that they did not, gave the subject of Highland emigration only a passing mention, and stressed incessantly the gain to the 'noble proprietor' which would result from the adoption of his schemes. While Pennant in 1775 had said that the old rents were scarce £1,200 a year, and the new rents expected from the divided farms £3,000, Headrick in 1807 said that the net rent, after defraying public burdens, was rather under £5,000, and that while it could not be increased under the prevailing system of management, and was indeed met from other sources than the produce of the land, such as smuggling, it could, if the island were put 'into a tolerable strain of improvement' be raised to '£15,000 or £20,000 per annum, and the people still be enabled to enjoy the comforts of wealth and independence'. By the people he could mean only the minority able to obtain leases. To the predicament of the others he seems to have been oblivious.

He did have one improvement to suggest not mentioned in the observations of Burrel. This was that above the head-dykes, which were built in Burrel's time to enclose the old infield and as much of the contiguous outfield as was deemed capable of cultivation, the 'whole hills and mountains should be lotted into sheep farms'. He did mention the 'inconsiderate rage' for sheep farming then prevalent in the Highlands as a cause of depopulation and deplored this, and he did suggest that if no farmers from a dis-

158

tance could be induced to embark on sheep farming on an extensive scale it could be conducted on a joint-stock system, with small tenants banded together in the ownership of flocks. But he had already contended during his criticism of runrig that joint ownership of stock made improvement by selective breeding impossible, and was clearly in favour of the imported sheep farmer with the new blackface and Cheviot breeds, recommending that the extent of hill grazing allotted to each flock should be divided into three hirsels, each with its separate shepherd. With that system of management, he contended, and cultivation increased by enclosure in the valleys, sheep could prove a source of increased population and prosperity. This is a remarkable statement in view of the great reduction in the number of cattle necessitated by his scheme, for he would have had the latter confined within the head-dykes. The attraction of sheep at the time was due not only to the boom in wool caused by the French wars of 1793 to 1815, but that as compared with cattle, sheep offered a greater return in proportion to the number of people involved in their management, and so enabled a greater proportion of the revenue from the land to go to its owner. Although Headrick was too exclusively preoccupied with the interests of the 'noble proprietor' to see it, sheep as an alternative to cattle did involve, even more than enclosure, a displacement of people from the land.

He made one other remarkable statement. 'Even the mountain pastures admit of considerable improvement, by burning the heath, which has been too much discouraged, from the foolish notion of preserving the game. Where the heath is burnt, on a dry bottom, ferns spring up, with a close pile of sweet grasses, and white clover below.' He seems not to have realised that the shoots of heather are an important item in the yearly diet of the sheep, nor that while excessive burning does indeed destroy heather, and cause ferns to spread, if by ferns we mean bracken, the latter is not edible by sheep or any other creature. And where bracken catches on it reduces the land beneath it to a mould of withered leaves. It is in fact a pest, and is spread not only by excessive burning of the heather, but by confining the hill stock to sheep. The drier areas of the hills, when grazed exclusively by sheep, become covered with a close mat of withered herbage in which the spores of bracken thrive. When cattle predominated on the hills, as they did before the Clearances, their heavy tread broke this up. The great plague of bracken over the island today, and over the Highlands and Islands generally, is a monument to the ideas of such as Headrick.

Burrel had failed to effect the changes proposed in his observations because to succeed he had to displace people from the land at a time when there were few opportunities for alternative employment, and emigration, either to the mainland or overseas, was difficult. At the same time the increasing use of the potato as a main article of diet was enabling more people to live off less land, and the population, in spite of the discouragement of his activities, was increasing. Unable to drive people into the sea, but determined to enforce competitive farming, he was obliged to allow much greater fragmentation of the old communal farms than he had planned, and of course the potato not only compelled this but made it possible. There was yet another difficulty. His plans for the replacement of communal by competitive farming involved the tenants who succeeded in obtaining leases in an awkward relationship with their deprived neighbours. Families who had originally worked together as a single community, taking the luck of the draw with each other as they shared the produce of their common labour, found themselves, some in a position to make a livelihood, and some deprived of the opportunity, yet still close neighbours in the old compact clachans. It is not surprising, and it is to their credit, that the more fortunate would not allow their neighbours to starve, and the surreptitious subsetting of ground, forbidden by the estate, and castigated as a bar to progress, occurred widely, so that the fragmentation of farms was even greater than that allowed. Yet although runrig was being disrupted little progress was being made towards enclosure and the division of the common grazings. Burrel achieved little in this respect beyond the establishment of head-dykes between the land considered capable of cultivation and the rough hillside beyond.

Yet enclosure and the division of the common grazings remained estate policy, and in the end were carried out, although in a way very different from that intended by Burrel, and under changed circumstances. Burrel had intended to divide the 100 or so communal farms in Arran into 250 enclosed holdings fairly equal in extent. When we consider the divisions which had been achieved by the time enclosure was reaching its peak, in 1837, we find that there were in the ducal estate alone some 448 holdings, of which 43 were fairly large, and the others small, varying from 40 to only 2 acres. Much of this distribution was organised in 1814, and is seen in a map of that date reproduced in the paper by Margaret Storrie already mentioned, which shows that the bulk of the very small holdings lay around the coast, at Tormore, Drumadoon, Corriecravie, Sliddery, Torrylin, Shannochie, Kildonan, Whiting Bay, Lamlash, Brodick, Corrie and Lochranza. On the whole the larger farms were less coastal, and had large areas of hill grazing, although there were a few large farms near the coast, notably those at Bennecarrigan, Clauchog, and Clauchlands. There were only two farms in the southern half of the island still nominally communal, in the Sliddery and Kilmory glens, but inland of these were areas listed for letting as special grazings which until then had been communal and were just about to be cleared. The farms of the north-west, between Machrie and Catacol, acquired from the Montgomeries by the Hamiltons in 1705, and not being in entail conferred by the 8th Duke on his natural daughter Anne Douglas, afterwards Lady Rossmore, were still communal, and remained so until reacquired by the Hamiltons around 1844. The farms of the north end, between Sannox and Lochranza, formerly Montgomery property also, which in 1783 the Duke of Hamilton intended to sell, remained communal, too, until the growing profitability of sheep led to a change in intention.

The pattern left by the enclosure of the farms and holdings in the ducal estate as determined by the reorganisation of 1814, and the white houses built apart from each other on the new holdings to replace the old compact clachans, make the landscape we know today outside the modern villages. There have since been amalgamations, as with the invention of more effective but more costly implements the size of farm required for their economic use has increased. And of course the great majority of the very small holdings, although their dwellings are occupied, are grazed by the animals of the contiguous larger farms. But these changes belong to a subsequent period. What concerns us now is the

1814

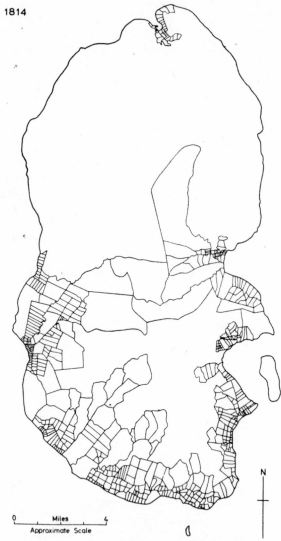

Map of divisions planned for the Hamilton lands in 1814

pattern established by the reorganisation of 1814, and why it differed from that intended by Burrel.

Of the factors which made enclosure and the division of the common grazings possible, two actually added to the effect of the potato in increasing the population. These were the development of fishing as a result of the extension of the bounty to inshore fishermen in 1787, and the boom in kelp during the French wars of 1793 to 1815, when foreign supplies of soda were unobtainable. Fishing and kelp began to offer more profitable employment both on the shore and at sea, and those who succeeded Burrel in the management of the ducal estate were able to absorb many of the people displaced by the enclosure of the more inland farms by the establishment of great numbers of small holdings in the coastal areas. The estate did not lose by this. The rents charged for the holdings were high, and in some cases at least the leases planned in 1814 obliged the tenant to supply a ton of kelp yearly, which was credited to the rent at two shillings per cwt, but if not made or of poor quality was charged against the tenant at four shillings per cwt, an interesting difference.

EMIGRATION

The great increase in the number of small coastal holdings, and in the number of families thus able to make a living from the combination of the potato, kelp, and fishing, had already absorbed all the displaced persons it could, and indeed raised the population to a new peak, in spite of some emigration, when the creation of extensive sheep farms, on the lines suggested by Headrick, was planned for the larger glens at the close of the leases initiated in 1814. This involved even more displacement, and was accompanied by the collapse of the kelp industry, owing to the withdrawal in 1823 of an import duty on Spanish barilla, imposed at the end of the French wars to keep the industry going. There might have been a repetition of Burrel's earlier dilemma, but by that time the problem had been solved by the development of Canada as a British colony at the close of the American wars. The 'inconsiderate rage' for sheep farming which was causing the Highland landlords to clear the glens of people, some of them ruthlessly with the help of troops and the fire-stick, and the general collapse of the kelp industry, acted together to make Canada the only alternative to the growing industrial towns of the mainland. Emigration to Canada began to be organised, partly by landlords interested in getting rid of their people, and partly by those who had acquired large tracts of virgin land in Canada and wished to have them peopled; and by the time the Arran leases of 1814 were expiring, it was in full swing.

Of the numbers of people displaced from Arran as a result of the establishment of the new sheep farms and the failure of the kelp, who went to the mainland to find work under the appalling conditions prevailing in the early years of the industrial revolution, there is no record. Nor is there any record of the emigrations to Canada of the people cleared from Margareoch, Glenree, Burican, Gargadale, Corriehiam, and Glenscorrodale in the Sliddery glen, or from Cloined, Aucheleffan, Strathgail, Ballygonachie, and Auchareoch on the Kilmory water, although the bulk of the people are said to have gone to Chaleur Bay, opposite Nova Scotia. But we do have a record of the clearances from the north end of the island, when all the people from the farms there, at South, Mid, and North Sannox, the Laggantuine, the Laggan, the Cuithe, and the Cock, were evicted in 1829 to make way for a single large sheep farm at Mid Sannox, and a smaller enclosed farm at the Cock.

This record is *Annals of Megantic*, a book written in 1902 by Dugald Mackenzie MacKillop, whose father and mother were among the emigrants. The people had early warning of their impending eviction, and started to make preparations for their journey early in 1829. They are said to have taken with them cooking utensils, an abundance of woollen clothing, a few articles of furniture, spinning wheels, tools, seed, and some books, the latter mostly religious, among them the Gaelic Bible. The emigration had been organised by the estate, and half the fare to Canada, which was £8 for an adult, or for three children under fifteen, was paid by the 10th Duke of Hamilton. The first wave of emigrants embarked at Lamlash on 25 April, on a copper-bottomed sailing vessel of 169 tons named the *Caledonia*, and it was perhaps fortunate that the skipper, Captain Donald Millar, was a native of the island. An Independent congregation had

164

been established at Sannox following an evangelical mission in 1800 by the brothers Haldane, and the minister, the Reverend Alexander Mackay, accompanied the people to Lamlash and preached a farewell sermon, on the text, 'Casting all your care upon Him, for He careth for you'. Twelve families sailed on the *Caledonia*, numbering in all eighty-six people. For five families, numbering in all twenty-eight, there was no room on the *Caledonia*, and four of these embarked on 5 June at Greenock, on the *Albion*, and the remaining family on the *Newfoundland*. The names of the ships have a curious pathos.

The *Caledonia* was two months at sea, arriving at Quebec on 25 June. There was much distress from a severe storm off the Irish coast, when all the passengers were violently seasick, otherwise the more interesting features of the voyage are that the unofficial leader of the group, Archibald MacKillop, held a religious service on deck every Sunday, and that a Paisley weaver was found stowed away. What might have happened to him in those days we can only guess, but the passengers held a *ceilidh* on board and paid his fare from the proceeds.

The *Caledonia* waited two days at Quebec, until Captain Millar made arrangements to have it towed up to Montreal, as the passengers were supposed to be bound for Renfrew County in Upper Canada. After disembarking at Montreal they remained at Point St Charles for two weeks, and during this period spread a huge washing along the shores of the St Lawrence. It was during this period, too, that they were approached by the Quebec immigration agent, who recommended that they should go to Megantic County in Lower Canada, instead of to the destination originally planned. His motive for the suggestion is said to have been that he wanted to have Megantic peopled by fellow Scots, as a means of securing votes when he stood for election as the county representative, and he did in fact contest the seat in 1832, unsuccessfully. Archibald MacKillop adopted his suggestion, however, and along with William Kelso went to view the proposed ground, on which they were able to report favourably, so the passengers took a barge back down the river to Point St Nicholas, about 15 miles from Quebec on the south side of the river. This cost two dollars a head. French-Canadian teamsters then transported them, at the rate of five dollars per horse-load of passen-

165

gers and luggage, over some 40-50 miles, a journey which took two days, to a ford on a river named the Thames, which lay close to the area in which the new land was to be allocated.

They arrived at the ford in the middle of July and set up their tents, but it was to be six weeks before a government agent arrived to allocate the land, which had been surveyed in 1819 and the 100 acre lots numbered. It is said that the heads of families, and sons over twenty-one years of age, had been promised a lot each. There was some disappointment when, although Archibald MacKillop got 200 acres, and the heads of families 100 acres each, the sons got nothing. They settled on their new land, which was virgin forest, on the first of September, rather late in the year to clear much of the land for the next spring sowing, and the six weeks lost at the ford were no doubt regretted. The stay at the ford was saddened also by an epidemic which caused the death of two of the children, Jane MacKillop, an infant of two, and Margaret Kelso, aged fifteen. But it was gladdened a little by the arrival of the families which had crossed the Atlantic from Greenock, so that by the time the tents were struck at the ford the company consisted of seventeen families from the north end of Arran, numbering in all 117 people. Later the Arran settlers in Megantic were to be joined by others from the island, for between 1830 and 1843, but mainly in 1831, seventeen more families arrived, mostly in small groups, so that by the end of the period the Scotch Settlement, as it was called, had a population of 222.

The severe Canadian winter was a shock to the settlers, and there were two deaths, of Neil Walker, who was over eighty when he sailed with his daughter in the *Caledonia*, and of the elderly widow MacKillop, who had sailed on the *Albion* with her six children. Meanwhile the forest had to be cleared, and work was held up by the intense frost, although some of the younger men took advantage of the break to earn wages in the timber mills at Ottawa. By February the average clearing was 4 acres, Archibald MacKillop having 20 to his credit. With the harvest from these the emigrants, apart from the wages earned in Ottawa, had their first income since their last Arran harvest of 1828, a gap of two years.

One wonders, in view of the contempt poured on the com-

166

munal farms by men like Headrick, how they managed to acquire the savings to pay their travelling expenses, maintain themselves between the two harvests, and stock their new holdings. The answer no doubt lies partly in the money obtained from the sale of their Arran stock, but it is clear that they cannot have been destitute. Nor were they enfeebled in constitution by intermarriage, as is sometimes suggested by people who, noticing the preponderance of MacKillops, Kelsos, MacKinnons, Mackenzies, and Kerrs, among the emigrants, fail to realise that among the Highland people a common surname implies no very close relationship. The hardships they endured from the long sea voyage and the drastic change in climate were great, but out of the 117 people involved in the first wave of settlement only four failed to survive the journey and the first testing winter, one of them a man over eighty and another a mere infant. Their very survival is a proof that they were hardy.

Nor did the emigrants have the benefit of the practices and implements of the improved agriculture to help them to establish themselves. At first the only enclosure was a fence round the cleared ground, and although each owned his own land the habit of communal working remained, perhaps in a modified form and under a new name, for we read of planting, sowing, bark-peeling, and spinning 'bees'. The plough first used was still the wooden one, and barley was pearled in a hollowed block with a pestle, a wooden version of the old husking-stone. The log houses, too, were built at first to the same plan as the blackhouses of Arran, with the hearth on the floor and the chimney of clay-plastered wicker. As a result some of the settlers were burnt out, and they eventually built chimneys of stone.

Until the first harvest there was some hunger, which the people were reluctant to admit to each other, and there was a distressing period when the clothes brought from home began to wear out, but the people soon got sheep and were able to make new clothes again.

Archibald MacKillop held services at his house until a log meeting-house was built in 1832, but after that there was a minister, Donald Henry, who had left Arran the year before. A school was conducted in the meeting-house also, the first teacher being another Archibald MacKillop, later known as the Blind

Bard of Megantic. He could teach Gaelic but the government would not allow payment for it. The policy was to let it die out. The second teacher was Catherine MacKillop, the daughter of the leader, and the third James MacKinnon. The names have a familiar ring in Arran today.

By 1840 the settlers had built a Congregational chapel. Although in wood, it had a striking resemblance to the Independent chapel built by the emigrants in 1822 before they left Sannox, which is now the Congregational church. The Haldane evangelists of 1800 had affected the Sannox people deeply, and the emigrants had carried with them their peculiar sectarian over-scrupulosity. It is recorded that they were at first troubled in Canada as to whether they ought to allow the bowls for collecting maple syrup to remain in position on the sabbath, although to remove them would lead to waste. The problem ceased to trouble them when they remembered that the Lord allowed the corn to grow on the sabbath, and they did not hesitate to accept the benefit. The problem of when to break the pond ice for Sunday's water, which was frozen in the bucket if carried in on Saturday, gave rise to two schools of thought.

RELIGIOUS FERVOUR

To relate the wave of religious fervour which swept the north end of the island on the occasion of the mission of the brothers Haldane in 1800, and the subsequent wave of fanaticism, psychotic in its intensity, which swept the west of the island in 1815, to the insecurity of the people during the period of impending eviction, seems the only way to explain them. This was a period of resistance to patronage all over Scotland, which developed into a conflict between the established church and the civil power over the respective spheres of their authority. It culminated in 1843 in the Disruption, when members of the Church of Scotland opposed to patronage walked out of the General Assembly and established the Free Church. It may well have derived some of its energy from the land policies then being pursued over much of the country. Any physical opposition would have meant prosecution and possible transportation, for in the days of Lord Braxfield, the Hanging Judge, it was considered

168

seditious to question the justice of a constitution which placed all political power in the hands of the landowner. It would seem that the fury of the people at the disruption of their lives, dangerous to express without disguise, was being channelled unconsciously into ecclesiastical protest.

Certainly in Arran there was a close link between resentment against eviction and the protest against patronage, for the first patronage dispute of 1758 arose when the congregation of Kilmory objected to the person appointed by the 6th Duke of Hamilton as assistant to the elderly James Stewart, a former catechist at Lochranza and minister of Kilbride, who was followed in that parish by his son Gershom, and later by his grandson John. The person appointed by the duke to assist the elderly James in Kilmory was himself a James Stewart, of Kilwhinlick, who had previously been minister of Kingarth in Bute. Stewart of Kilwhinlick, in the course of an argument with an elderly female tenant who had been served a decreet of removal and had refused to budge, threatened to burn down her house if she did not leave it, whereupon she took the tongs and handed him a peat glowing from the fire. Unwilling to have his bluff called, he carried out his threat, and earned such unpopularity that he had to leave his parish. The Duke of Hamilton then appointed him assistant to his namesake in Kilmory, probably intending him to succeed when the latter died. A majority of the presbytery of Kintyre sustained the presentation, although two ministers appealed to the synod of Argyll, and old James Stewart, who had been unable to attend the presbytery, appealed to the General Assembly.

A further meeting of the presbytery took place, when with a fuller attendance the voting on the issue was equal, with the moderator, the Reverend Gershom Stewart, among the objectors. Ignoring the appeals and the result of the second vote, three ministers proceeded to admit Stewart of Kilwhinlick, but as the opposing party had taken possession of the church, the ceremony had to be held in the open air. The General Assembly censured the three ministers not only for being high-handed, but also for the irregularity of the ceremony, and suspended the leader, the Reverend John Hamilton of Skipness, for three months. Of Stewart of Kilwhinlick we hear no more, but on the death of

169

old James Stewart in 1761 it was John Hamilton who succeeded him in the parish, evidently without objection on the part of the congregation; for it was under John Hamilton that the church was rebuilt in 1785, and it was he who wrote the article on the parish for the *Statistical Account*.

The part played by the Reverend Gershom Stewart in this first Kilmory patronage case can be explained only in terms of filial loyalty. The elderly James probably saw that his only hope of retaining his congregation lay in objecting to his unpopular assistant, and his son must have felt obliged to support him. He was in no danger of offending the 6th Duke, who had died immediately after presenting Stewart of Kilwhinlick, and was to be followed by two minors. But Gershom Stewart was himself loyal to the improvement policies, although his personal contribution was a minor one. It is recorded in Burrel's diary that he offered £5 a year for the fresh water fishings of Arran, promising to improve them by prohibiting the liming of hides in the pools, which polluted them to the detriment of trout and salmon.

The second patronage dispute on the island, also at Kilmory, came in 1815 on the death of the Reverend Neil MacBride, son of a Patrick MacBride who had farmed at Auchencairn. In his concluding years the parish had reached the peak of its religious fanaticism, and on his death the congregation wanted as his successor a man of equal fervour, Angus MacMillan, who was catechist at Lochranza. The 9th Duke of Hamilton presented Dugald Crawford, who had formerly been assistant in the parish to John Hamilton, and was now minister of Saddell. The congregation would not have him, and under the leadership of one William MacKinnon they deserted the parish church, and during the six years of Dugald Crawford's ministry worshipped in the cave on the shore below Kilpatrick. Dugald Crawford was drowned while crossing from Greenock to Arran when the boat in which he was making the passage foundered in a squall. He was succeeded by the minister originally preferred by the congregation, Angus MacMillan, who on the occasion of the Disruption left the parish church, and while a new church and manse were being provided for him held services in the parlour at Clauchog farm, and lived in a cottage there, although not for long. He was in poor health, and died the same year.

Possibly the most significant feature of the opposition to Dugald Crawford was that the man who led it, William MacKinnon, had previously been deprived of his farm as a consequence of enclosure and reduced to the status of a cottar. There seems a probability here at least that ecclesiastical protest was an unconscious outlet for repressed political fury, and his case cannot have been an isolated one, or he would have been unable to exercise leadership.

Yet all the bitterness was not channelled into the protest against patronage. Some of it was turned inwards against the people themselves. Unable to blame their superiors for their misfortunes without feelings they had to repress, they became easy victims of the doctrine that their misfortunes were the consequence of their own sins, and since their misfortunes were great, their sense of sin became morbid. One of the Cook brothers, two Free Church ministers who spent their boyhood in the Kilmory area during the wave of fanaticism there, and who left a volume of letters, wrote that he considered the death of his infant daughter a just punishment for the fact that he had idolised her, setting her above God himself. The over-scrupulous sabbatarianism of the Megantic settlers can be passed off as amusing, but the letters of the Cook brothers show that the wave of fanaticism which rose from the strain of the enclosure period had its darker and more tragic side.

THE MACMILLANS

Of some interest is the link with the Arran clearances of the publishing branch of the Arran MacMillans. Malcolm Mᶜmillan, the grandfather of Daniel, the founder of the firm, lived all his life on runrig farms. He was born on such a farm, in the Lochranza area, and lived for a long time at North Sannox, rearing most of his family there before becoming tacksman of the more northerly of the two runrig farms in the Cock area, close to the site of the steading built shortly after the clearances and now a ruin. His daughter Janet married Alexander Mackay, the first minister of the Independent congregation at Sannox, who preached the farewell sermon to the Sannox emigrants, among whom were two of Janet's cousins, Malcolm and James

McMillan, and their widowed mother. But by the time of the clearances Janet's brother Duncan, the father of the original publisher, had already left the island with his family. Born at North Sannox, he had in 1793 married Catherine Crawford or MacGraffin, as the Crawford surname was rendered in those days, and gone to live with her on her father's runrig farm at the Achag, situated on the hillside at Corrie above the modern house called Thirlstane. The Achag was one of three divisions made in the original Corrie farm in 1773 by Burrel, all however let to a single tacksman, John Robertson, who must have sublet.

William Crawford, Catherine's father, was still alive in 1793 when Duncan M°millan or McMillan (both spellings are on record) married her and went to live and work with him. A map prepared in 1811 by Robert Bauchop, who surveyed the whole island in preparation for the divisions planned in 1814, shows three buildings at the Achag, one obviously a long black-house and the other two probably cots. The census enumerator's return for 1801 shows that there were then three households on the farm : that of William Crawford, his wife, two sons, a daughter and a male farm servant; that of Duncan M°millan, his wife, a son and three daughters; and that of Isabell Crawford, who lived alone. William Crawford died in 1805 and was succeeded as tenant by his son Daniel, who erected the gravestone to his memory which can be seen in Sannox graveyard. Daniel is listed in the census of 1801 but not included in the list of William Crawford's family in *Annals of Megantic*. The latter is, therefore, incomplete. The M°millans continued to live beside him, and his nephew Daniel, the future publisher, was born in 1813. Following 1814 the Corrie farms were again subdivided and although Daniel Crawford retained the tenancy of the Achag it was probably deprived of much of its hill grazing. At any rate he would be obliged to enclose and run it as a single tenant. Duncan M°millan, unable to farm runrig with his brother-in-law any longer, left with his family in 1816 to join two of his older sons, Malcolm and William, who were already in Ayrshire working as carpenters on a new school being built at Irvine, now the old Irvine Academy. He became a carter, taking coal from the new pits to Irvine harbour for export to Ireland.

Thomas Hughes, the author of *Tom Brown's Schooldays*, in his

Memoir of Daniel Macmillan, records that four little girls of Duncan M^cmillan's family died at the Achag in the course of an epidemic. This, and the references throughout the book to Daniel's tuberculosis, have been used to support the view, mentioned earlier, that the Arran people were so enfeebled by intermarriage, starvation, and insanitary living conditions, that their removal was a kindness. It has to be remembered that Duncan M^cmillan's family of twelve, reared not in a blackhouse but a small cot, was rather larger than the average even for that period. The average size of family involved in the Sannox emigrations was six. And it was not in Arran that Daniel contracted tuberculosis, but in Glasgow, where he had gone to work after serving his apprenticeship to a bookseller in Irvine, and where living conditions were such as to make an Arran blackhouse a paradise. The spread of tuberculosis over the Highlands and Islands came later, when the first victims of the disease in the industrial towns returned to their homeland to recuperate in the cleaner air of the country.

To realise how appalling conditions in the towns became we have to remember that by the time Daniel Macmillan went to Glasgow the poorer people of the Highlands and Islands, who had been crammed into small coastal holdings and then displaced from them by the collapse of the kelp industry, and who could not afford to go to Canada, were pouring into Glasgow and other industrial towns by the thousand; and they were to be followed, before the enclosure period in Arran and elsewhere came to a close, by thousands of starving emigrants from Ireland, driven out by the potato failure and encouraged to think that they would find employment in Scotland by the unscrupulous advertising of the shipping companies, in whose overcrowded vessels many of them perished by suffocation.

The mills and factories were increasing, but they could not absorb all the labour, and were able to offer wages inadequate for bare subsistence, certain that these would not be refused, and that when one wave of labour was exhausted by malnutrition another would be available. Yet between 1815 and 1846 the Corn Laws prevented the import of corn unless the price rose to 80s a bushel. Critics of runrig have frowned on the employment of children to herd the cattle from the crops on the open

173

fields. Until 1842 children under thirteen were employed for over ten hours a day not only in factories but underground in pits. As for Glasgow's housing, the Chief Constable reported in 1840 that 'in the centre of the city there is an accumulated mass of squalid wretchedness, which is probably unparalleled in any other town in the British Dominions'. It was soon to be paralleled in Edinburgh, where by 1861 there were 1,530 single-roomed houses in the city, with six to fifteen persons living in each; and 121 of these houses were merely cellars without windows. Any historian, crammed with the propaganda written for the landlords by the established clergy, who pretends that the enclosures and clearances were effected to provide the victims, albeit against their will, with a higher standard of living, is singularly blind to the obvious motive, and to the wider historical context.

And anyone who denies that there was a racist as well as a class element in the exercise need only read *An Account of the Island of Arran*, written in 1837 by John Paterson, one of the Arran factors involved. For this essay he received a silver medal of the Royal Highland and Agricultural Society. This was the man who deplored the fact that the people were so foolish as to waste their resources on their displaced neighbours when they could have employed them in the improvement of their holdings. He believed, as did Headrick, that there could be no progress on the island until the Gaelic language was stamped out, and in describing the native inhabitants drew attention to their physical peculiarities with the detachment of a zoologist. Of their feet and limbs he said they were, 'especially of the females, very clumsy, the former being large and flat, the ankles thick, and the heel projecting considerably beyond the limb'. There is less detachment in his comment that 'although generally honest in their dealings with one another they frequently, like the Jews, think it no great crime to get as much as they can from strangers, or those in a situation above them in rank'.

THE RESORT TO TOURISM

URING the century which followed the Arran clearances agriculture steadily changed its function of providing mainly for the subsistence of those who lived on the land, to that of providing food for export to the rapidly expanding industrial towns. To produce the growing surplus for export it was necessary that increasing productivity should be achieved by a diminishing labour force, and the introduction of more effective implements and methods made this possible. The iron plough, iron harrows, the reaping machine, the horse rake, the seed drill, the ridging plough, and the potato digger, all made it possible to produce greater crops while employing fewer people. Productivity was increased also by seed hay and turnip husbandry, and by the introduction of improved breeds of farm animal: notably the Clydesdale horse, a heavy animal which could cope singly or in pairs with the new implements; and the Ayrshire cow, which gave a heavier yield than the earlier breed, but as a beef animal was of little value; and was less hardy, although this was not considered important, since it was deliberately excluded from the hill grazings in favour of blackface sheep. The existence of the new manufacturing towns on the mainland made it possible to displace people from the land without creating the problem which had baffled Burrel, and as the new farming techniques were adopted the number of people on the farms declined steadily and rapidly.

ISLAND INDUSTRIES

Attempts to establish industries continued. In the earlier half of the nineteenth century there were carding mills at Brodick and Burican, a flax mill at Lagg, and a wauking and dye mill at Monamore. With the increasing manufacture of cotton on the mainland a mill for the manufacture of bobbins was established at Pirnmill. There was a clay drain tile manufactory at Clauchog. The textile mills failed when water power elsewhere gave way to steam, and the bobbin and clay drain enterprises failed with the exhaustion of their raw materials. In 1793 there had been three licensed distilleries on the island. In 1836 the last of them, at Torrylin, had closed, and the Arran barley was sent to Campbeltown. A similar contraction due to more efficient plant reduced the number of meal mills from the five plotted by Bauchop around 1811 to two in 1878: one at Shedog, whose ruin is still visible, and the other, a distinguished red sandstone building with crow-stepped gables, situated downstream from the dye mill at Monamore. Further improvements in plant elsewhere made milling uneconomic on the scale possible in Arran and by 1909 the Shedog miller was superintending both mills until they closed a few years later. The lovely Monamore mill, a striking feature of the landscape even in ruin, became unsafe and was demolished in 1967.

The mining of coal and quarrying of slate in the Lochranza area did not survive into the nineteenth century, but the quarrying of white sandstone and limestone continued at Corrie, above the Port and below An Sgriob, and of limestone in the Clauchan glen. Local limestone was burnt in kilns both at Corrie and Shiskine. Imported white Irish limestone was burnt at Clauchog. During the First World War a very pure limestone was quarried beside the Coire nan Larach burn, about a third of a mile NNW of High Corrie, and a tram line conveyed it to the Corrie Sandstone Quay. The quay, built originally in 1882 to serve the red sandstone quarry further south, was connected with that quarry by a light railway. Red sandstone was quarried also at Brodick, Cordon, and Monamore, and there was some quarrying of building stone in the schists at Lochranza and in quartz-porphyry at Glenree and Brown Head. The red sandstone quarries were the longest in use, but by 1928 were being abandoned. Barytes was first mined at Sannox in 1840, and between 1853 and 1862 nearly 5,000 tons were produced, but the mine was closed by the 11th Duke on the ground that it spoiled the solemn grandeur of the scene. After the First World War it was reopened, and a wooden pier and light railway built, and by 1934 the output had risen to 9,000 tons; but the vein petered out in 1938. The pier and light railway were demolished at the close of the Second World War.

Fishing on a fairly wide scale continued throughout the nineteenth century. In 1840 there were 100 wherries at the herring fishing, with almost the same number in 1847, there being twenty-three boats at Lamlash, nine at Brodick, eight at Corrie, twelve at Lochranza, nine at Whiting Bay, with the others spread along the west coast. By 1914 there was herring fishing only from Lochranza and Pirnmill, and by 1928 it was almost extinct. The cause of the decline was the increasing cost of the most economic type of vessel, and the growing centralisation of markets.

Apart from mining and quarrying, which maintained the bulk of the population of Corrie and Sannox from the time of the clearances until just before the opening of the First World War, and fishing, which employed a fair number of people in the main villages throughout the nineteenth century, the industries of the island did little to provide work for the people displaced from the farms by improved methods, and the island might have been seriously denuded of people had not inventions making for more comfortable, speedier, and cheaper travel brought country and seaside holidays gradually within easier reach of those obliged to spend the greater part of the year in the unpleasant environment of the new industrial towns. Yet it was some time before manual workers and labourers could afford holidays and even when, with the extension of the franchise and the growth of trade unions, wages began to rise in the mills and factories, Arran was beyond reach of all but the middle classes and the aristocracy, and it was as a resort for such that it developed in the latter half of the nineteenth century.

The first holidaymakers on record seem to have come just after the middle of the eighteenth century, by the weekly sail packet from Saltcoats, to drink goat's milk, then fashionable as a health beverage, in a 'commodious slated house hard by the castle of Brodick', which must refer to the building now known as the Cladach, said to have been built by the Duchess Anne early in the eighteenth century for her physician, and afterwards extended and converted for use as an inn. It is said to have been the first slated house in Brodick, and was for a long time known as *Tigh an Sgleat* for that reason. There is evidence also that Paisley weavers, a prosperous class of men before the power loom

177

reduced them to penury, came to the blackhouses in the old
clachan of Glenrosa during the same period, to drink goats' milk
and ramble in the glen and about the slopes of Goatfell. Goats'
milk not only went out of fashion but became, as a result of the
discouragement of the goat by the improving factors of the nineteenth century, difficult to obtain, and the fashion which brought
the succeeding wave of holidaymakers was that for romantic
scenery.

<h2 style="text-align:center">EARLY TOURIST LITERATURE</h2>

Like many other fashionable tourist resorts in Scotland, Arran
derived some benefit from the attentions of Sir Walter Scott, who
in 1814, before abandoning verse and turning his attention to the
novel, published *The Lord of The Isles*, in which the events
described in Barbour's *The Bruce* were used as the framework
for a characteristic romance. The island itself was treated for the
first time as scenery, something to be looked at; not with under-
standing of how it came to be, or of the influences which moulded
the character of its people, but in terms of composition, tone, and
colour, a vision rather than a reality, whose purpose was to elevate
the soul. In effect this meant not only a highly artificial style of
language, and an obvious straining after effect, but much ludic-
rous distortion. Nevertheless the style became popular, and later
visitors thrilled to the idea that in the vicinity of the old mediaeval
chapel of St James, now hardly visible in a field beside Ballarie
farm, they were on the site of the nunnery of St Bride, where
the sister of Bruce had spent her days in prayer, having renounced
forever the love of a man whom she considered betrothed to
another.

The *Lord of the Isles* was published in 1814, the year in which
the second major division of the Arran farms was being planned,
and many people were to be displaced from their homes. The
next poem about the island came in 1828, the year before the
Sannox clearances, and just before the days of the steamboat. Its
author was none other than the Reverend Dr David Landsborough, and his *Arran, a Poem in Six Cantos*, is in the style of
another poet associated with the fashion for scenery, William
Wordsworth. This is so at least in respect of language and some

178

of the subject matter, but he was divided in his models, some of his content being suggested by Burns. There is a description of an open-air communion at Lamlash, obviously suggested by Burns' *Holy Fair*, but in the Landsborough version everything is seemly, and indeed there is only one Arran record to suggest that he might have been wrong—of a woman found at Brodick on the Monday following the sacrament, 'drunk behind the tents'.

It is impossible to say if Landsborough's poem was widely read, or helped to stimulate interest in the island as Scott's certainly did, but in 1847 the same author published a prose work, *Excursions in Arran, with reference to the Natural History of the Island*, with a reprint of the poem added. This work proved popular, and another series of *Excursions* followed in 1852. The Reverend David Landsborough junior continued the work, and in 1873 a volume was published containing edited extracts from his father's works, with a memoir and other chapters of a miscellaneous character written by himself. These constitute the earliest works in the class of tourist literature written about the island, and were added to in the nineteenth century only by George Milner, who in 1894 published *Studies of Nature on the Coast of Arran*, which in spite of its title is simply a delightful account of a summer holiday spent at Corrie.

To the Landsboroughs, therefore, is due almost the sole credit for providing Arran visitors, in the developing years of the island's holiday trade, with something useful to read, either in anticipation of their visit, or while confined to their lodgings by inclement weather. In parts the *Excursions* are unreadable today, because of wearisome repetition in the botanical lists, and a compulsion to grasp every possible excuse for the preaching of a sermon. Yet we cannot withhold admiration from the two men, in spite of their pedantry and fervour, for they were men of vigour. They established a fashion for strenuous open-air holidays still followed by some of the regular visitors to the island. Their activities included scrambles to the summits of the northern peaks, expeditions to the most remote lochs, picnics in the glens, usually beside the larger pools where a bathe was possible, and inshore fishing in the evenings from sailing or rowing boats. The island will never have anything better to offer.

The senior Landsborough had a lively curiosity, and besides

179

investigating the natural history of the island, for which he was qualified, took pains to learn what he could about its human past, and to note any antiquity encountered during his excursions and record what was said of it. Much of his historical information is inaccurate, and was vitiated further by his tendency to indulge in the imaginative reconstruction of any scenes which he thought picturesque, to the extent that history was drowned in fiction. His views on the antiquities, too, and those of his son, having been acquired from the islanders in the days before scientific archaeology, which was unknown in the island until Thomas Bryce conducted his investigations for the first volume of *The Book of Arran*, now seem absurd. Nevertheless the Landsboroughs' interest in these various aspects of the island helped to attract others who could investigate with greater prospect of success, and for this they deserve our gratitude.

Partly because they were unable to communicate with the islanders in their own language, and partly because they identified themselves with the gentry, the Landsboroughs tell us little of how the local people lived. The senior, referring back to the year 1841, some twelve years after the Sannox clearances, when elderly people who had not left the island, but had lost access to land, were lingering on in poverty in the decaying old blackhouses, said the latter were the poorest dwellings he had seen inhabited by human beings. There were a few rather less uncomplimentary references, as that to the little inn at Urinbeg, Lochranza, run by Mrs MacLarty, who 'notwithstanding her inauspicious name, was kind, and cleanly, and did everything in her power to render us comfortable'. For the benefit of non-Scottish readers it should be explained that 'clartie' is Scots for 'dirty'. They do give us a few glimpses of island life out-of-doors, of open-air services and communions, and the bustle of the fishing community on the Lochranza shore, but they remain onlookers, cut off from the people by barriers of race, language, and class. Nor do we obtain from the Landsboroughs much insight into the lives of the contemporary island aristocracy, although the Hamiltons, after the marriage in 1843 of the Marquis of Douglas and Clydesdale, later 11th Duke of Hamilton, to Princess Marie of Baden, visited Brodick castle much more frequently than ever before in their history.

180

The 11th Duke was the William Alexander Anthony Archibald whose statue stands today in the playground of Brodick school. Towards him and his successor, William Alexander Louis Stephen, the 12th Duke, the Landsboroughs were on no closer terms than are implied by a complimentary reference or a dedication. Their attitude was one of distant respect, mingled with gratitude for favours granted to members of the Stoddart family, to whom they had become related by marriage. For any idea of the kind of people the landowners were, and of the lives they led, we have to depend on works of a reminiscent character written in the following century: *Victorian Sidelights*, by A. M. W. Stirling, published in 1954, and *Marie and the Duke of H*, by Doris Langley Moore, published as recently as 1966.

THE VICTORIAN DUKES

The earlier 9th and 10th Dukes, who flourished during the most active period of enclosure and clearance, seem to have been like all their feudal predecessors except the Duchess Anne, absentee landlords, who administered the island through their factors. If they visited the island it was to hunt, and they were content with the rough accommodation offered by the castle as it was left by the Cromwellian garrison. Lord Cockburn, a Scottish judge, who in 1842, just after the Ayr railway had been built, made a trip to the island on one of the early steamboats, was shown over the castle by the caretaker, and described it in *Circuit Journeys* as 'a strong thing, with antiquity, site and trees, sufficient to have enabled its noble owner, if he had chosen to spend a little of the gilding he had wasted on the weavers of Hamilton, to have easily made it a fine place'. This of course the 10th Duke did in just two years, to provide a seat for his son William Alexander Anthony Archibald and his new daughter-in-law Princess Marie, and it was from the time of the building of the Victorian wing in 1844 that the link between the Hamiltons and their island estate became once again, as it had been briefly in the days of the Duchess Anne, personal.

Victorian Sidelights, the book which tells us something of

William Alexander Anthony Archibald, who became 11th Duke in 1852, is based on the papers of a lady named successively Marion Hamilton, Jeanie Hering, and Mrs Adams-Acton. The approach to her parentage is decidedly oblique. After giving a few pleasant glimpses of the 11th Duke's legitimate daughter, Mary, driving through Brodick in the tiny pony and trap presented to her by her godmother, Queen Victoria, or making omelettes in the Bavarian summer-house in the castle gardens, the book goes on to describe the lot of another little girl, Marion, said to be the daughter 'of a Scottish nobleman and a very lovely girl, Elizabeth Hamilton, who was known locally as the Belle of Brodick'. We are left to guess that the noble father was the 11th Duke himself, and in fact most local people take this view. Some, however, perhaps anxious to deny the little girl her ducal descent, attribute her existence, not to Elizabeth Hamilton, but to Princess Marie of Baden, the alleged father being Mr Hering, originally Baron von Heringen, a German, who had come to Britain and was establishing himself as a landscape painter. He had been invited to Brodick castle in the hope that he would find inspiration there, and he and Princess Marie, having in common their German origin and their craze for landscape gardening, became close friends. That they were such close friends as to start having a family in the duke's own home is not very likely, for although the duke was very often absent in Paris, Mrs Hering was present always. Mr Hering, however, did become little Marion's father, by adopting her, for it seems that before coming to Brodick castle he and his wife had lost their only child, and so had a void in their lives waiting to be filled. They justified themselves for taking the little girl from her mother by offering to obtain skilled treatment for a lameness from which she suffered and which could not be cured in Arran. They renamed her Jeanie Hering.

That the 11th Duke was the child's father best explains the reason why he built for the Herings the large red sandstone villa on the outskirts of Brodick, which is still known as Ormidale. This became the holiday home first of the Herings, and then of Jeanie when later she married Adams-Acton, the most successful portrait sculptor of his time, whose sitters included Queen Victoria herself. Adams-Acton (the hyphen and the Acton were additions made to his name because plain Adams did not seem to have the style appropriate to a sculptor looking for clients in the most exalted circles) had his studio in St John's Wood, then a fashionable outer suburb of London, and Jeanie there acted admirably the part of hostess to his famous sitters. There can be no doubt that it was through her connection with Ormidale, which she inherited on the death of Mr Hering and where she spent part of every summer, that many fashionable people were attracted to the island, for she never failed to sing its praises, persuading many of her friends to visit it, and sometimes letting her house. In the wake of her fashionable friends others of the same class followed, and for a period towards the turn of the century many well-known figures, some artistic, some literary, and some political, came to Arran on holiday.

One at least of the famous, Robert Browning, visited the island when the Hering step-parents were still alive, and several times walked over from Blairbeg, in the Lamlash area, to visit them at Ormidale. This was in 1862, the summer after the death in Florence of his wife Elizabeth Barrett. The poet had known Mrs Hering before her marriage, when she was still Katie Bromley. Sir Noel Paton, Queen Victoria's limner for Scotland, whom Jeanie described as so handsome that when he entered a room he conferred a favour by his mere presence, holidayed in Arran with his family year after year, in houses too numerous to detail, but principally at Alltachorvie, now a guest-house of the Holiday Fellowship.

It was in pursuit of Noel Paton that in 1871 Professor Charles Dodgson, later to become famous as Lewis Carroll, first visited the island. He had seen Noel Paton's *Quarrel of Oberon and Titania* in Edinburgh some years earlier, and when contemplating the publication of *Looking Glass House*, later to be entitled *Alice Through the Looking Glass*, was keen to have Noel Paton as his illustrator. Calling at Edinburgh and finding that the artist was in Arran he followed him there, and leaving his bag at the little inn by Lamlash quay called on him where he was lodging, on that occasion at Glenkill. The Noel Patons had arranged an expedition to watch the laying and taking up of a long sea-line, and Dodgson was invited to take the place of a member of the party who had sprained an ankle. He did so, giving up his plan of returning to the mainland that afternoon, and enjoyed the

183

experience, there being several charming little girls in the party to compensate for the disappointment of the catch, which was negligible. The trip included also a visit to the 'hermit's cave' on Holy Isle. When he left at six o'clock the next morning, having slept at the inn, he had failed to persuade Noel Paton to become his illustrator. He made subsequent visits with no better result and suffered bad weather in addition. Noel Paton eventually excused himself and recommended Tenniel.

Jeanie Hering, who continued to use her 'maiden name' after her marriage as a *nom de plume*, for she wrote children's stories, novels, and plays, claimed rather ingenuously to have some responsibility for the marriage of Henry Herbert Asquith to Margot Tennant. She had written but not posted a letter agreeing to let Ormidale for the summer to an unspecified applicant when she received a request for the house from Asquith. She felt tempted to refuse the first applicant in Asquith's favour, then felt it would be unfair, and refused Asquith. He took instead a house at Lamlash where the drains were bad, and Mrs Asquith contracted typhoid and died. She is buried in Kilbride graveyard. Jeanie claimed that if she had let Asquith have Ormidale, where of course the drains were flawless, the first Mrs Asquith would have lived, and the subsequent marriage to Margot Tennant could never have occurred.

Asquith had another link with Arran, for John MacKinnon Robertson, who was born at Low Glencloy in 1856, was Parliamentary Under-Secretary to the Board of Trade in his last administration. Robertson, who in the 1890s edited the *National Reformer* and the *Free Review*, played as a humanist and political radical an important part in the controversies of his time. He seems to have inherited his radical outlook and controversial vigour from his grandfather, John MacKinnon, who was known locally as the Baron, for he believed himself the lineal descendant of the MacKinnons who had held Sliddery in early feudal times as hereditary or 'kindly' tenants of the crown: a class of men who in the reign of James IV seem to have held their farms in Bute and Cowal in feu, and were known in these areas as 'barons'; but that a similar system of tenure applied in Arran has the authority only of local tradition. By the time of James IV most of Arran had passed to the Hamiltons, and they also could

184

have let their farms in feu, but there is no official record of this. The Baron, when there was dissatisfaction with a certain Brodick parochial schoolmaster, is said to have opposed him by setting up a school of his own, which was well attended.

In Arran Jeanie Hering is still remembered for her famous walk with her six young children, two maids, and a curious three-wheeled perambulator, from London to the Broomielaw, where in those days boats left for the island. The idea was suggested in the summer of 1886, when the Adams-Acton family was contemplating its annual holiday at Ormidale, by the news that a family on holiday in Dorset had walked there from London. Jeanie, who had been writing about her perambulator for a children's publication called *Little Wide-Awake*, thought a walk from London to the Broomielaw with the perambulator as the centre-piece would make wonderful copy, and after some conflict with her husband, who refused to accompany her, and many of her friends, she set out on the journey which resulted in due course in her book *The Adventures of a Perambulator*.

Perhaps the most significant event of the journey, since it establishes Jeanie as a born aristocrat, occurred when the nurse Ellen discovered on arriving at St Albans that she had left her travelling bag at South Mimms. She had to walk the six miles there and back the next morning before the normal time for starting the journey onward, and continue without any rest, for Jeanie would permit no departure from her timetable. It was Ellen who pushed the perambulator, loaded with luggage in addition to the one-year-old child, most of the way from London, although at the end of the journey it was Jeanie who received the acclaim. Ellen married an Arran man, John Sillars, for a time gardener at Ormidale before becoming tenant of West Mayish farm (plate p 89). She died at West Mayish in 1958, in her ninety-sixth year, and was buried in Brodick graveyard, where Adams-Acton and Jeanie Hering, too, are commemorated, by an impressive sculptured stone.

William Alexander Anthony Archibald, the 11th Duke of Hamilton, was always mentioned by Jeanie Hering with an admiration close to reverence. It was during his tenure of the dukedom that the old village of Brodick was moved from the vicinity of the castle and planted across the Rosa burn in the

lower reaches of the Cloy, and there is evidence of a more responsible attitude to the island people in the fact that in 1856 he
built Douglas Row and Alma Terrace to house those displaced
from the older cottages removed to provide the environment of
park and woodland considered appropriate to the extended and
embellished castle. The attractive row of houses at Catacol was
built also in the 11th Duke's time to rehouse people displaced
by the belated clearances in the north-west. These were to make
way for deer, not for sheep, for the profit was going out of the
latter; and since in 1849 Queen Victoria had initiated the custom
of royal holidays at Balmoral, and grouse shooting and deer
stalking had become a rage, the north end of the island was being
developed as deer forest, and much of the rest as grouse moor.
Shooting lodges were built to exploit the fashion, at Dougrie
and Dippen. The schools built by the 11th Duke will be discussed
later.

The 11th Duke died under rather dubious circumstances in
Paris. According to *Victorian Sidelights* he had been gambling
in a company which included Prince Louis Napoleon. He and
the prince had a disagreement, and on the prince becoming
aggressive he left the room. The prince followed him to the landing outside, there was a disturbance, and when the rest of the
company joined the prince it was to find the duke at the foot
of the stairs, fatally injured. The matter was hushed up, but
there seems to have been some suggestion that the duke did not
fall by accident. Of his successor, William Alexander Louis
Stephen, the 12th Duke, Jeanie Hering says little, except that he
sometimes visited her at Ormidale and listened to her stories of
old Arran, which she may have picked up from her mother's
people, if her mother was indeed Elizabeth Hamilton. They were
about the Sannox clearances, which Jeanie says took place in
the days of a 'cruel factor', by name Burrel. In this, as in most
of her island history, she was rather muddled. Burrel may have
been callous enough, but the Sannox clearances took place in
the days of the factor John Paterson, whose son of the same name
officiated in her own day from the Whitehouse in Lamlash in
what was still a fairly oppressive régime.

Jeanie suggests that the 12th Duke had less interest in Arran
than his predecessor, and this is borne out by what we read of

him in *Marie and the Duke of H*, a book on the diarist Marie Bashkirtseff by Doris Langley Moore. In 1872, when Marie as a girl of thirteen was doing the round of fashionable European resorts with her Russian parents, she saw the young Duke of Hamilton at Nice and fell in love with him. Although she never actually spoke to him she recorded in her diary, with considerable excitement, every occasion on which she either caught sight of him or even heard news of him, and we learn much about the sort of life he led. His glamour for Marie lay in his fabulous pedigree, his many titles, his income of about £140,000 a year from rents and mineral rights, his skill with yachts, horses and guns, his bachelor condition, his good looks, soon to be lost as he stoutened into middle age, and the suggestion of wicked virility conveyed by the fact that he maintained at Nice a stylish and expensive mistress, Amelia Gioia. The news of the duke's engagement to the nineteen-year-old daughter of the Duke of Manchester, which reached Marie in October 1872, was a tremendous shock, for Marie had herself resolved to marry him, and had gone to ridiculous lengths to bring herself to his notice. She was so distraught that she confided in her diary that she would have preferred him to go on even with Gioia, and indeed feared that the abandonment of that relationship, which had taken place before the duke's courtship of his future bride began, might prevent him from ever revisiting Nice, so that she might never see him again. His yacht *Thistle* did not in fact appear again at Nice while Marie was there, and she had to record with some jealousy not only that Gioia seemed to prosper in spite of her abandonment, but that the duke's marriage was successful, for his bride was by birth, upbringing and personality an admirable hostess for his deerstalking, fishing, steeplechasing, and yachting parties. The deerstalking parties were of course entertained in Arran, and included many members of the British and several foreign royal families.

That the 12th Duke may have left his Arran tenants too much at the mercy of his factor is suggested by the need felt, in September 1881, to defend him against certain calumniators. In the Arran estate office, preserved as a curiosity, is a petition signed by all his farm tenants, by the ministers, innkeepers, merchants, teachers, and even by the inspector of the poor, the steamboat agents, and the owner of the steamer *Brodick Castle*, which reads:

May it please Your Grace,

We, the undersigned, Inhabitants of Arran, have observed, with feelings of deep indignation, the recent public attack made on Your Grace as an unjust and tyrannical landlord.

Such attacks are alleged to be made upon information supplied by us, and made with our concurrence and on our behalf.

Lest our silence be misconstrued, we beg to repudiate all such statements as imply that we are at all discontented—on the contrary we desire to tender to Your Grace our heartfelt thanks for the just and kind manner in which we have invariably been treated, and we feel assured that should any just causes for complaint arise we shall receive at Your Grace's hands the greatest consideration.

It is our fervent wish and prayer that Your Grace may long be spared to prove as kind and liberal a landlord to us in the future as Your Grace and noble Ancestors have been in the past.

We are,

Your Grace's obedient servants

The words of the petition are on a separate sheet. Enclosed with it in a round case are the sheets of parchment containing the signatures, all stuck together top and bottom to make a continuous roll. Who initiated the petition we cannot be sure. One suspects the factor, John Paterson junior, whose own unpopularity was in no doubt from the memories of him handed down among the oldest inhabitants. But although he may have initiated it to save the duke's reputation from the consequences of his own harshness, it seems likely that it was Dr John A. Jamieson, a local physician, who superintended its circulation; for in the left-hand margin, against the signature of Duncan MacMillan of 'Bolary', obviously Ballarie farm at Lochranza, is a note reading 'See letter to Dr Jamieson of 3 Oct 1881 withdrawing', followed by a note in the right-hand margin reading 'See letter of 8 Oct 1881 adhering and explaining'. That the 12th Duke attached some value to the petition seems obvious from the fact that the case containing it is covered elegantly in black morocco leather and lettered in gilt. Yet what, in the circumstances of the time, was it worth? Any tenant causing offence by saying he was discontented could presumably be told that he could go elsewhere, as Duncan MacMillan of Ballarie may have been to make him so quickly change his mind. Patronage had been abolished in 1874, and it might have been possible for a minister to express dissent, if he felt it right to do so, but even ministers were still dependent on the landowners: the conformists for their salaries and the heritors' share of manse and church maintenance, for teinds were not abolished until 1921; and the non-conformists for security of tenure. Even the owner of the steamboat would have to consider the advantage of access to the new wooden pier at Brodick, built as recently as 1872 and an estate property.

There are further indications of discontent in the days of the 12th Duke in books by two local men which, unlike those of the holiday visitors or summer residents, tell us something of the lives of the ordinary island people. John Sillars, who was born in the Corrygills area and lived most of his life at Lamlash, published several novels set in Arran, most of them with period settings. Although the scenery of Arran figures pleasantly, the social background of most of them, that of a community of small independent landed proprietors, is not appropriate to Arran, and was probably borrowed from the works of S. R. Crockett, whose influence on his novels is obvious, not only in respect of social background, but also in choice of incident, characterisation, and style of dialogue.

But in the last of his novels, *The Desperate Battle*, published in 1925, Sillars ceases to be derivative, and not only captures the rhythms of real speech, but introduces characters closely observed from living originals, and builds his story from incidents characteristic of Arran life. The story is obviously autobiographical, and covers the lives of three generations of a family which had taken to the sea, as so many did, when displaced from the land. There is no better record than this novel of the shifts to which the people were put by the need to adapt to the new conditions created by agricultural improvement, developing trade, and the growth of the holiday industry. The story ends at the close of the First World War in a blaze of rather hysterical patriotism, and has the blemish of some rather materialistic aspirations too neatly fulfilled; yet apart from its ending and one or two earlier touches of melodrama it is a genuine record of Arran life, written with humour and compassion, striking a note of real tragedy in an account of a shipwreck, and achieving in its central character, based on the author's mother, a triumph of portraiture. The desperate battle of the title is her struggle to rear her family.

Although the subject is not stressed, the grip of the factor on the people of the period is apparent, summed up in the alliterative phrase, 'for in those days the fear of the factor was the foundation of fortune'. This fear figures again as 'the terror of the Whitehouse', which was of course the home of the Paterson factors, in a slightly later book by James Inglis, written sometime shortly after 1929, entitled *Brodick Old and New*. This is a work of reminiscence, written by the descendant of a mainland farmer introduced during the enclosure period to set local tenants an example in the new farming methods. Beginning at Corrygills it covers the whole of the Brodick district from there to the castle, taking each of the old communal farms in turn and describing the changes which had taken place between their disruption and the development of the village of Brodick as it was in the author's own time. The detail is profuse, and the book is difficult for the stranger because it assumes considerable local knowledge, not only of places but of people; but apart from its strictly local interest it has value as a record of the innovations which accompanied the change from the old life to the new, and made it possible.

EARLY STEAMBOATS

There are details of early steamboat services, with anecdotes of notable trips evidently handed down in local tradition. The particulars given sometimes conflict with those given by Mackenzie in the second volume of *The Book of Arran*, and it is wise to check them both against the facts supplied by James Williamson in *The Clyde Passenger Steamer*, published in 1904, or by Andrew MacQueen in *Echoes of Old Clyde Paddle-Wheels*, published in 1924.

Mackenzie's account starts with a voyage made by the *Helens-*

burgh from Greenock in August 1825 to Rothesay, the Kyles of Bute, Lochranza, Brodick, Millport, Fairlie, Largs, and Helensburgh, the trip starting at 8 AM and finishing at 9 PM. By 1829 the Castle Company ran two steamboats a week, the *Toward Castle* leaving Glasgow every Tuesday for Brodick and Lamlash, and the *Inverary Castle* every Saturday, the vessels returning from Arran on Monday and Wednesday mornings respectively. From 1832 to 1864 the MacKellar Company ran the *Jupiter* and the *Juno* on the Arran route, also from Glasgow, but after the construction of the Ayr Railway which took Lord Cockburn to the coast in 1842 there were sailings from Ardrossan, by the *Hero* and the *Leven*, the former owned by the MacKellar Company and the latter by Robert Jamieson of Arran, a brother of the Dr Jamieson already mentioned as involved in the petition to the 12th Duke.

The above sailings were in summer only, but in 1847 the Ardrossan Steamboat Company built the *Isle of Arran* for the winter run, to supersede the schooner *Brodick* of the twice weekly sail-packet mail service, conducted first from Saltcoats and later from Ardrossan. In 1860 the *Isle of Arran* was itself superseded by the *Earl of Arran*, built for the same company. Unlike its predecessors, which were built of wood, the *Earl of Arran* had an iron hull. Later the 12th Duke himself entered the business with the *Lady Mary*, Mackenzie says in 1868, which indicates that it was named after the duke's sister Mary Victoria, who a year later married the Prince of Monaco, and not after his future bride, Lady Mary Montagu, who did not become engaged to him for another four years and would at the time be only fifteen years of age. The *Lady Mary* was so successful that after only two years a new and faster vessel was built to replace her. This was the *Heather Bell*, and accounts kept in the estate office until she was sold after proving a failure cover the period 1871-4. After being sold she went into service in the Bristol Channel. The *Lady Mary* was brought into service again but eventually failed also, and the Arran traffic passed into the hands of William Buchanan, owner of the *Rothesay Castle*, and later of the *Brodick Castle*, mentioned earlier in connection with the petition to the duke. The Buchanan steamer *Scotia* succeeded the *Brodick Castle*, then the traffic passed into the hands of the Glasgow and South-

Western Railway, whose first steamboat was the *Glen Sannox*, first of three to bear that name.

In 1890 the Caledonian Steam Packet Company, associated with the Caledonian Railway Company, which by now also had a line to the south-west coast, entered the traffic with the *Duchess of Hamilton*; so Lady Mary Montagu did have a steamboat named after her, but under the title she acquired by marriage. Another Lady Mary, the 12th Duke's daughter, later to become the Marchioness of Graham and then Duchess of Montrose, also had steamboats named after her, under both titles. It was she who inherited the Arran estate when in 1895, on the death of the 12th Duke without male issue, the Hamilton title passed to a descendant of William Douglas, the 3rd Duke and husband of the Duchess Anne. Eventually, after much hectic competition not without its dangers to passengers, and much amalgamation of railways, the steamboat services over the whole Clyde area were themselves amalgamated under the Caledonian Steam Packet Company, which functioned until recently as a subsidiary of British Rail.

All the vessels so far named were paddle boats, but after the successful trial of the turbine *King Edward* on the Greenock to Campbeltown run in 1901, turbines were introduced widely, although in many cases they retained the names of the vessels they replaced. The three vessels successively named *Glen Sannox* illustrate almost completely the evolution of the ships of the Clyde passenger fleet, the first a paddle boat, the second a turbine, and the third, which entered the Ardrossan to Arran service in 1957, a motor vessel with a car deck and hydraulic lift.

The pier at Brodick, first of the wooden piers to be built on the island, was completed in 1872. Previously passengers had been landed from the steamboats by rowing boat at small stone jetties, and this practice continued elsewhere on the island until parliamentary orders for further piers were obtained: for Lamlash in 1883, Lochranza in 1886, and Whiting Bay in 1897. From the passing of the orders a few years elapsed before the piers were built and in use. Mackenzie says that the last of the wooden piers, that at Whiting Bay, was not in use until 1901. The small stone jetties, most of them built by statute labour, which will be discussed later, continued in use for cargo boats.

These too had progressed from sail to steam; and it is interesting to learn from Inglis that one of the earliest of the small steam cargo boats or puffers in the Arran trade was built on the island. This was the *Glencloy*, built in the corner of a field at Low Glencloy from timber mainly of local growth. It was launched in 1895 and was the first of the puffers of the Cloy Line, founded by Adam Hamilton and his sons George and Gavin. These were the son and grandsons respectively of James Hamilton, skipper of the *Brodick*, built by Fife of Fairlie about 1832 as a sloop, but later converted into a schooner and sailed regularly between Brodick and Ardrossan, the last of the sail packets to carry the mails or to ship cattle from the island. The Brodick-built *Glencloy* was followed by the *Invercloy* and the *River Cloy*, both built elsewhere, and finally by a new and larger *Glencloy*, on the earlier vessel of that name being sold to Irish owners. Apart from the Hamilton puffers those most commonly associated with the Arran trade have been of the Hay Line, with names such as *Trojan*, *Spartan*, *Tuscan*, and *Cretan*. Some of these, such as the *Roman*, have lately been owned by small local syndicates, and although the last named sailed out of the Port at Corrie in December 1957 to be broken up at Troon, one or two of the others are still to be seen about the island.

INTERNAL DEVELOPMENT

With so much progress in the means of transport to the island, it was inevitable that something should be done to accommodate the kind of people who were coming to it on holiday. The naturalists and geologists who had come in the earlier half of the nineteenth century, and vigorous trampers like Milner and the Landsboroughs, might have been content with simple cottage inns such as that run at Urinbeg by Mrs MacLarty; but those of the Adams-Acton and Noel Paton sets, while willing enough to overflow at times into cottage accommodation, preferred comfortable living in hotels and villas. There were two main waves of hotel and villa building, the first in the days of the 11th Duke, around 1856, coinciding with the building of the rows, terraces, and shooting lodges already mentioned, when the Douglas Hotel took the place of the Cladach; and the second, according to

Inglis, when the 'terror of the Whitehouse' vanished in 1881, that is, when the second of the Patersons ceased to be factor. One sign at least of a new influence at work is that a year before the 12th Duke's death in 1895 Hamilton Terrace was built at Lamlash to rehouse people from the old whitewashed row which until then stood on a site slightly seaward of it. No doubt the property would be made to pay, but its provision was a service, although the 12th Duke was less fortunate than the 11th in his architect. Yet it was not until the death of the 12th Duke that building restrictions were really eased, and leases given freely, which could be converted into feus after a dozen years, and it was in the period immediately following 1895 that the bulk of the dressed red sandstone villas, shops and boarding-houses were built in Brodick and over the island generally.

It would seem from hints dropped by Inglis that in the days of the 12th Duke, when deer and grouse had taken precedence over sheep farming, visitors were not really welcomed, and those who did come were forbidden to bring dogs. Tenants of estate houses such as Douglas Row were not for a long time allowed to accommodate visitors, until the fear that poverty might make them a public charge led to a relaxation. They were then allowed to take visitors provided they paid an increased rent. According to Inglis, when the news of this relaxation was announced an old woman ran up and down Douglas Row shouting 'Hooray! Hooray! We've got oor leeberty noo! We've got oor leeberty noo!'

The earliest visitors of the railway and steamboat era, such as Lord Cockburn, had to make their expeditions into Glen Rosa and Glen Sannox either on foot or horseback, but in 1863, during the period of the amalgamation of the very small farms established by the divisions planned in 1814, one MacBride lost his land when Peter MacDonald, lessee of the Douglas Hotel, became tenant of the new enlarged farm of Brandon Bank and combined farming with his innkeeping. Reduced to the status of a cottar, MacBride imported a wagon from the mainland and ran it for hire. It was the first spring vehicle to be seen in Arran, but was unfortunately lost at sea when being taken to Irvine for repair. Later in the century its journey would have been unnecessary, for there was at least one family of coachbuilders on the island, the Mackenzies of Shiskine, some of whose vans, beautiful pieces of craftsmanship, can still be seen lurking behind more modern vehicles in the Victorian premises of some of the island's butchers and grocers.

Until about 1930 horse wagonettes still met the steamboats at the piers, although the first motor car had come to the island, on the PS *Jupiter*, as early as 1897, and caused a sensation by travelling from Brodick to Sannox, a distance of seven miles, in thirty-five minutes. The first bus on the island was bought from the Albion works by Colin Currie of Balmichael, who had carried mail, goods and passengers to the west of the island throughout the days of wheeled horse transport. Asked about payment for the bus, he drew the necessary cash from his pocket. Further bus enterprises developed along mail routes served by Ernest Ribbeck and Donald Stewart to the north and south-west respectively. Ernest Ribbeck, one of two brothers, saddlers by trade, who had come to Brodick in the days of Princess Marie of Baden and were favoured because of their nationality, became postmaster at Brodick in 1871. He brought a horse vehicle into service and took over the delivery of mail from Brodick to the post-office at Corrie from Robert Douglas, the postmaster there, who had hitherto made the journey on foot. Ernest's daughter followed him in Brodick post-office, which in 1913 was moved to the building which is now Pelligrini's café, and his son Kaspar on the Corrie mail route. The latter in the 1920s developed a bus service on the Corrie route, and this, with the others mentioned, initiated a burst of enterprise which was to reach its peak in 1962 when seven bus companies, functioning from Brodick, Lamlash, Whiting Bay, Kildonan, Blackwaterfoot, Machrie, and Pirnmill, were run respectively by Ribbeck, Gordon, Lennox, Stewart, Bannatyne, Weir, and MacMillan.

The telegraph was first installed in 1872, when several gentlemen staying at the Douglas Hotel sent a congratulatory telegram to Sir William Thomson, later Lord Kelvin, himself a fairly frequent visitor to Arran, and famous as a pioneer of the Atlantic and other long distance submarine cables. The telegraph was soon extended all over the island, and a permanent linesman appointed in 1886. The first telephone on the island was installed in 1891, when a private line was laid between Brodick castle and Dougrie Lodge, and the first telephone link with the main-land came with the building of the post office in 1913. By 1962 the island had ten exchanges, nine of them automatic, twenty-five kiosks, and three call offices, and today there are more telephones per hundred of the population than in Britain as a whole. Since the beginning of the Second World War trunk calls have been transmitted partly by beam wireless.

Electricity was first generated privately by the estate during the First World War and supplied some forty or fifty houses, but it was not until 1933 that the Arran Light and Power Company was established, which generated electricity at a station beside Brodick Pier. This was taken over in 1946 by the North of Scotland Hydro-Electric Board, and the service extended into every corner of the island. Since 1965 power has come from the grid by means of a cable laid between Carradale and Balliekine.

The first aeroplane landed in the Corrygills district sometime around 1929. It probably created an even greater sensation than the first motor car, but no greater than would be created today if the feat were repeated, for Arran's record of air transport has since been limited, after some use in the 1930s of a small airstrip at Shiskine, to the use of the helicopter, mainly in cases of medical emergency.

HOLIDAY AMENITIES

Coincident with the relaxation of restrictions which followed the end of the Paterson régime there was, in addition to the acceleration of the building of shops and villas, some attempt to provide amenities. The Invercloy Improvement Trust was formed in 1892, on the initiative of Inglis, to make what was to become the heart of the new Brodick more attractive to visitors, and shortly afterwards the need was felt for a village hall. Inglis tells how, just before the death of the 12th Duke, a deputation of three leading citizens made its way to the castle to obtain his permission, already promised through an intermediary, to form a limited liability company to build and run the hall. Henry Ribbeck, the second of the two German brothers already men-tioned, who had developed from saddler to general merchant

196

and built himself the shop now owned by the Alexanders, led the deputation, the remaining members of which were Robert Hamilton and the baker Alexander Wooley, the latter a descendant of a veteran of Waterloo who had come to Arran in the preventive service. Henry Ribbeck, being more fluent in German than in English, asked his companions if he might speak in that language, and when the interview took place neither of them knew what was being said. The company was formed and the new hall built in 1895, and about the same time the directors laid out a golf course on the slopes of West Mayish, but the estate replaced this in 1913 by its own course on the present site between Ormidale and Strabane. The hall directors also laid out a bowling green, which was formally opened in 1908 by a summer visitor of some fifty years standing, and a clubhouse was added in 1927. Tennis courts followed some ten years after the bowling green.

There was no Inglis to record how the other villages compared with Brodick in the provision of amenities, but Alexander Hamilton of Lamlash, who holds the unusual distinction of being an honorary sheriff in the county, is convinced that his own village was slightly ahead with most of them. He mentions a story told by his friend John Kerr, in 1968 just ninety years of age, of how as a senior pupil he was allowed out of Lamlash school early on spring afternoons to go to the new golf course and tramp down the greens. The golf course must, therefore, have been made before 1892, nine years before the clubhouse was opened. The date of the building of Lamlash 'parish hall', said to have been the best hall in Arran before Brodick hall was built, is also given as 1892. Although nominally a church hall, it was made available to the whole community, because donations towards its cost had been accepted from people outside the established church.

Whiting Bay, now one of the three main villages of the island, was the last of these to be developed, having been the last to get a pier.

8   THE GROWTH OF DEMOCRACY

IN considering the innovations which accompanied the rise of
the holiday trade on the island, we have so far confined our
attention almost entirely to those effected by private enterprise.
We come now to consider for the century following the clearances
the development of the services supplied by local government
bodies. It is largely a story of the growth of democracy. Before
the extension of the franchise began with the Reform Act of
1832, only persons holding 'forty shillings land of old extent' from
the crown, or freeholders of land worth 400 pounds Scots a year,
had the right to vote in the counties. The maintenance of law
and order, and the provision of roads, harbours, and bridges,
were the responsibility of justices of the peace who were
appointed, and controlled in respect of their expenditure, by
commissioners of supply, themselves nominated from among the
principal landowners of the counties. This meant that as far as
Arran was concerned the Duke of Hamilton had virtually
absolute power. In 1790, of twelve persons entitled to vote in
the county of Bute, which being small had a representative in
parliament only after every other election, nine were 'parchment
barons', or persons granted by the owner the nominal superiority
of a piece of land worth 400 pounds Scots a year, on condition
that they voted as he wished. The three persons in the county
of Bute entitled to vote by virtue of genuine ownership of land
would obviously include the Duke of Hamilton and the Marquis
of Bute. The other may have been Fullarton of Kilmichael. The
nine 'parchment barons' or fictitious voters would be henchmen
of the two larger proprietors. The commissioners of supply would
certainly be the Duke of Hamilton and the Marquis of Bute, and
the justices of the peace men of their choice. A paper included
with the census enumerator's return for 1801 shows that in Arran
then there were two justices, William Stevenson and John
Stoddart. William Stevenson was the duke's factor, and John
Stoddart his physician, and the latter was appointed on the
suggestion of the former. So in Arran the maintenance of law

198

and order, and the provision of roads, harbours and bridges, were virtually in the hands of the factor.

As far as these last were concerned, the labour was supplied by the tenants and their able-bodied dependants, who from 1719, and this explains why roadmaking was first recorded in the days of the Duchess Anne, had been obliged by statute to provide six days labour a year, and a clause inserted into the Arran leases early in the nineteenth century exacted three days more. Tenants could instead of supplying labour compound for a money payment fixed by the justices of the peace, and Mackenzie suggests that such monies bought the tools and equipment used and paid the wages of the overseer, in which case the roads cost the landowner nothing. Of course the upkeep of such tracks as were adequate before the introduction of wheeled vehicles would involve little effort; but as better roads were required from about 1807 onwards, when according to Headrick small carts were being introduced to the south end of the island from Ayrshire, the island factors felt the compulsion to exact statute labour with increasing strictness, and this being inadequate, began to augment it by imposing fines of road labour for breaches of estate rules. This practice continued until statute labour was abolished in 1878, and for by-roads, according to tradition, throughout the period of the Paterson régime, which did not end until 1881; and it seems to have been resentment against the imposition of road labour for breaches of estate rules, rather than the pressure of exorbitant rents, which lay behind the hatred felt towards the Patersons, and the discontent suggested by the need felt by the 12th Duke's adherents to organise the petition quoted earlier in the previous chapter.

As the nineteenth century progressed statute labour proved inadequate to turn the old pony tracks into roads suitable for the increasing cart traffic, and although the system was the basis of road maintenance until its abolition, it had to be augmented for purposes of road construction. In 1810, at the joint expense of the government and the landowners, a road suitable for wheeled traffic was constructed between Gortonallister, south of Lamlash, and Brodick. It was known as the Parliamentary Road, and its construction no doubt gave some employment to people displaced from the land by the division of the communal farms. Seven

years later the road was continued from Brodick across the island
to the shore at Blackwaterfoot. This length of road, known as
the String, was planned by Thomas Telford, the famous Scottish
road engineer, and built and maintained by a contractor at an
annual charge to the duke of from £40 to £80. In 1817 a
branch road was made from Brodick to Sannox, and in 1821-2
the Ross Road was built from the Parliamentary Road at Lamlash
to Bennecarrigan by the Monamore and Sliddery glens. At the
same time detached stretches of road were made at Kilpatrick,
Largybeg, and Auchencairn. Between that time and 1843, when
the road from Sannox to Lochranza was built over the Boguille,
these various stretches of road were joined up. Illustrations in
such books as Ramsay's *Geology of Arran*, published in 1841,
show the roads of the period to have been narrow cart tracks
interrupted by gates at farm boundaries. Most waters and burns
were crossed at fords, and bridges were wooden, usually for
pedestrians only.

It was not until after the passing of the second Reform Act of
1868, which gave the vote to proprietors of land or property
valued at £5 a year or more, and tenants paying annual rents of
£14 or more, that statute labour was abolished. The first Reform
Act, which gave the vote to proprietors of land valued at £10
a year or more, or tenants paying annual rents of £50 or more,
had meant little in Arran, as it increased the Parliamentary voters
on the island by no more than a few tenants of the recently
created large farms, like Captain Shannon of Bennecarrigan,
Robert Stoddart of Sannox, Lieutenant MacKirdy of Bennan,
and Major MacAllister of Springbank. The Reform Act of 1868,
however, ensured that the majority of the reasonably substantial
farm tenants qualified for the franchise, and although they might
not be willing to provoke the hostility of the factor by openly
adopting political attitudes not approved by him, they would
be more than willing, with the newly enfranchised farmers all
over the country, to abolish statute labour, not necessarily
because it would make the provision of roads cheaper for them,
for of course they had to pay rates, but because of the
indignity associated with it, in spite of the provision for
opting out.

A third Reform Act followed in 1885 and gave the parliamentary vote to all male adults, irrespective of wealth in land or property; and shortly afterwards popularly elected county councils took over the provision of roads and bridges, although not of harbours, from the commissioners of supply and justices of the peace and appointed county road boards for the purpose, with delegation of powers in many cases to district committees, of which there was one for Arran. It was under the Arran District Committee, which functioned until 1929, when local government was again reformed, that the first stone bridges were built in Arran, and most of these survive until today. It was after the passing of the third Reform Act also that the police administration passed from commissioners of supply and justices of the peace to police committees of county councils, although until 1929 the commissioners of supply continued to function as collectors of revenue, and shared control of county expenditure with the county councils, having equal representation with them on standing joint committees for that purpose. The first Arran policeman, who is said by Inglis to have lived at Strathwhillan, the home also of the first recorded Fullarton crowner, seems to have come to the island around 1863, when farm amalgamations were taking place in the area. This was in the days before popularly elected county councils, so he would be subject to the commissioners of supply and the justices of the peace, virtually the duke and the factor.

EDUCATION

The duke and the factor had considerable control also over the other local government functions of the pre-democratic period, which were the responsibility of the parish kirk sessions, for under the system of patronage the landowner appointed the minister, and over the lay members the factor could assert himself firmly. The two local government functions for which the established church was responsible after the Reformation were education and poor relief. An Act of 1698 had made it compulsory for heritors or landowners to establish and maintain a school in every parish, and they were allowed to make their tenants pay half the 'stent' or rate agreed for this purpose. Neither landowners nor tenants were anxious to assume the burden, in spite of the misappropriated church lands from which many of the former drew revenue, and as the kirk sessions responsible for administering the schools had no way of forcing them to do so, except by moral persuasion, it was almost a century after the passing of the act before John Knox's ideal of a school in every parish was realised. The position in Arran does not seem to have been as bad as in other parts of Scotland, although in the early eighteenth century it would appear that although education was provided, it was without help from the landowners or tenants, and was paid for almost entirely out of session funds, obtained partly from church collections, and partly from 'mulcts' or fines imposed upon certain types of delinquent for breaches of moral law.

There is a record of 1704 for Kilmory parish of a school building ordered, at a cost of 40 pounds Scots, from the latter source. It was to be a simple building, of stone and clay, 'without divot except one going or two upon the top of the wall thereof', 42 ft long by 13 ft broad, with three gables and two doors; which suggests that it was to be in two parts, one the schoolroom and the other a single-roomed dwelling for the schoolmaster. 'Sufficient lights' were stipulated, which probably meant that there would be unglazed windows on opposite sides of each apartment, with shutters which would be manipulated according to the direction of the weather, as in the blackhouses already described, and the building, again like the blackhouses, would be thatched with divot and heather, and would have its hearth on the floor. There seems to have been a similar school building at Kilbride, in the Blairmore area beside the old church of St Brigid, in 1709, some of the stone for which was removed from the Dunan Beag cairn, and in 1715 Kilbride session ordered another similar building for the Glenashdale district, although the intention was that the Kilbride parish schoolmaster had to pay his Glenashdale assistant from his own salary. Apart from these schools there seem to have been others, conducted in schoolmasters' houses or in barns or caves, financed partly by the sessions, partly by the parents, and partly from the fees paid for each subject taught. Besides paying fees the children took peats to school in winter for the fire, and on St Bride's day, 1 February, presents of money to the schoolmaster, the boy and girl giving the largest amounts being crowned king and queen for the day with paper crowns, before all marched off, sustained by a dram of toddy supplied by the schoolmaster, for a holiday.

Matters were improved by an Act of 1803 which made provision for 'side schools' in parts of each parish too remote to be served by the main parochial schools, and laid down for the principal schoolmasters maximum and minimum salaries, to be paid by the landowners and tenants, who had to supply also, for the principal schoolmasters only, a house of not more than two rooms. There was talk at the time of 'palaces for dominies'. The act, therefore, gave recognition to the side schools already in existence, making them a proper charge on landowners and tenants. Accommodation does not seem to have improved immediately, for there is a record of as late as 1845 of an accident in a side school at Feorline, where the walls of a potato barn being used as a schoolroom fell during the thaw following a severe frost and crushed five little girls to death. This tragedy seems happily to have been an isolated circumstance, and by the time it happened Arran had no fewer than eight parochial schools, four in each of the two parishes.

The salaries of the eight parochial schoolmasters seem to have been met in each parish by dividing among them, in proportion to the number of their pupils, a single maximum salary. Thus in Kilbride parish the salaries were for Lamlash £19, Brodick £16, Corrie £4, and Lochranza £6, although the last was a joint school with Kilmory, from which the schoolmaster had a further payment. About the same time the salaries for Kilmory parish were for Kilmory £17 10s, Shiskine £15, Imachar £5 16s and Lochranza £10 10s, the last again only a part payment. All the parochial schoolmasters on the island, except at Imachar, had a free house with garden and 'glebe'. By this time the main schoolhouses, although still thatched, were built of stone and lime, had chimneys in the gables, and were whitewashed. In both parishes, as in other parts of Scotland, children still paid fees, those for Kilmory being, for reading 2s, for reading and writing 2s 6d, for these plus arithmetic 3s, for Latin 5s, all per quarter. Bookkeeping and navigation cost respectively £1 and £1 10s. It was stipulated that all teachers in the parish should be able to teach Gaelic, although Paterson, who was for the abolition

203

of the language, suggests that this was not so, and that it was taught only in the extra-parochial schools set up by the General Assembly under a scheme of 1823. Gaelic would of course be necessary for the teaching of English, which probably explains the discrepancy. Finally, it was stipulated that no teacher should be appointed to the main parochial school at Kilmory who could not teach both Latin and church music. Mackenzie says that the largest school on the island could draw no more from fees than £14 a year, and the smallest not more than £5, which even if we assume that the fees went to the schoolmaster in addition to his salary means that most were little better off than farm servants, and worse off than skilled workmen such as masons or carpenters; for in 1840 the former earned from £6 to £8 in the half year, and the latter from 3s to 3s 6d a day. Each of the parish ministers had a free manse and glebe and more than three times the income of the best paid teachers.

Generous as was the provision of parochial schools as compared with that in many other parts of Scotland, it was insufficient for the needs of an island with such scattered communities, and in addition to its four parochial schools Kilbride had at least two others, one at Whiting Bay set up by the General Assembly, and the other a private school, maintained at the expense of the parents, in Lamlash. Kilmory, still the more populous parish even in the 1840s, had in addition to its four parochial schools eight others, two of them set up by the General Assembly, and six private. After the Disruption of 1843 the Free Church established its own school at Balmichael, a successor to that conducted, in the earlier days of the patronage disputes, in the cave at Kilpatrick.

The system remained unchanged until the passing of the Scottish Education Act of 1872, but before that date, in the days of William Alexander Anthony Archibald, the 11th Duke, because of the keen interest of Princess Marie of Baden in the welfare of both teachers and children, the building of greatly improved schoolhouses accompanied that of such estate housing enterprises as Alma Terrace and Douglas Row. The red sandstone Victorian schoolhouse forming the principal part of the curious complex of buildings devoted to education in Brodick today is a fair sample of the improved schools built by the 11th

Duke. Inglis says that although 1854 is the date on the building it was not opened until 1856. Such delays are commonplace nowadays, and cannot detract from the merit of the 11th Duke in providing the building which replaced the old whitewashed school beside the smiddy at Rosaburn.

By the Scottish Education Act of 1872, which set up the Scottish Education Department and made education compulsory between the ages of five and thirteen years of age, the administration of the schools was taken out of the hands of the kirk sessions and made the responsibility of school boards elected by the ratepayers of each parish. Fees were still charged, but those unable to pay were given assistance from the rates. Schools became subject to government inspection and grants were paid if the pupils reached a prescribed standard, a system which led to much abuse of the tawse. In 1883 the school-leaving age was raised to fourteen, and was to remain so for another sixty-three years. In 1888 the leaving certificate examination, which was to become accepted as the gateway to the universities, was established. In 1891 fees for children between the ages of five and fourteen were abolished.

The parish school boards established in 1872 took over such schools as were built by the 11th Duke and were, therefore, adequate to the standards of the time and built others similar in style, substantial and fairly elegant stone buildings with slated roofs, each with a schoolhouse and classrooms, as at Lochranza. According to Inglis the 12th Duke refused to part with the buildings at Brodick, Corrie, and Auchagallon. It may be that these had been built by the 11th Duke without call on the tenants, and could, therefore, be regarded as estate properties. Inglis says they were retained and run by the 12th Duke until his death in 1895. For the other existing Victorian schools, presumably built under the terms of the 1803 act with the tenants paying half the cost, the estate exacted payment for the surrender of its interest, the schoolhouse at Kildonan costing the Kilmory school board £250. New leases of ninety-nine years, subject to annual payments of ground rent, were granted to the school boards at the time of the takeover, and similar leases in respect of the Victorian schools subsequently built. As these leases run out the buildings still subject to them revert to the landowner, but schools built recently, as at Lamlash and Whiting Bay, or substantially extended, as at Brodick and Shiskine, are on ground acquired by outright purchase. That the 12th Duke held on to the schools built at the sole expense of his predecessor would seem to indicate that he was hostile to the growth of democracy. In the pre-democratic days of the kirk session schools the schoolmasters' salaries had been fixed jointly by the factor and the minister, and no doubt this suited him better.

The Victorian school buildings still stand at Kildonan, Kilmory, Sliddery, Shiskine, Machrie, Pirnmill, Lochranza, Corrie, Brodick, and Lamlash. One at Whiting Bay has recently been demolished and replaced by an intriguing glassy building fronted by a row of lozenge-shaped gables. That at Kildonan is the headquarters of the travelling library. Those at Machrie and Sliddery have been sold for other purposes. That at Lochranza was allowed to revert to the landowner and stands empty, while the Lochranza children attend school at Pirnmill. That at Lamlash was superseded by Arran High School, completed in 1941, but used until the end of the Second World War as a billet for the Navy, and not opened, as a junior secondary school, until 1946, since when it has been upgraded and extended piecemeal. The old school and school house now accommodate the sheriff and justice of the peace courts, and the offices of Arran District Council and of the subcommittees of Bute County Council, and will no doubt continue as local government offices when these councils are abolished in 1975.

An Act of 1908 introduced compulsory medical examination and made it possible for the school boards to provide cheap school meals and free books and stationery, but in the absence of records it is impossible to say if these voluntary powers were used in Arran. Certainly school meals are a recent innovation. Free books and stationery may not have been provided until the Scottish Education Act of 1918 replaced the parish school boards by education authorities elected every three years on a county basis. The intention of this Act was to put an end to the inequality of the schools provided by comparatively wealthy towns and poor country parishes. In 1929 the Scottish Local Government Act replaced the specially elected education authorities by education committees nominated by county councils mainly from among their own members. The intention here was said to be to enable the county councils to plan education in the wider context of county development. Differences in the services supplied by the various counties were reduced when an act of 1946 made all counties pay the same scale of salaries to their teachers. The same Act fixed 1947 as the year for raising the school-leaving age to fifteen, and provided for grants to parents of children who continued at school beyond that age. The increases in government grant necessitated by the 1946 act have tended to place control of education more and more into the hands of the central authority, and it is now only partially a local government function.

POOR RELIEF

This applies even more to the other local government function performed in pre-democratic times by the kirk sessions, poor relief, now entirely in the hands of the central authority. There is a record of 1746 that Kilbride session served out badges to 'real objects of charity' which enabled them to beg without molestation, but in the main provision for the poor was made from church collections, and besides the local poor, of whom there seem to have been few during the runrig period, probably because the system itself catered for the elderly and disabled, travellers of various sorts were given assistance, as 'a stranger awaiting a fair wind', or 'a poor passenger's five children', or 'a poor passenger who was Robed by the privateirs and was for a considerable space in france'. Mackenzie notes also payments by Kilmory session to funds for 'the propagation of Christian knowledge in the Highlands', for 'the supply of the Presbyterians of New Castle', and for 'the relief of distressed Protestants in Lithuania'. Clearly the unofficial relief of poverty by 'country charity' or neighbourly help was sufficient to allow the sessions to exercise benevolence from the church collections on an almost global scale. The session clerk and the beadle obtained their wages from the same source, as did some of the early side schoolmasters, and on the occasion of old James Stewart's ordination, when he came from being catechist at Lochranza to become minister of Kilbride, there was paid from the collection taken at the sacrament a sum for the ministers' dinner equal to about a quarter of the total amount paid to the poor of the parish in a whole year. But the dinner need not have been an extravagant one. The amount paid to the poor was not large, since they were then so few in number.

Mackenzie comments on the increase in the numbers on the parish poor rolls subsequent to Burrel's onslaught on runrig. In 1793 there were twelve poor on the Kilbride roll out of a population of 2,545, and forty on the Kilmory roll out of a population of 3,259. By 1835 the figure for Kilbride was fifty out of a population of 2,397, and for Kilmory seventy-five out of a population of 3,779. By 1850 the figure for Kilbride was sixty-eight out of 2,786 and for Kilmory seventy-eight out of 3,455, but by this time the system had changed. By 1845, a time of much poverty in the mainland towns crowded with Highlanders displaced from the land, and inevitably referred to as 'lazy and useless', the system whereby the poor were relieved by the churches from the voluntary contributions of its members had become inadequate; and although the church had been authorised to levy an 'assessment' for poor relief this, like the 'stent' for education, was not easy to enforce, and in the majority of parishes, and certainly in Arran, never was enforced, although as far as the Arran landowners are concerned it is only fair to say that their personal servants seem in old age to have been given allowances, for there are occasional references to the 'duke's pensioners'.

Over the country as a whole, however, the old system had been strained beyond its limits and in 1845 the responsibility for poor relief was vested in parochial boards elected on the basis of a property qualification. Some public health duties were also imposed on these parochial boards, and in 1857 district boards, of which there was one for Arran, were set up to take care of lunatics. The relief of the poor on a parochial basis would work quite well in Arran, where the proportion of poor to the population of each parish was not overwhelming, but on the mainland, where some industrial parishes had a high proportion of poor, the system was inequitable. This was in no way overcome by the next change. In 1894, five years after the setting up of popularly elected county councils, popularly elected parish councils were set

208

up also, which in addition to other functions took over poor relief from the parochial boards. Poor relief, therefore, continued on a parochial basis, although the public health functions of the parochial boards were taken over, like roads and bridges, by district committees, the latter consisting in Arran of representatives of the county and parish councils. With the passing of the Scottish Local Government Act of 1929 poor relief was at last put on a county basis, and was administered in Arran by a local subcommittee of Bute County Council, which employed a separate inspector of the poor for the island. By this means the burden on the parishes with a high proportion of poor was partially eased, but there were still differences in the burden as between the counties, and in 1948 the relief of the poor became a function of the National Assistance Board, and the local government inspector of the poor in Arran left the island to take up an appointment with that board on the mainland.

PUBLIC HEALTH

It was when the Arran District Committee, set up by the Act of 1894, took over public health duties from the old parochial boards, that the first hospital was built in Arran. An isolation hospital for people suffering from infectious diseases, it was built of corrugated iron, and stood near the head of the Blairmore burn, almost quarter of a mile south-east of the summit of the road between Lamlash and Brodick, on a site still marked by a group of beech trees. The next isolation hospital, opened after the passing of the 1929 Act by the health committee of Bute County Council, was in a converted house called Ardmhor at Whiting Bay. Although it continued to function until the passing of the National Health Act of 1947 it was considered inadequate to the needs of the island, and was complemented in 1923 by the specially built Isle of Arran War Memorial Hospital, which was paid for by voluntary subscription. Its ownership was invested in a board of trustees whose chairman was the 6th Duke of Montrose, and administered by a board of management whose chairman was the Duchess of Montrose, the 12th Duke of Hamilton's daughter. The two hospitals functioned side by side until they were taken over by the Board of Management for

Arran Hospitals, which functioned from 1947 until 1974. The Ardmhor Hospital was closed but the War Memorial Hospital continued and has since been considerably improved and extended. It is now managed by the Ayrshire and Arran Health Board, one of fifteen boards in Scotland whose members are appointed by the Secretary of State. Tom Alexander of Brodick has been appointed a member. The old folks' home at Arnhall, Whiting Bay, the first institution of its kind on the island, was also an adapted private house. Opened in 1948 by the welfare committee of Bute County Council, it has since been administered by Arran District Council, which acts as a county welfare subcommittee for that purpose, and will do so until 1975. The home has for some time been considered unsuitable for its purpose, and is being replaced by a specially designed building sited at Brodick.

THE LAND COURT

There was one other sphere in which the gradual extension of the franchise led to a transfer of authority from the landowner to elected representatives of the people, and that was the land itself. The distress caused in the west Highlands by the policies initiated during the Clearances led eventually to agitation. Conditions were investigated in 1883 by the Napier Commission, a report was submitted, and in 1886 the Crofters' Act gave the crofter greater security of tenure at a fair rent. The Napier Commission did not visit Arran, and the County of Bute was excluded from the area to which the act applied. Peter MacKinnon, who held a small lot at Strathwhillan after having been evicted from the Burican, led an agitation to have the island included in the area, and secured the signatures of 281 of the island tenants, an overwhelming majority, but the petition was unsuccessful. It was not until the Land Court was set up under the Small Landholders (Scotland) Act of 1911 that distress in Arran was alleviated. The Land Court visited the island in 1912 and 1913 and considered appeals in respect of 120 holdings. Rents were substantially reduced, and 78 per cent of the arrears cancelled.

W E have seen that the Hamilton lands in Arran passed
on the death of the 12th Duke of Hamilton to his only
child, the Lady Mary Louise, who in 1906 married the
Marquis of Graham, later to become the 6th Duke of Montrose.
On her death in 1957, which followed only three years after
that of her husband, Brodick castle and policies became the
property of the Treasury in part payment of death duties, and
the Treasury presented them to the National Trust for Scotland.
The present Duke of Montrose is now farming in Rhodesia,
associated there with the fight to maintain white supremacy, and
the greater part of the former Hamilton lands in the island has
been divided among other members of the family. The Lady
Mary Boscawen inherited Dougrie estate in the north-west of the
island, but sold it to Mr S. C. Gibbs, a member of a London
banking family, in 1971. The Lady Jean Fforde inherited Strabane estate, in the vicinity of Brodick, and Lord Ronald Graham
Drumadoon estate, which includes lands in the Shiskine and
Blackwaterfoot districts. Sannox estate, at the North End, was
inherited by Mr Charles Fforde, the Lady Jean's son, on his
twenty-first birthday, and five years later, in 1974, he acquired
in addition the stretch of land from Merkland to Corrie.

Some parts of the old Hamilton lands have been either gifted
or sold. Eleven years before the death of Mary, Duchess of
Montrose, twenty-five acres in Glen Diomhan were presented to
the Nature Conservancy, to ensure protection of the Arran service trees. After her mother's death the Lady Jean Fforde presented 7,000 acres in the Goatfell and Glen Rosa area, contiguous
to Brodick castle policies, to the National Trust. Some 15,500
acres in the south-east of the island and at the north end have
been sold to the Forestry Commission. Dippen Lodge with some
farms in its vicinity, together forming an estate of some 2,545
acres, were sold to Mr A. E. Martin, a London dealer, but he
soon parted with the estate and it is now fragmented. King's
Cross Point and Holy Isle were sold to Mr Stewart Huston, an

American descendant of the Reverend Gershom Stewart, who figured with his father James in the first of the Kilmory patronage disputes, and wrote the account of Kilbride parish for the *Statistical Account*. On Mr Huston's death the Holy Isle was bought by the Universities Federation for Animal Welfare, which has successfully introduced Soay sheep, some thirteen animals having increased to thirty-two between 1971 and 1974, but two badgers introduced have apparently failed to breed. King's Cross Point was bought by a Glasgow business man with a holiday house in its vicinity. Several local farmers are now owner occupiers. Further fragmentation of estates is likely to take place when the legislation promised to end feuing in Scotland becomes law. The present Duke of Hamilton, who holds no land in Arran, still holds the earldom of Arran as a subsidiary title along with those of Angus and Lanark. The Earl of Arran who figures as a journalist and broadcaster has no connection with the island. His family surname is Gore and his title is given in *Burke's Peerage* as 'Earl of Arran of the Arran Islands'. The islands in question are the Aran Islands off Galway in Ireland.

The Kilmichael estate of the Fullartons has been fragmented also. The family is now represented by Mrs Brown-Fullarton, the Fullarton surname having been hyphenated, not for the first time, owing to the failure of male heirs, with that of the husband of the heiress. Mrs Brown-Fullarton now holds sixty acres, 1,500 acres having been disposed of in 1952 to the Forestry Commission. She has no children, and the Fullarton link with the island, initiated shortly before 1371 with the grant of Knightsland by Robert, the High Steward, is likely to cease with her.

AGRICULTURE

The principal cause of the fragmentation of the island estates was of course the impact of death duties, first imposed in 1894 to prevent the great inequality of wealth and opportunity which unrestricted inheritance of land and property made inevitable. The imposition of death duties, and the increasing application of the principle of graduating taxation according to wealth, had, with the control of rents by the Land Court, the effect of reducing the landowner's will and ability to provide the fixed capital of farming and to finance schemes of improvement, and it was some time before the state stepped in to take the landowner's place. This gap coincided to a great extent with a decline in the profitability of home farming, due to the increase in the amount of cheap produce made available by the development of mass mechanised farming in the dominions and colonies, and apart from the war periods, when home-produced food was again in demand owing to the submarine menace and the shortage of shipping space, farming at home was in the doldrums. Even during the First World War farming in Arran declined as a result of shipping difficulties, and until the period of the Second World War can be said to have declined fairly steadily almost from the beginning of the century, leaving a legacy of abandoned smallholdings, decayed steadings, neglected hedgerows, fences and drains, and sour land. There was also a growing deterioration of hill grazings owing to the spread of bracken, a legacy from the clearances. This neglect of the land was due mainly to the fact that the legislation which effected it was framed by a democracy in which power was in the hands of the urban voter, possibly vindictive towards the landowner because of the sins of his fathers, and indifferent to the plight of the rural worker, isolated and unable, like the urban worker, to exert pressure, by means of lightning strikes, to better his pay and conditions.

During and after the Second World War there was a change of heart, and now the government has far surpassed the landowner in performing the functions which came to be regarded as the latter's responsibility in the early days of improvement. This it has done by organising advisory, instructional, and research services, by a variety of schemes for the improvement of farm buildings, stock and crops, and of the land itself, and by granting subsidies or ensuring guaranteed prices. Early in the 1950s dairying was put on a secure footing by the establishment by the Scottish Milk Marketing Board, a government-sponsored body, of a creamery at Torrylin. In 1973 the creamery manufactured some 300 tons of cheese, 80 per cent of it sold in large 40 lb blocks, and 20 per cent in small round cheeses, marketed as Isle of Arran Dunlop Cheese in attractive cardboard boxes. The cheese itself is of a type first associated with the Dunlop district of Ayrshire and the milk of the Ayrshire breed of cattle, now the

213

common milk breed in Arran. It is a good table cheese if not allowed to dry after cutting, and an excellent cooking cheese. The red variety is coloured by a vegetable dye which in the days of Dunlop farmhouse cheese was obtained from the marigold. The creamery employs only five people, but its importance is due mainly to the numbers it employs in keeping it supplied with milk, of which its average daily intake in 1973 was 2,200 gallons.

There was some slight improvement in farm dwellings from a now obsolete provision of the Hill Farming Act of 1946, and a farm improvement scheme of 1957 led to an improvement in farm buildings, notably in the provision of large barns for the storage of fodder. Other provisions enabled roads to be improved in stock-rearing areas, as in Glenrosa, at Auchencairn, at Levencoroch, and on Sliddery Moor. The emphasis is on the rehabilitation of the hill grazings. Arran is classified as an upland farm area and as such benefits from current hill land improvement and winter-keep schemes which in conjunction with subsidies for breeding ewes and for beef cows kept in regular breeding herds on hill land, and for their calves also, induce the farmers to drain the hill grazings, eradicate bracken, and rear hardy beef cattle in addition to sheep. These schemes have been contrived as a belated corrective to the damage done by neglect during the long period of depression and by the policy followed from the time of the clearances of confining the hill grazings to sheep alone. Even the hardiest of hill cattle cannot be returned at once to bracken-infested hills, but once re-established they will help to keep the bracken in check.

There was some fear that the increasing emphasis on hill cattle might lead to a decrease in milk production, and so reduce the output of the creamery, but the introduction of bulk storage tanks in 1969 led to an increase in milk supplies, although among the larger producers only. The reduced cost of milk collection enabled these farmers to lay out more on ploughing for heavier crops of hay or silage and so to increase their dairy herds.

A distinct threat to milk production did come, however, in 1973, when the European Economic Community achieved its 'butter mountain'. A Dairy Herd Conversion Scheme was introduced, which made a generous grant available to farmers who

214

kept eleven or more dairy cows, provided they undertook to give up supplying milk or milk products for four years and switch from dairying to the rearing of beef cattle or sheep. Since the creamery can seldom supply local retailers in the holiday season with all the Arran cheeses they need, and caterers on the north of the island are sometimes compelled to put tinned milk on the tea table, it is fortunate that few Arran dairy farmers were seduced by this inducement, and now that the EEC has achieved a 'beef mountain' it will surely be withdrawn.

Artificial insemination has been introduced as a government service to improve dairy cattle, and the farmers encouraged to produce a proportion of cross-bred calves more suitable for rearing as beef animals than pure Ayrshires, whose bull calves, unless outstanding enough to develop into useful sires, are useless except for veal. A popular cross is Ayrshire cow with Galloway bull, to produce an animal hardier than the Ayrshire but with a better milk yield than the Galloway. This makes a good hill mother. Hereford and Aberdeen Angus bulls are in turn crossed with this and other crosses, as Ayrshire x Friesian, Shorthorn x Irish, and Aberdeen Angus x Highland, to improve weight. Apart from these crosses a few animals of breeds hitherto seldom seen in Arran, as Jersey, Charolais, and Simmental, have been brought in during the 1970s, some with a view to the rearing of pure-bred stock.

Rising freight costs and the growing emphasis on hill cattle have caused some change in island farming since the publication of the *Third Statistical Account* in 1962. Potatoes are no longer grown for export. There has been a steady decline in this trade since the more active years of the late Donald MacKelvie, who between 1908 and 1947 introduced many new varieties, all with names prefixed by that of the island. He became known locally, if we can judge by an affectionate vernacular poem addressed to him by James Nicol in *A Book of Arran Verse*, as Tattie Mac-Kelvie, and for his contribution to food production during the Second World War he was awarded the OBE. Many of the Arran varieties are still widely grown, although not in their place of origin. Arran people today buy their Arran Pilots, early in the year before the local potatoes are available, from their village grocer, who imports them from Cyprus. The varieties mainly grown on the island today, entirely for local consumption, are Epicure, Pentland Dell, Kerr's Pink and Golden Wonder.

Most arable crops today are grown for stock feeding, the traditional rotation being oats or barley, followed by potatoes, turnips or marrow-stem kail, oats or barley, hay, and two or three years' grass. By 1973 barley had begun to replace oats as the grain crop, there being 454 acres of barley to 248 of oats. Arable crops are declining as farmers increasingly sow to grass immediately after ploughing. This policy, in conjunction with improved seed and heavier dressings of fertiliser, enables them to produce heavier crops of hay and silage, and so maintain more stock. According to the *Third Statistical Account* of 1962 the island carried 32,000 sheep, said to have been double the figure for 1851, 5,200 cattle, said to have been an increase of 10 per cent in ten years, and an average of 300 pigs on each of several farms. In 1968 the island carried, according to figures supplied by the Department of Agriculture and Fisheries, 35,984 sheep, 3,741 dairy cattle, 2,632 beef cattle, and 56 pigs. The figures are not strictly comparable, since those of 1962 are less precise, but it appeared in 1968 that in spite of forest planting, which had started in 1952, improved husbandry had led to no diminution in the number of sheep, and it was likely that the increase of about 1,000 in the number of cattle had resulted from the policy of returning beef cattle to the hills. The decline in the number of pigs was due partly to government policy based on its view of national requirements, but mainly to the increasing freight costs, which in a factory type of farming involving the import of feeding stuffs and the export of the finished product, made competition with mainland producers more and more difficult.

Figures issued for 1973 are in turn not strictly comparable with those for 1968, since holdings requiring 'less than 40 standard man-days per annum' are no longer required to make returns to the Department, and therefore many of a kind common in Arran are unrepresented. But on the 134 holdings obliged to make a return there were 3,161 dairy cattle, 4,854 beef cattle, 33,427 sheep, and 9 pigs. No more can safely be deduced from these figures than that since 1968 there has been a rise of at least 2,000 beef cattle, and that pigs have almost disappeared from the island.

The decline of 2,557 in the number of sheep between 1968 and 1973 seems slight in view of the continued forestry planting. This may be accounted for by a recent increase in parkland as opposed to hill sheep husbandry.

Agricultural exports, apart from cheese, are of stock. Wether lambs and cross-bred cattle reared on the island are exported to the mainland to be finished on the richer farms there for the butcher. Blackface ewes whose teeth have become worn on the tough heather of the hills, usually by their fourth year, are drafted and sold to the mainland also, where they can be kept for a further two years on grass and crossed with Border Leicester rams to produce heavy lambs. Such crossing to produce heavy lambs is practised in Arran, too, but there is little killing on the island either of sheep or cattle, and that mainly in the west. There is little export of eggs or poultry, although poultry farming is practised both by intensive methods and on free range. To compare Department figures for 1968 and 1973 in respect of poultry would be even more misleading than in respect of sheep or cattle, since much of the poultry rearing on the island is on a cottage basis. One would expect the 1973 figures to be lower, and they are except in respect of turkeys, which show a slight increase. In 1968 there were 3,838 fowls, 58 being reared for the table, with 64 turkeys. In 1973, on the reduced number of farms obliged to make a return, there were 2,104 fowls, with 40 being raised for the table, and 74 turkeys. The eggs and table birds produced are sold locally, the eggs from free range being in great demand by summer visitors.

The improvement in farm techniques introduced since the Second World War was accompanied during the same period by increased mechanisation, which having started during the war accelerated in the 1950s until by 1961 about 98 per cent of the farmers had tractors. Most farms, too, since the establishment of the North of Scotland Hydro-Electric Board in 1946, have steadily acquired electrical appliances. These changes must have led to a dramatic increase in the output per worker. They could therefore have been expected to increase the rate of decline in the numbers employed on the land. Decline is in fact continuing, in the number of farmers as well as in the labour employed. In 1968 there were 219 holdings worked in Arran as against 226

217

in 1965. The labour employed in addition to that supplied by the farmers and their families amounted to 90 persons in 1968 as against 106 in 1965. These figures include casual workers.

It was thought that the number of holdings might be reduced still further by various farm structure schemes introduced between 1967 and 1973, but none of these was quite tailored to Arran's requirements, and few amalgamations took place. This was unfortunate because most of the very small holdings in Arran are no longer worked by their occupiers, and although most of them are grazed by the stock of neighbouring farmers they cannot meanwhile be improved, and are in an appalling state of neglect. If they could be absorbed by the larger holdings and improved it would make these more viable without reducing substantially the number of people actively employed on the land. It would in fact slow down the ultimate rate of decline by affording better prospects to the remaining occupiers. Lately the island factors have been offering small landholders outright ownership of their cottages, hitherto held on a ground-rental basis and inalienable from the holding, in return for a cash payment and the surrender of their land, and this may help towards the creation of more viable units.

It will be seen that although the steady modernisation of farming has led to a decline in the number of holdings on the island, and the amount of employment available on the land, there has been an overall increase in production. In many ways farming on the island has an excellent record. It was part of the first area in Britain to become attested, or declared free of bovine tuberculosis, is free of brucellosis, and hopes soon, when the other parts of Bute and Argyll catch up, to become accredited in this respect. In the eradication of these sorts of troubles the schemes of the Department of Agriculture and Fisheries played an important part.

The Forestry Commission started planting in Arran in 1952 at Glenrickard on the Kilmichael estate, but now owns land widely almost throughout the island. Not all will be planted. Pockets of low land will be left for agricultural use, although the commission has in Arran only two part-time holdings of the kind established in the Highlands to enable men to combine forestry work with crofting. Areas unsuitable for planting, such

218

as those above the tree line, will be let for grazing provided the cost of fencing is not prohibitive. It is estimated that 10,400 acres are assured and that 11,500 may be attained eventually. Planting has settled to a rate which in 1974 employs ten men full-time. The number similarly employed in 1963 was twenty-eight. The decrease is said to be due to the policy now adopted all over Scotland of replacing unskilled men using traditional tools with highly trained men using new power equipment. The policy was compelled not only by the need for increased efficiency to reduce costs but by the difficulty of keeping men in the remote areas on the agricultural minimum wage. In addition to the ten men it employs full-time the commission in Arran employs an agricultural contractor to plough and drain the land for planting. Work on road construction has ceased, but may be resumed later.

Thinning will begin about twenty-five years after planting, 1977 in the case of Glenrickard. Felling of mature trees will begin after fifty years, in 2002. It is likely that in Arran only the timber close to the forestry roads will be thinned and grown on to mature, while the timber further from the roads, and so more difficult to haul, will be cut unthinned for pulp. It is likely to be shipped direct from Arran to a pulp mill at Workington in Cumberland. The cutting and felling are likely to be let out to contractors, who may of course make use of local labour if that is available. Although it puts the land to use and may even be necessary to regenerate hill land which has deteriorated too seriously under sheep to be rescued by other means, forestry may not seem, in terms of the number of men it employs, to contribute greatly to the economy of the island. Yet it should be remembered that ten full-time jobs, small as the number may seem, may mean ten families reared on the island, and so may help more to preserve the community than would forty jobs in the holiday trade for three months every summer.

TOURISM

The holiday trade in Arran, which as we have seen began to develop rapidly with the advent of the steamboat and the railways, and the provision of wooden piers in the main villages, is now the most important factor in its economy. The main line

219

of communication today is from Ardrossan to Brodick. The *MV Caledonia*, a stern-loading vessel of Scandinavian origin, which can take 40 cars and 650 passengers, makes four double trips each weekday except in winter, when the number is three. The summer schedule would be impossible with one ship if it had to call at more than one island pier on each of its trips, and in any case both Lamlash and Whiting Bay piers were closed some years ago, the former in 1954 and the latter in 1957, partly because they had become too expensive to maintain, and partly because passengers could save time and shorten the sea trip, often in winter quite rough, by disembarking at Brodick and making their way to Lamlash and Whiting Bay by bus or car. The two villages concerned put up some resistance, but in each case Arran Piers Limited were successful in obtaining a statutory order from the Ministry of Transport authorising closure, and the piers have since been demolished.

The Brodick sailings are augmented in winter by a late boat on Fridays and Saturdays and by midday and late boats during the Christmas, New Year, and Easter holiday periods. In winter there is also a late afternoon boat from the island on Sundays. In summer the augmentations are naturally much greater, there being five double trips daily between the end of the third week in May and the end of August, with a very early Monday-morning boat, known to its patrons as the Death Ship, and very late boats on Fridays and Saturdays. From the end of the third week in May until 1 September there are four double trips on Sundays, with three between 1 September and 5 October. There are extra sailings also at the middle and end of each month, when fortnightly or monthly visitors cause a rush. Until the advent in 1970 of the stern-loading *Caledonia* these rush periods were chaotic. The first car ferries introduced to the Brodick service, the *MV Arran* in 1954 and the much larger *MV Glen Sannox* in 1957, were equipped with hydraulic lifts. Although these were a great improvement as a means of disembarking cars, on a couple of rather springy planks, they were nevertheless slow when the state of the tide left a deep gap to be negotiated between the car-deck and pier levels. When loaded during busy periods with its full complement of forty cars the *Glen Sannox* could not keep to its time table, and long delays were experienced in which travellers had to wait in places with few amenities and exposed to inclement weather. That the island survived as a holiday resort was a great tribute to its popularity.

The advent of the stern-loading *Caledonia* ended these delays, but the new service was not without its teething troubles, for Ardrossan harbour is difficult to leave or enter in stormy weather. Caledonian-Macbrayne, the company which under the Scottish Transport Group took over from the Caledonian Steam Packet Company in 1972, having converted the piers at Brodick and Ardrossan to meet the needs of the new stern-loading vessels, thought it had spent enough, with the result that if the *Caledonia* is unable to take Ardrossan harbour it has to sail to Gourock, the nearest alternative harbour suitably equipped. This more than doubles the sea voyage, and passengers waiting at Ardrossan to embark when the boat arrives from Brodick have to be taken from Ardrossan to Gourock by bus, a distance of some thirty miles. Often it is not known at Ardrossan, until the boat sails from Brodick, which route is to be taken, and the inability of the poor pier employees to provide this information leads to much blind fury. Fortunately for visitors these experiences are less frequent in summer than in winter, but in winter they occur too often. Many islanders sigh for the good old days when the boat could use the now abandoned Fairlie Pier (not far up the coast) when Ardrossan was stormbound, but most would acknowledge that when the present service is running smoothly it is the best they have ever had. And a new Arran Lounge has been built at Ardrossan harbour to make long waits less miserable.

Lochranza pier, although never officially closed, has been abandoned since boats ceased to call on their way to and from Campbeltown in Kintyre. Since 1972, however, there has been a concrete slipway at Lochranza, from which there is an hourly sailing, except in winter, to Claonaig in Kintyre, just opposite, by a bow-loading vessel capable of taking five cars and fifty passengers. The voyage lasts half an hour, and the ferry makes eight double trips each weekday, with seven on Sundays, between the end of April and the beginning of September. From the beginning of September to 5 October, when the service ends for the winter, the number is reduced to seven. In 1972 the ferry carried 11,226 passengers, 2,781 cars, and 38 other vehicles. In

Finance) (Scotland) Act of 1964 gave the district council power of 6,400 cars compares interestingly with the car figure for the Ardrossan to Brodick ferry for the same period, of 10,600. The ferry is considered a considerable success in spite of its frequent interruption by bad weather, and is likely to continue. It gives motorists touring the Western Highlands a delightful opportunity to substitute a tour of Arran for the alternative approach through the ugly industrial belt of Scotland.

The cruises which at one time were a principal feature of a Clyde holiday are almost a thing of the past, and are likely to remain so. Only one is available from Arran now, a short trip round the Holy Isle in the *TS Queen Mary II*.

Public transport within the island itself has shrunk considerably since the 1950s, when the number of motor cars on the island increased rapidly, accelerating after the advent of the car ferries. The increase in the number of island car owners, and the number of holiday visitors who brought their own cars, led to a drastic reduction in the numbers making use of the buses, and by 1967 bus services in winter had been reduced to less than might reasonably be considered even a skeleton service. For many years an attempt had been made to ensure that even in winter people wishing to travel to or from Brodick for the departure or on the arrival of the boat could travel by bus, but as the number of passengers decreased the bus companies were allowed by the transport commissioners to cut the uneconomic services, and for several days in the week travellers from the outlying villages who did not own cars had either to hire them or abandon their journeys. Similarly services which had once been run to take workmen from outlying villages to their work elsewhere were discontinued, which had the effect of causing a gradual movement out of these villages mainly into Brodick, but in some cases over to the mainland.

This movement was resisted by many, attached to their homes, who bought the only kind of car they could afford, third or fourth-hand and short-lived, and this itself created a problem which has so far not been tackled : the disposal of wrecks. Here and there on the island are unsightly dumps of 'cannibalised' cars, unfortunate in an island visited by holidaymakers mainly for its scenic beauty. The Local Government (Development and

1973 the figures were 11,000, 6,400, and 270. The 1973 figure to solve this problem, but no advantage was taken. There was similarly an opportunity for the county council, under the Transport Act of 1968, to restore the missing bones to the skeleton bus service in winter, so that public transport of some sort would be available in connection with the main daily sailings; but since this would have involved a subsidy paid partly out of the county rate, it was never, in a county dominated by car owners, seriously considered.

Public transport in summer is more adequate, and most sailings to and from Brodick are served by buses which link that village with the other main eastern villages of Lamlash and Whiting Bay. Services to other villages are less frequent. Everywhere on the island they end early in the day, and it is difficult for a walker reaching the road in a remote part of the island after a long day's excursion into the hills, or round a long isolated stretch of the coast, to find transport back to his quarters. Walkers who have cars to take them to where they start an excursion have to return to the same place at its close unless they can persuade a friend to act as chauffeur, and those who cannot, lose much freedom which public transport could provide. On the evidence of hill tracks once clearly visible and now overgrown it seems clear that those who keep up the Landsborough tradition, and willingly face a ten-mile tramp along the main road after a tiring day on the hills, are growing scarce. But in the nineteenth century the main roads must have been much more peaceful to frequent. For those without cars who wish to explore the island without unaccustomed exertion, coach tours are less varied than formerly – the single remaining bus company having dropped the central Arran tour, the only one which included the Ross Road.

Accommodation in the island is offered in some seventy-six hotels and boarding-houses, of which thirty are licensed. The licences are spread fairly evenly around the villages of the island, only Pirnmill being without one. This was not always so. The parish of Kilmory, predominantly agricultural and rather rigid in outlook, was for a long time without a licence by virtue of local veto, but an increasing interest in the holiday trade caused a change in attitude, and in recent years licences have increased, and the west of the island is little less alcoholic than the east.

223

The larger hotels are scattered fairly widely, too, although the largest is at Brodick, close to the pier. This is the Douglas, with which is now incorporated the St Denys, the two having been joined together by a multi-levelled passage which at night has something of the atmosphere of a Kafka novel. This hotel, with six single bedrooms and forty-seven double, all fifty-three with hot and cold water, and nineteen with bath or shower, adds a service charge, has accommodation for cars, offers reduced terms for children, welcomes dogs, has a night porter, has telephones in bedrooms, employs someone who speaks French and at least one other European language, may be booked through travel agents, offers diabetic or vegetarian dishes on request, has heaters in bedrooms, and has a sauna bath. This type of information, taken from the 1974 Accommodation Register of the Isle of Arran Tourist Association, is available for all accommodation on the island, from the Douglas Hotel to the very smallest boarding-house, North Sannox Cottage, which has three double bedrooms, accommodation for cars, offers reduced terms for children, welcomes dogs, offers diabetic or vegetarian dishes on request, has heaters in bedrooms, and lists itself as a farmhouse.

Besides its seventy-six hotels and boarding-houses, which as indicated vary from large licensed hotels to small cottages letting rooms with attendance, the island has 140 furnished houses to let without attendance. The accommodation register gives particulars of these also, listing the number of bedrooms, of beds whether single or double, of what are called reception rooms, and of bathrooms. Here again accommodation varies, from the largest house of seven bedrooms, three reception rooms, and one bathroom, to the smallest with one bedroom, one reception room, and a shower. These furnished letting houses are of course most plentiful in the largest villages, but are spread throughout the island and include many farmhouses. They are made available by their winter occupiers moving into summer quarters either in miniature cottages built at the same time as the main house to form a planned unit, or in lean-to additions or converted outbuildings.

The furnished houses let without attendance are popular with young couples rearing a family, and many are taken year after year by such guests, who often book for the following year before they leave. They are difficult to obtain for the peak months of July and August, and anyone who delays application until after February runs the risk of being disappointed. Those in outlying parts of the island, off the main road and especially on farms, offer the ideal holiday for young children, with safety from traffic, freedom to roam in open ground with burns and woodland and within easy reach of the shore, and with farm animals and wild creatures to delight in. In the farmhouse and outlying cottage accommodation there is some chance, too, of obtaining really fresh garden produce and newly laid eggs, although only in the cottages let with attendance can home-baked scones and pancakes, home-made jams and jellies, and rare luxuries like comb honey, be obtained in addition. The quality of the food in the larger hotels and boarding-houses varies greatly. No classification is attempted in the accommodation register, nor would it be right with limited experience to discriminate here, but it can fairly be said that the most consistent reputations for good food have been achieved by hotels and boarding-houses not subject to constant changes of management, and these tend to be fairly small and privately owned. They generally have their own kitchen gardens and offer really fresh salads and greens, otherwise really fresh vegetables are not readily available, and there has been criticism of the fact that so few vegetables are grown on the island commercially, only a quarter of an acre, for instance, in 1973.

It is, however, doubtful if the largest hotels would use fresh vegetables even if they were available, as their preparation takes a great deal of labour and is therefore expensive. Visitors in letting houses can obtain fresh vegetables from cottage gardens in most villages, but it is noticeable that apart from lettuces and spring onions they use dried or tinned vegetables to save themselves trouble. As far as the island can be said to have any distinctive gastronomic delights they are of the simple kind already mentioned, with excellent mutton broth in some of the farmhouse quarters, fresh sea-trout where the hotel proprietor has the netting rights, a haggis rather too infrequently made by the butcher at Corrie, and various delicacies, most of them with venison as a main ingredient, put on the market a few years ago by the Lady Jean Fforde, which are in great demand beyond the island. Excellent bread and rolls are baked in Brodick daily.

It is difficult to estimate just how large the holiday trade bulks in the island's economy. In 1971, the latest year for which figures are available, it employed with the ancillary trades 62 per cent of the island's working male population, as against 23 per cent employed in agriculture and forestry, but the ancillary trades include shopkeepers, tradesmen, electricity and postal workers, who serve both the agricultural community and the elderly, and the latter today account for just under 25 per cent of the total population. The majority of women work in the service trades, but much of their employment is seasonal.

The part played in the island's holiday trade by hotels and boarding-houses on the one hand, and letting-houses on the other, has been completely reversed since 1968. In that year the hotels and boarding-houses had accommodation for 1,311 guests, and the letting-houses for 2,219, not far short of double the number. In 1974 the hotels and boarding-houses had accommodation for 1,549 guests, a small increase on the 1968 figure, but letting-houses had dwindled to the point of being able to accommodate only 905 guests. These figures reveal more than a change in the balance between the different kinds of accommodation offered. They indicate a continuing decline in the total accommodation offered by the island exclusive of caravan sites and holiday houses, i.e. houses owned by people from the mainland who retain them exclusively for their own use. Before the days of accommodation registers the only indication of the capacity of the island to accommodate holiday visitors was given by the official census of 1921 (see table on page 240). This was taken in June instead of in early spring (the customary time), and therefore in the holiday season, although not at its height. This suggested that the population of the island at the height of the season, probably a little higher than in June, would in 1921 be a little more than double that of the winter population. In 1968 the same applied, there being 3,530 beds available and an estimated winter population of 3,135. Yet in 1921 the winter population was over 4,500, well over that of 1968. Since in 1974 the island offered only 2,454 beds, it would appear that the shrinkage continues, although some allowance must be made for the fact that forms sent out by the tourist association to people letting houses are becoming increasingly elaborate, and those who dislike filling in forms, but have no difficulty in letting their houses year after year, are becoming increasingly uncooperative.

Caravan sites and holiday houses have so far been excluded from these calculations. In 1974 there were twelve caravan sites on the island, more than ever before, but offering a total of no more than fifty berths, with twelve touring pitches. The number of holiday houses can be given as yet only for 1971, when the figure was 210, as against 1,308 houses occupied throughout the year. It will be seen later that the number of holiday houses is likely to have increased considerably since 1971.

The increases in the hotel and boarding-house trade, and of wealthy visitors who own second homes on the island, has been accompanied by a change in the character of the island shops and catering establishments. The distinctive Arran shopping experience, offered by the general stores in the outlying villages, usually also sub-post offices, still holds pride of place. In these often shadowy and rambling emporiums there is little that cannot be purchased, from paraffin, waterproofs, gum-boots, jeans, books, sweets, jam, bread, cakes, tools and patent medicines to cosmetics. Not all the shopkeepers are as unpleasantly eccentric as the old lady at Lochranza who was alleged to have refused to sell bread to strangers she did not fancy – one delightful old lady in Shannochie is known to have sent twopence change by post to a customer she found she had overcharged. But these interesting old people are dying out, and today, apart from such ordinary shops in the larger villages as butchers, grocers, bakers, chemists and stationers, and a couple of small department stores, there has arisen a plethora of craft shops, specialising often in the products of particular craftsmen, as wood-carvers, candlemakers, jewellers, potters, weavers, leather-workers, and dressmakers. Many of the shops sell the work of local craftsman only, but there are several which sell imported craft goods also. Some of the island craftsmen produce work of real artistic distinction. There has been an increase also in grills and bars in old boathouses, barns, and blacksmiths' shops, most with names suggestive more of the Cornish Riviera than of Arran. The food offered is sometimes both sophisticated and wholesome, and the bars usually offer a fair selection of both Highland and Island malt whiskies.

Other services offered to holidaymakers are bicycles for hire in all the main villages, cots and prams in Brodick and Lamlash, television and radio sets in Lamlash, and boats in all villages, but increasingly and in connection with sea angling at Brodick and Lamlash. Lamlash also has a sailing school. Ponies for trekking are available at Brodick, Blackwaterfoot, and Auchereoch, the last in the new forest at the head of the Kilmory Water. Pony trekking and sea angling, as opposed to inshore fishing with a hand-line, are recent developments, and the island is likely to develop both considerably in the near future. An Arran branch of the Sea Angling Association has been formed, and sea-angling festivals have been held at Lamlash. At one of these a British record was achieved with a catch of 7 tons of fish by 300 anglers in 3 days. During these festivals free fresh fish is available to any holidaymaker who cares to collect it. At other times most white fish available has come from Aberdeen.

Mention has already been made of amenities provided for visitors by village improvement trusts or associations and similar groups. There are eighteen-hole golf courses at Brodick, Lamlash, and Whiting Bay, a twelve-hole course at Blackwaterfoot, and nine-hole courses at Lochranza and Sannox, the last in a superb setting of towering peaks. There are tennis courts in all the larger villages and bowling greens at Brodick, Lamlash, and Whiting Bay. Entertainment is provided in village halls throughout the island in the form of film shows and dances. In the larger village halls of Brodick, Lamlash, and Whiting Bay, professional bands are employed at the height of the season. For some years now these have included well-known pop groups, extremely popular with the younger visitors but condemned by the older inhabitants, who regard the hairy pop musicians with undisguised revulsion, and their bare-navelled and tight-jeaned female followers with a mixture of avid curiosity and histrionic outrage, and maintain firmly that the pop groups have ruined the island. Apart from film shows and dances entertainment cannot be said to be lavish. Some concerts are staged in summer for local charities, in which amateur singers and drama groups perform. Most villages arrange sports for children in the summer months, and Highland games are held in Brodick during the first week in August. Races are organised by the Arran Yacht Club, and a motor-sports weekend is held in July. Sheep-dog trials are held in Machrie in June and July, and annual agricultural and flower shows at Lamlash in August. Coffee mornings and sales of work are organised by the various village churches.

SOCIAL AND RELIGIOUS LIFE

Social life in the summer is governed almost entirely by the activities of the visitors. People mix on the beaches, on picnics, at dances, in cafés and grills, and at barbecues, on tennis courts, golf courses and bowling greens, and during pony treks. Sea anglers fraternise in some of the larger boats hired out to parties, and visiting yachtsmen may join the Arran Yacht Club. The churches, too, welcome visitors and organise appropriate activities, including in Brodick particularly a beach mission by young visiting evangelists whose aim is to offer the pop-group enthusiasts an alternative to the attractions of drink, drugs, and sex, in the form of coffee and discussion in the church hall. This seems to cause good-natured amusement rather than resentment and indeed, even during the last weekend in September, when there is a great influx of young people, mainly students having their last holiday before the beginning of the winter term, there is little evidence of vice. Spirits are high, and occasionally there has been some silly practical joking in which properties such as weighing machines have been moved during darkness into surrealist settings, but little real damage is done, although a section of the press looks on the occasion hopefully as a possible source of news, and tries hard to stimulate exhibitionism. Extra police are drafted into the island to cope with the expected trouble, but are able to admit with relief almost every year that the young people have been, on the whole, very well behaved.

The social life of the permanent population, almost dormant during the summer, stirs during the winter, although in the smaller villages it is organised chiefly for women, and the sociable male has to resort unreluctantly to the hotel bar. In all the villages there are branches of the Scottish Women's Rural Institute, which hold monthly meetings during the period of the full moon, and offer talks on a variety of improving subjects, and some competition in womenly skills. Some villages have branches of the Church of Scotland Women's Guild, and some women's work parties of the Free Church. Some villages have music or drama clubs, or form choirs for the purpose of taking part in the island musical festival. Community drama festivals have lately ceased. They were very popular just after the end of the Second World War, when as many as twenty-one teams, drawn from every village in the island, used to compete in the course of a week, some of them producing plays with a local setting or by local men, among them the late Ernest Ribbeck, grandson of the original of that name already mentioned. Although the festival has ceased some villages still present amateur dramatic productions in summer for fund-raising purposes. The musical festival has shown rather less decline, and a recently formed branch of An Comunn Gaidhealach should increase the number of Gaelic entries. Brodick, Shiskine and Kilmory have recreation clubs, Lamlash and Lochranza badminton clubs, Brodick, Lamlash, Shiskine and Lochranza bridge clubs, and Brodick a poultry and pigeon club, social in its winter activities. Brodick, Lamlash, and Whiting Bay have Thursday or Friday Clubs run by the fairly young for the elderly, which have meetings on Thursdays or Fridays in church halls, and Brodick has a Young Wives' Club. Guides, Brownies and Cubs flourish, but Scouts are few.

Organisations with an island rather than a village basis have developed with the increase in car ownership. Although the Red Cross Society and the Royal Lifeboat Institution have representatives in every village for the purpose of their annual collections, they function as island units. Other organisations in this category include a very active Junior Agricultural Club of some years' standing, and recently formed Camera, Subaqua, and Gun Clubs.

The most popular and active cultural organisation in the island is probably the Isle of Arran Film Society, founded in 1961. It offers eight programmes a year at monthly intervals, usually in a Brodick hotel, but with at least one meeting a year in the Whiting Bay and Kinloch Hotels, the last at Blackwaterfoot. The films shown are mainly Continental and *avant garde*, which during the interval, spent by many members pleasantly in the bar, arouse considerable discussion, much of it puzzled, and some of it outraged, although as the years pass the members' capacity for outrage grows steadily weaker. The Arran Music Club, another fairly new venture, holds recitals of classical music from records, and organises several concerts at which visiting professional musicians perform in the drawing-room of Brodick castle, by courtesy of the National Trust for Scotland. In this the club has the support of the Scottish Arts Council.

The religious life of the island still retains some of its nineteenth-century character of sectarian division and strict sabbatarianism, but this is more apparent in winter, for the impact of the holiday trade has led in summer, in the eastern villages at least, to something approaching a mild version of the Continental sabbath. Many visitors to the island, particularly those who favour the west and the north, are regular churchgoers, and popular preachers attract large congregations, yet it would take more than another revival to strain the accommodation offered by the superfluity of churches built on the island in the nineteenth and early twentieth centuries. This superfluity is not simply the result of falling population or declining faith. It reflects the series of sectarian dissensions initiated by the Disruption of 1843.

Within two years of that event Free Church buildings were being erected at Brodick, Bennecarrigan, Shiskine, and Lennymore, and before the end of the century others followed at Kildonan, Whiting Bay, Lamlash, Corrie and Lochranza. In the same period the Church of Scotland renewed its existing buildings and added others at Whiting Bay, Brodick and Corrie, and the Congregational denomination at Sannox, which had been deprived of most of its members by the clearances, erected a building at Corrie. Then in 1900 came the union of the Free Church with the United Presbyterian, the latter without a congregation on the island, to form the United Free Church, and the refusal of many Free Church members to participate led to conflict for the ownership of the existing Free Church buildings. In the end seven new churches had to be built, at Brodick, Whiting Bay, South End, Bennecarrigan, Shiskine, Pirnmill, and Lochranza, to accommodate the new United Free congregations. To be fair to the native inhabitants it should be said that the money for this orgy of sinful display would not have been available if visitors who shared their convictions had not encouraged it by contributing extravagantly. In 1929, by which time patronage and teinds had alike been abolished, and the root causes of the original dissensions removed, the United Free Church merged with the Church of Scotland, and some of the buildings of these two denominations, having become more than redundant, were abandoned and either demolished or used for secular purposes.

The Free Church persists, and some of its buildings, too, have been demolished, although in three of these cases, at Brodick, Shiskine and Whiting Bay, the demolition has been accompanied by replacement. The Church of Scotland now has eight parishes: Lochranza & Pirnmill, Shiskine, Kilmory, Kildonan, Whiting Bay, Lamlash, Brodick, and Corrie. Shiskine and Kilmory, Kildonan and Whiting Bay, and Brodick and Corrie, are linked charges. All parishes are now in the presbytery of Ardrossan, having with the exception of Lochranza & Pirnmill been transferred from that of Kintyre in 1929. Lochranza & Pirnmill followed in 1956. The Free Church has four charges: Lochranza, Shiskine and Southend, Whiting Bay, and Brodick and Corrie. All are vacant except Shiskine and Southend. The Congregational Church at Sannox is also without a resident minister, but visiting ministers conduct services there in summer. A retired Scottish Episcopalian clergyman holds services in his home at Whiting Bay throughout the year, and Roman Catholic services, a recent innovation, are conducted in the summer in Brodick public hall.

POLITICS

Arran is now part of the parliamentary constituency of Bute and North Ayrshire, and for many years now has returned a Conservative representative, the present MP being Mr John Corrie. Its local government structure, established in 1929, is being phased out, and will be replaced by a new two-tier structure in which the island will have no separate unit of local government with powers to rate.

Under the 1929 scheme Arran was a landward district of the county of Bute. The island had six electoral areas: Lochranza, Shedog and Dougrie, Southend, Whiting Bay, Lamlash, and Brodick and Corrie. Elections were held every third year and each area elected a county and a district councillor. Arran

District Council consisted of twelve county and district councillors. Bute County Council consisted of six Arran members, four members from the landward district of Bute, one from the landward district of Cumbrae, eleven from the burgh of Rothesay, and three from the burgh of Millport. In the small minority of purely landward issues Arran could, therefore, command a majority of six to five, but in the great majority of issues, in which the burghs too were concerned, it was in a minority of six to twenty-five. These figures were originally related to the populations of the various landward districts and burghs concerned, which in 1961 were as follows : Burgh of Rothesay, 7,687; Burgh of Millport, 1,593; Arran District, 3,712; Bute District, 2,125; Cumbrae District, 53. Arran was, therefore, well represented in proportion to its population, as was Cumbrae also.

In the exercise of its functions the county council had special committees for education, health, child care, welfare, planning, roads and road safety, finance, and probation, some of these having members co-opted or *ex officiis*. The county council appointed licensing and licensing appeal courts, and for purposes of valuation and weights and measures was paired with Argyll, and for police with Renfrew. For fire prevention it was represented on a western area joint committee. Both county and district councils sent representatives to their respective local authority associations.

On the county education committee of twenty-two members Arran had six, normally four county councillors and a teachers' representative, with periodically a co-opted lady or clergyman, all appointed by the county council. Similarly, the health and child-welfare committees of eleven had three Arran members, the welfare committee of ten had three, the planning committee of fifteen had two, the roads committee of twelve had three. On occasion Arran county concillors might sit on some of these committees *ex officiis*, by virtue for instance of the chairmanship of a committee with a related function, or of the convenership or vice-convenership of the county.

Arran had special subcommittees for the various county functions. That relating to education, curiously named the Arran Sub-Committee for the Management of Educational Establishments in the County of Buteshire, was concerned mainly with the

233

maintenance of school buildings, but included among its other concerns school attendance, the fixing of Arran school holidays, the granting of free school meals, and the fixing of the times and stopping places of the school buses. It consisted of the Arran members of the county education committee, two members appointed by the district council, two appointed by parents from each of the two civil parishes of the island, and two appointed by Arran teachers. This subcommittee, although much more widely representative of the Arran community than the Arran membership of the county education committee, had no statutory duty to make representations on behalf of the island on matters of educational policy, and its right to do so was denied by the parent body.

Arran health subcommittee consisted of the six Arran county councillors, as did the planning subcommittee. The Arran roads subcommittee consisted of all twelve members of the district council. The latter also had delegated powers in respect of special rating districts established to provide services such as lighting, drainage, scavenging, and for some time water, and in respect of running the old folk's home and the care of the island graveyards.

Apart from the care of the elderly, roads, and graveyards, in respect of which its powers were delegated to it by the county council, Arran District Council acted as an independent authority, with power to levy a district rate, in respect of such powers as were conferred upon district councils by statute. Until the passing of the Physical Training and Recreation Act of 1937 these were negligible, and even then were by nature such as could be exercised without financial strain only by the councils of the large, densely populated, industrial districts of the mainland. In districts such as Arran, with a small population scattered widely in a large number of tiny villages, powers to levy a rate for the provision of halls or sports grounds were difficult to exercise, for to cater for every village would have been costly, and to cater for only a few would have been unfair. The situation was the more difficult in that some of the villages, favoured by a high summer population of generous visitors, had already provided these amenities by voluntary effort. At first councillors from the villages which already had halls and sporting facilities voted against aid to those who had not. A similar situation existed in relation to powers given to district councils in 1958 to erect bus shelters, for several villages, notably Whiting Bay, had already supplied these also by voluntary effort.

Then in the 1960s came legislation empowering district councils to fulfil functions more appropriate to rural districts dependent on the holiday trade. At first Arran District Council showed no great inclination to take advantage of the new powers. Part of the trouble lay in its composition, in which county and district councillors were equal in number. Since only a county councillor could preside over a county subcommittee, and since the district council functioned as a subcommittee of the county council in respect of the greater number of its duties, the chairman of the district council was inevitably a county councillor, and his right to a casting vote put the district councillors in a minority. The district council became thirled to the idea of itself as a county subcommittee, and only in respect of such matters as liaison with the shipping and bus companies did it function as an independent unit of local government. It spent no money in the exercise of its independent statutory powers.

The powers conferred on it by the Caravan Sites and Control of Development Act of 1960 did not alter the situation. Councillors who were hotel or boarding-house keepers or farmers tended to regard campers as a threat to their livelihood or as vandals. The Local Government (Development and Finance) (Scotland) Act of 1964 did alter the situation. This Act enabled district councils to levy a rate to contribute to the cost of running their districts as holiday resorts. County and burgh councils had long possessed this power, and in the islands of Bute and Cumbrae the burghs of Rothesay and Millport had exercised it. Arran had been compelled, in contrast, to run its holiday trade on an amateur basis on money raised by voluntary subscriptions. The county council could have come to the rescue in respect of its landward districts, but Arran county councillors, although they could have commanded a majority of one if the issue had been raised, were shy of compelling· the landward districts of Bute and Cumbrae to pay a rate mainly in the interests of Arran, fearing that it might create hostility between Arran and the other islands, and invite a grudging or retaliatory attitude when expenditure was being considered on the wider county functions, such as education, in respect of which Arran county councillors were in a decided minority. For nine years prior to 1964 Arran District Council pressed, through the District Councils' Association for Scotland, for the right to rate for the purpose of running its holiday trade, and other district councils joined in the campaign, but they met opposition from the County Councils' Association for Scotland, presumably jealous of any extension of powers to the lesser authority, and more surprisingly from the Scottish Tourist Board, piqued at the time because of some well deserved criticism of its shortcomings.

The power was eventually granted, and the district council made use of it at once. By 1974 the Arran Tourist Association, a voluntary organisation on which the district council is represented, was receiving an annual grant from district council rate of £2,000. The Arran Tourist Association publishes an excellent illustrated brochure and the accommodation register already mentioned deals with enquiries reaching the island on holiday matters, and runs an information bureau at Brodick pier, the last as a result of constant agitation by Miss Bess Macmillan, who was recently awarded an MBE for her many and varied services to the island.

The habit of rating in respect of its own statutory powers having once been established, the district council not only made some use of the powers hitherto neglected, making contributions to many villages in need of help in the erection or extension of halls, but used also an opportunity afforded by the Act of 1964 to contribute to the cost of repairing some of the small stone jetties on the island, whose value to visitors with small pleasure craft is obvious.

The district council was thus beginning to extend its functions on the island, and indeed to regard itself as having a right, as the distinct island unit of local government, to look beyond its statutory limitations and consider the island's special problems and by representations, sometimes through the District Councils' Association for Scotland, and sometimes direct to the appropriate body, to effect remedies, especially in matters such as education and tourism, in which the conflicting interests of Arran and Bute made representation to the county almost pointless. In the meantime, however, an event had occurred which threatened the district council's existence, the publication in 1963 of a white paper called *The Modernisation of Local Government in Scotland*, and although this did not lead to a slackening of its effort, it gave added significance to a new body established on the island in 1965, the Isle of Arran Council of Social Service.

This has persisted and in 1974 consists of representatives of some fifty-one voluntary organisations, eight churches and nine miscellaneous bodies concerned with the welfare of the island, among which are three trade unions, four employers' organisations or concerns employing labour, and such bodies as the Brodick Public Hall and Recreation Company, the National Trust for Scotland, and the Arran Society of Glasgow. It had representatives also from each of three statutory bodies, Bute County Council, Arran District Council, and the Board of Management for Arran Hospitals, although these last will be phased out by 1975. Its executive committee of fourteen is elected by these representatives, from among their own number, by postal ballot. It is, therefore, democratic, but in a different sense from the local authority bodies, whose members are directly elected by those of the adult population sufficiently interested to record their votes. The vote in the case of the council of social service is virtually confined to those who participate in some corporate activity, and in the case of its executive committee to those who have achieved leadership in such activities, either as chairmen, secretaries, treasurers, or committee members. It is claimed that this type of constitution, by removing from the members both of the council and the executive committee the necessity to offer themselves as candidates at popular elections, at which they have to convince the public that they are better than their opponents, offers opportunities of service to men and women of ability and experience who are too modest to praise themselves in public, and too polite to denigrate others. It is said also to ensure a council and an executive committee with a wide range of interests and abilities.

The council of social service is government-sponsored to the extent that it is financed mainly by the Development Commissioners, and has assessors appointed to it by government departments. It cannot, like the district council, raise money for its purposes by levying a rate, but the power of the district council is limited as we have seen to certain mainly minor statutory functions, and where it has dared to raise its voice on the wider issues affecting the island it has been faced, like the education subcommittee, with the attitude that it has no right to discuss matters other than those allocated to it by statute. This at any rate has been the attitude taken by the county education committee and the county council, and although it confuses a duty imposed with a right allowed, it is ingrained in local government thinking. The council of social service, by virtue of the very fact that it is not a statutory body, is free to raise its voice on any subject relating to the island's welfare, and to conduct any activity beneficial to the island which is not prohibited by law. The extent to which it succeeds varies, of course, with its leadership, and it was under Tom Alexander that it made its greatest impact.

From the outset it devoted its attention to the main problem of depopulation. It cooperated with the district council in investigating the possibilities of establishing local industries, of raising a fund to finance possible industrial development, and of employing a projects officer. But its most important single act was to commission and publish a study of the depopulation problem itself. The population of the two civil parishes had decreased steadily from the period of the clearances until the advent of the steamboat and the railway, when a temporary halt in the rate of decline occurred in the western parish, and a steady rise began in the eastern, due to the development of the holiday trade (see table, page 240). This change occurred around 1881, and although the downward trend continued afterwards in the western parish, the increase continued in the eastern, and the population of the island as a whole remained comparatively stable until about 1951. Then a steep decline followed, in the eastern parish particularly, and by 1961 the island population had fallen by 944, a decrease of 20·3 per cent in ten years.

Both Arran District Council and the Isle of Arran Council of Social Service became concerned, and the latter commissioned Margaret Storrie, of Queen Mary College, London, whose paper *Landholdings and Population in Arran from the Late Eighteenth Century* has already been mentioned, and her husband, C. I. Jackson, of the London School of Economics and Social Science, to conduct a detailed study and prepare a report. It was pub-

lished in 1967 under the title *Arran 1980-81: 2,021?*, and fore-
cast that under certain assumptions based on present trends, and
unlikely to prove false unless these were radically altered by some
unforeseen contingency or by effort difficult to envisage, the
population of the island by 1981 would be just a score above
2,000. The report, a thorough, closely argued, and authoritative
document, startled even those who had been concerned with
the problem since the 1961 census.

It had been assumed that just as the rise in the eastern parish
which began about 1881 had been due to the railway and the
steamboat, the fall which began about 1951 had been due mainly
to electricity and the internal combustion engine. We have seen
that the North of Scotland Hydro-Electric Board, established on
the island in 1946, had carried electricity into every corner, and
that in the 1950s 98 per cent of the farmers acquired tractors,
and there was an increase in the ownership of motor vehicles.
These reduced labour requirements on the farms, in the hotels
and boarding-houses, and in the trades and transport. There is
no doubt that without this modernisation a drift from the island
would have occurred in any case, since every activity on the island
would have become uneconomic, but modernisation without
expansion to absorb the labour made redundant by it led
inevitably to population decline. This was the factor which had
operated from the time of the clearances until the rise of the
holiday trade, and had operated in the mainly agricultural
western parish even then. It was now operating over the island
as a whole, but particularly in the eastern parish, to an extent
quite unprecedented, and at a rate greater than that even in the
crofting counties.

It had, however, been assumed that when the island eventually
became saturated with electrical and mechanical appliances and
motor vehicles the population would steady, at a lower level than
before, but with a higher standard of living, and at a higher level
than would have been likely if the island had stagnated. But as
labour became redundant it was the younger people who left,
partly because they were less entrenched, and partly because life
in the cities had for some time offered a greater variety of jobs,
higher wages, more entertainment, and enhanced possibilities of
sexual selection and marital fulfilment. In Arran especially the

239

POPULATION TABLE

	Kilbride Parish	Kilmory Parish	Arran	
1801	2183	2996	5179	
1811	2274	3430	5704	
1821	2714	3827	6541	
1831	2656	3771	6427	
1841	2786	3455	6241	
1851	2512	3414	5926	
1861	2408	3148	5556	
1871	2290	2778	5068	
1881	2153	2580	4733	
1891	2298	2482	4780	
1901	2469	2297	4766	
1911	2451	2177	4628	
1921	5293	3001	8294	June census
1931	2658	1874	4532	
1941	2800	1750	4550	Estimated
1951	3158	1498	4656	
1961	2532	1181	3577	'Final resident' Census
1965	—	—	3145	Enumeration
1968	—	—	3162	Enumeration
1971	—	—	3332	Enumeration

The figure of 3,332 is also the 'corrected final resident' figure, based on the 'provisional final resident' figure of the 1971 official census, all that is yet available from that source.

effect of the last of these considerations was aggravated by the situation created by the provision from 1946 onward of grant-aided senior secondary education. Although made available, it could be obtained in Arran only by sending children away from the island, not merely to the mainland, but from 1955 onward to Bute. We shall discuss this question more fully later, but there can be no doubt that with the growing redundancy not only young people left the island, but middle-aged couples who had growing children. The population left on the island of an age to reproduce itself decreased radically, until the point at which the population as a whole might be expected to steady was likely to be delayed, and the figure at which it might do so reduced, by a subsequent fall in natural replacement. The danger stressed by Storrie and Jackson was that before the population could steady it might fall below the figure necessary to enable the island to maintain a reasonable level of essential services, and if that did happen the decline would not just continue, but accelerate.

The paper went on to consider ways of halting the decline,

no doubt that without this modernisation a drift from the island culture and forestry, by establishing industry, and by encouraging a residential population. It was argued that although there were distinct possibilities of an extension of the holiday trade, such an extension was most feasible in such enterprises as large hotels, motels, holiday camps, and caravan and camping sites, which were more likely to add to the imported summer labour force than to the number employed on the island throughout the year. Agriculture was likely to develop increased production through further amalgamation of uneconomic farms and increased output per man, both unlikely to halt population decline. The industries which seemed feasible were few in number in view of the difficulties created by freight costs and the lack of island raw materials. A residential population of commuters was unlikely in an island comparatively difficult to reach, but there was a possibility of attracting a fair number of retired people, and this seemed to the authors of the paper to be the island's main hope.

In reviewing the possibilities of creating employment, the authors considered how far the government's development schemes, as revealed in white papers, might establish more favourable conditions, but saw little hope except in one instance. The terms of the Highlands and Island Development (Scotland) Act of 1965, passed to aid economic and social development in the crofting counties, made it possible for the Secretary of State to extend its application to contiguous areas of similar character. Bute County Council and Arran District Council had applied for the inclusion of their respective areas in that covered by the Act, and had met with rejection. Storrie and Jackson pressed for the inclusion of Arran, chiefly on the ground that the power to give financial assistance by loan or grant to any person proposing to establish an industrial or commercial enterprise would enable Arran to overcome the main difficulty encountered by Arran District Council, and the Isle of Arran Council of Social Service, in their attempts to promote industry. Although pressure for inclusion was continued, it has only now succeeded.

Storrie and Jackson had acknowledged that the provision of employment would not necessarily halt the population decline. A reasonable social environment would have to be created also. They saw some prospect of improvement in this respect in another impending government project, the reorganisation of local government.

The principal defect in the life offered by Arran to people rearing families was that the children streamed for senior secondary education had to go to Rothesay. Until 1967 they went straight from the primary schools at the age of eleven or twelve; subsequently the intention was that they should go, after two years of comprehensive education at Arran High School, at the age of thirteen or fourteen. The journey to Rothesay was a long and awkward one, since the children had to sail to the mainland, travel by bus to Wemyss Bay, and sail again to Bute. In winter the reduced services enabled them to return to their homes at the weekend only once a month. While in Rothesay they had to stay in lodgings, and unless parents were able to pay more than the recognised lodging-rate, which was determined by a grant made by the county education committee, these could not without loss to the landlady be generous either in their catering or facilities.

The system had various obvious disadvantages. It meant that parents were deprived of their natural desire to contribute fully to their children's development during an important formative period, and that the contribution of the more gifted children was withdrawn not only from the community life of Arran High School but from that of the island villages. It is true that the more gifted children are almost certain to have to leave the island in any case after completing their education, for few professional posts are available on the island, but their presence in the school and village communities would have been valuable not only for the leadership they could have given but for their opportunity to exercise it. It was argued that such opportunities were open to them on an even greater scale in the urban community of Rothesay, but to plunge children into town life in lodgings from rural homes involved a considerable effort of social adjustment, while the school community itself required such an effort, for it was segregated in terms of ability, and yet composed largely of pupils already familiar with the town environment, and at first strangers to the newcomers. There was the further fact, disturbing to children, that their tenure of lodgings was never secure. A suitable age for such demands of social adjustment is surely in the later teens, when the children have had time to recover from the

considerable effort of personal adjustment required from them by
the onset of puberty.

When local government was last reorganised in 1929 there was
a proposal that the county of Bute should be abolished and the
islands forming it distributed among neighbouring counties. Arran
was to become part of Ayrshire. Rothesay, however, was unwilling
to surrender its prestige as a county capital, and Arran, forgetting
that it meant more to the economy of Ayrshire than to that of
Bute, feared that as a small district in a large county it would
suffer neglect. Both islands campaigned for the survival of the
county, and their campaign prevailed. It was a sad mistake, for
even then it should have been realised that the county was an
anachronism.

When the area had first been established as a sheriffdom in
the twelfth century, sea routes had been short, and Arran was
linked with the upper Clyde mainly through Bute. Rothesay was,
therefore, a reasonable centre for administration. But by the
time county councils had been set up after the third Reform Act
of 1884-5 the railways from Glasgow to Wemyss Bay and to
Ardrossan respectively had been in existence for a quarter of a
century, and roads, too, had been established on similar routes.
Rothesay had long ceased to be the centre through which any
traffic passed between Arran and the outside world. It gained at
first no benefit from being the county capital beyond the business
it secured as the seat of county administration, yet having at
least half the population of the county in its boundaries it had
to bear at least half the cost of county services in as far as these
were paid for out of rates and not taxation, and the proportion
paid for out of rates was higher then than it is today. A view
developed that Arran was 'a millstone round Rothesay's neck',
and where the interests of the two islands conflicted Bute felt
justified in using its majority on the county council to curb expenditure in Arran.

Relations did not become really strained, in spite of Arran's
much greater mileage of roads, one of the earliest county functions, until the provisions for education demanded by the Welfare
State established after the Second World War caused an astro-
nomical rise in expenditure. There was a great increase in the
number of pupils, owing partly to the raising of the school leaving

age to fifteen, partly to the post-war bulge in the child population, and partly to the fact that the payment of bursaries to the children of poorer parents, and of travel and lodging grants to pupils attending school away from home, enabled many children to have secondary education who formerly would have been sent out to work. As long as the numbers able to afford secondary education had been low, and the cost to the county also, Arran senior secondary pupils were allowed by an inter-county arrangement to attend school at Ardrossan, from which they could return easily at the weekends. But as the number of pupils increased everywhere Ardrossan Academy was required for Ayrshire pupils, and the Bute county education committee, on the burning down in 1955 of the old Rothesay Academy, by then an inadequate building, firmly settled on a policy of bringing Arran and Cumbrae pupils to Rothesay, and built the new Rothesay Academy as the single county senior secondary school.

There was little demur from the Arran members of the county education committee, most of whom had the same attitude to the Welfare State as the 12th Duke had shown towards democratically elected parish school boards, and thought the Arran children fortunate to be educated anywhere, especially after the compulsory school-leaving age, at the expense of the ratepayers. They accepted the view that a senior secondary school on Arran was absurd in view of the small number of pupils available, the high cost to such a small county, and the national shortage of teachers. The name of the one Arran member who did not share this view, the late Tam MacArthur of Merkland, deserves recognition here.

The Arran parents were less satisfied, estimating that a reasonable provision for senior secondary education on the island would cost slightly less than the provision of hostel accommodation in Rothesay, and such accommodation was provided, for pupils removed from their homes, by all other counties with islands. They drew attention also to the fact that there were then several successful senior secondary schools elsewhere in Scotland of the size required in Arran. They were not impressed by the idea that Rothesay was carrying Arran on its back, for although at least half the money paid from rates for county services came from Rothesay, more than half the total county expenditure was

POLITICS

being met from national taxation in the form of equalisation grant and grant aid. As for the county's rating burden, in 1967-8 the total Bute county rate of 18s 11d (95p) was exceeded in fifteen of the thirty-three counties of Scotland. Although the cost of education was high in the county owing to its island character, at £199 12s 11d (£199·65) per pupil as against a figure for Scotland as a whole of £155 1s 1d (£155·05), it was by no means the highest in Scotland, that being the figure for Sutherland of £310 7s 8d (£310·38). And while equalisation grant was much higher in Sutherland it was calculated according to the resources of the county on a system designed to give the ratepayers in all counties a service as nearly as possible equal for an equal rate, and Bute was in terms of property, on the value of which rates are levied, a comparatively wealthy county. As for capital debt per head in the county, it was below average, £138 4s 7d (£138·23) as against a Scottish figure of £253 16s (£253·80)

At the time of the publication of the Storrie and Jackson report the only hope of easing the educational difficulty seemed to lie in the inclusion of the island, for purposes of education, in a local government area which included the adjacent mainland. Arran children qualifying for senior secondary education would then be able to attend school on the opposite coast close to the main line of communication between Arran and Glasgow, where the shorter journey and better services would make weekend breaks possible throughout the year. There was also the hope that a more generous attitude to the provision of hostel accommodation might prevail than at Rothesay.

As it turned out, the parents achieved their objective of a senior secondary school on the island before the reform of local government took place. After the upgrading of Arran High School to 'O' Grade the members of the parents' association, encouraged by what Rothesay councillors called a 'vociferous minority' and the director of education, more flatteringly, a 'skilfully led pressure group', determined to keep their children on the island until they took their 'O' Grades, even if they were considered fit to proceed further eventually. The director of education circulated a letter advising them that to send their children to Rothesay after the second year was 'educationally desirable', but by that time most of the Arran parents had ceased to consider him credible. It was

245

then found necessary to make the school virtually a four-year comprehensive, and eventually, when in 1973 the school leaving age was raised to sixteen, the establishment required for the school was so little short of that required to provide senior secondary education that resistance crumbled, although two pig-headed Rothesay bailies maintained to the bitter end that nothing had ever been wrong. The skilful leadership of the 'pressure group' was again supplied by Tom Alexander, and the island's main protagonist within the county education committee was Evelyn Sillars of Mid Mayish, a daughter-in-law of the maid Ellen, who pushed the Adams-Acton perambulator from London to the Broomielaw.

The gradual upgrading of Arran High School has been one of the most important factors in the change which has taken place in the population trend since the publication of the Storrie and Jackson report in 1967. The council of social service, anxious to keep a close watch on the situation, agreed that Dr Storrie should be asked to conduct an enumeration exercise every third year, and until 1971 this was done with the help of adult volunteers. In the absence of Dr Storrie in 1974 the exercise had to be carried out by senior pupils of Arran High School, under the supervision of their headmaster, himself a geographer, but it has not yet been completed. The 1968 and 1971 figures, along with the provisional figures of the 1971 official census, are so far the only ones available on which to speculate.

It appears that the population of the island, although lower in 1971 than in 1961, was in 1965 and 1968 even lower (see table page 240). Between 1965 and 1968 there appeared to be a halt in the decrease, and between 1968 and 1971 there was a real increase. This was found to be due, not to natural increase—there having been more deaths than births on the island—but to an excess of immigration over emigration, 200 people having left the island in the three-year period, but 400 having come in. Of these about 60 per cent were under forty-five years of age. There was a change also in the age structure of the population, the number of young adults, or people between fifteen and forty-four, had increased both absolutely and relatively to other age groups. This is likely to lead in a few years to an increase in the number of children born on the island, and the age structure may improve still further.

This change has obviously not been due solely to the influx of retired people thought possible by Storrie and Jackson, although retired people coming to the island now, except for the burden of the comparatively high prices resulting from freight charges, have more prospect of comfort and happiness now than in 1968. Before the solution of the educational problem they had to depend on the services of a dwindling number of elderly tradesmen, and the atmosphere was geriatric. Now the number of young tradesmen with growing families is increasing.

There were, of course, other factors at work than the upgrading of Arran High School, but without that improvement these would have had less effect. Some were due to efforts made by the islanders themselves. The council of social service, the district council, and the tourist association combined to form a development association, and for some time had a full-time project officer to guide enterprise to the island. Nothing spectacular was achieved, but several small rural industries and craft workshops were established, many with the help of grants or loans, and in the climate created came a wave of young people anxious to find an alternative to the increasingly impersonal computerised society breeding ugly discontent on the mainland. Among other developments may be mentioned the cannery started by the Lady Jean Fforde, now being taken over for expansion by a company in which Lord Bute and the new laird of Dougrie are interested; a wrought ironwork plant at Monamore; a new printing office at Whiting Bay which produces an island newspaper; and, most recent of all, a nature centre which provides a fascinating opportunity for visitors to brief themselves for their rambles about the island.

Among other factors behind the halt in the population decline are the new weekend commuters, increasing with the development of industrial conurbations on the adjacent mainland, although a proportion are professional people from Glasgow. These increased with the policy pursued until recently by the government and county councils of making improvement grants available for second homes. This policy, and the feeling that land and property are safer than money during a period of high inflation, probably account for the displacement of the poorer local people from their cottages into council houses, and the consequent decrease in letting-houses mentioned earlier. There has, however, been an increase in private as well as in council-house building, and an increasing interest in the island by developers. Although commuters and holiday house-owners do not add to the permanent population they do call for more permanent residents to provide services. So far mass-chalet and caravan-site developments of a kind likely to cause an imbalance between the permanent and the holiday population have been resisted successfully, but greater vigilance may be needed when the new local-government structure comes into force in 1975.

In this, Arran is in the Strathclyde Region for major planning, police, fire, education, social work, and general recreational services, and in the Cunninghame District for minor planning, local recreational, and all other services. Arran is a ward for the purpose of electing a district councillor, but only part of an electoral division which elects a regional councillor. It will therefore have one resident member only on the new district council of twenty-four members, and most probably seldom or never any resident member on the regional council. Now that this has come about there is a surprising consternation, which argues considerable apathy when the change was mooted. The consternation may be to some extent misfounded. Arran is much more closely linked economically with Glasgow and the Cunninghame district of the mainland than it ever was with the island of Bute. Its main lines of communication to the outside world are through Ardrossan and Glasgow. That is how its trade flows, in goods and even cattle and sheep if not altogether in motorist visitors. And although the island will no longer have a distinct unit of local government with power to rate for specific functions, it has been seen that under the 1929 structure the old district council had few of these, and was inhibited in its attempts to suggest solutions for major problems by being told they were not its business. Under the new structure, largely due to the efforts of Mr J. S. Campbell, for a long time honorary secretary of the District Councils' Association for Scotland, it will be possible for small distinct communities, such as Arran, to have a community council. This will have as its primary function the making of representations, on any matter affecting the welfare of the island, to the district and regional councils, and presumably to the Scottish Office, or through the local MP to parliament. Since it will have to be set up and financed by the new district council, it may run into difficulty if it ever dares to differ from the higher body. For this reason it may be too early yet to suggest that when Arran achieves its community council its council of social service should be wound up.

BIBLIOGRAPHY

The works are listed under separate chapters. Where the name of an author only is given, followed by a figure in brackets, the latter denotes the chapter under which the work is first listed.

CHAPTER I

BRYCE, J. *Geology of Clydesdale and Arran, embracing also the Marine Zoology and the Flora of Arran, with complete list of species.* Glasgow 1859

GEIKIE, SIR A. 'The Building-Up of the Island', *The Book of Arran,* Vol 1. Arran Society of Glasgow, 1910

HEADRICK, REV J. *A View of the Mineralogy, Agriculture, Manufactures and Fisheries of the Island of Arran.* Edinburgh 1807

HUTTON, J. *The Theory of the Earth,* Vol 1. Edinburgh 1795

HUTTON, J. *The Theory of the Earth,* Vol 3. London 1899 (Written in 1795, this was now edited by Sir Archibald Geikie, author of *Founders of Geology.* It contains the first complete account of the geology of Arran ever written)

JAMESON, R. *An Outline of the Mineralogy of the Shetland Islands and of the Island of Arran.* Edinburgh 1798

MACCULLOCH, J. *A Description of the Western Islands of Scotland,* Vol 2. London 1819

MACGREGOR, M. *Excursion Guide to the Geology of Arran.* Geological Society of Glasgow, 1965

RAMSAY, SIR A. C. *The Geology of the Island of Arran from Original Survey.* Glasgow 1841

TOMKIEIFF, S. I. Geologists' Association Guides, No 32, *Isle of Arran.* Colchester 1961

TYRRELL, G. W. Memoirs of the Geological Survey, *The Geology of Arran.* Edinburgh 1928

For a complete geological bibliography to 1928 see Tyrrell, p 277, and from 1928-61, Tomkieiff, p 33.

CHAPTER 2

BALFOUR, J. H. *Account of botanical excursions made in Arran in 1869.* Printed for private circulation, 1870

250

Brodick Castle and Gardens. The National Trust for Scotland, 1968
Brodick Gardens and Policies. The National Trust for Scotland, 1968
BRYCE, J. (1)
DARLING, F. FRASER. *Natural History in the Highlands and Islands.* Collins, London 1947
GIBSON, J. A. 'The Birds of the Island of Arran', *Transactions of Bute Natural History Society,* Vol XIV. Rothesay 1955
GRAY, R. *The Birds of the West of Scotland.* Glasgow 1871
LANDSBOROUGH, REV DR D. *Excursions to Arran, with reference to the Natural History of the Island.* Edinburgh 1847
Second series of above, 1852
LANDSBOROUGHS, THE. *Arran, its Topography, Natural History and Antiquities.* (An edition of the senior Landsborough's works revised and edited by his son, the Rev D. Landsborough junior, with a memoir) Ardrossan 1875
MACWILLIAM, J. M. *The Birds of the Firth of Clyde.* London 1936
MARTIN, M. *A Description of the Western Islands of Scotland.* (Visit to Arran 1695) London 1703
MONRO, D. *A description of the Western Isles of Scotland, called Hybrides.* (Visit to Arran 1594) First printed from the MS by Auld, Edinburgh 1774
New Statistical Account of Scotland, The. Vol V. Edinburgh 1840
PENNANT, T. *A Tour in Scotland and Voyage to the Hebrides.* (Visit to Arran 1772) Leathley, Dublin 1775
Statistical Account of Scotland, The. Glasgow 1793
Third Statistical Account of Scotland, The. Vol XI. Collins, Glasgow 1962

CHAPTER 3

ATKINSON, R. J. C. 'Fishermen and Farmers', *The Prehistoric Peoples of Scotland.* Edited Piggot, S. Routledge and Kegan Paul, London 1962
BRYCE, J. (1)
BRYCE, T. H. 'The Sepulchral Remains', *The Book of Arran,* Vol 1
COLES, F. R. 'Cup and Ring-Marked Rocks', ibid
DANIEL, G. E. 'The Megalith Builders', *The Prehistoric Peoples of Scotland.*
HEADRICK. (1)
LACAILLE, A. D. *The Stone Age in Scotland.* CUP, London 1954
MACARTHUR, J. *The Antiquities of Arran.* 2nd edition 1873, Black, Edinburgh. First published 1861

BIBLIOGRAPHY

MARTIN. (2)

PENNANT. (2)

PIGGOT, S. 'Traders and Metal Workers', *The Prehistoric Peoples of Scotland.*

ROY, A. E. 'A New Survey of the Tormore Circles', *Transactions of the Glasgow Archaeological Society*, Vol XV, Part II, pp 59-67

SCOTT, J. G. Regional Archaeologies, *South-West Scotland.* Adams and Mackay, London 1966

CHAPTER 4

BALFOUR, J. 'Viking Burials', 'Fortified and Domestic Sites', 'An Irish-Celtic Monastery', 'The King's Cave', 'The Holy Isle', *The Book of Arran*, Vol 1

BRATE, E. 'Runic Inscriptions in the Cell of St Molaise', ibid

BREMNER, R. L. 'Norse Place-Names of Arran', *The Book of Arran*, Vol 2. Arran Society of Glasgow, 1914

BRØNDSTED, J. *The Vikings.* Translation 1965, Penguin, Harmondsworth. Copenhagen 1960.

BRYCE, J. (1)

CAMERON, REV J. K. *The Church in Arran.* Grant, Edinburgh 1912

CHADWICK, NORA K. *Celtic Britain.* Thames and Hudson, London 1963

CHADWICK, NORA K. and DILLON, M. *The Celtic Realms.* Weidenfeld and Nicolson, London 1967

CURRIE, R. *The Place-Names of Arran.* Smith, Glasgow 1908

ECCLES, F. C. 'An Effigy of an Abbot at Shiskine', *The Book of Arran*, Vol 1

FIRSOFF, V. A. *Arran with Camera and Sketchbook.* Hale, London 1951

HAMILTON, J. R. C. 'Forts, Brochs and Wheel-Houses in Northern Scotland', *The Iron Age in North Britain.* Edited Rivet, A. L. F. EUP, Edinburgh 1966

HEADRICK. (1)

JONES, G. *A History of the Vikings.* OUP, London 1968

KENDRICK, T. D. *A History of the Vikings.* Methuen, London 1930

LYTTEIL, W. *Landmarks of Scottish Life and Literature.* Miller, Edinburgh 1877

MACARTHUR. (3)

MACBRIDE, M. *Arran of the Bens the Glens and the Brave.* Foulis, Edinburgh 1910

MACKENZIE, W. M. *The Book of Arran*, Vol 2

MARTIN. (2)

PENNANT. (2)

POWELL, T. G. E. *The Celts.* Thames and Hudson, London 1958

POWELL, T. G. E. 'The Coming of the Celts', *The Prehistoric Peoples of Scotland.*

RADFORD, C. A. R. 'From Prehistory to History', *The Prehistoric Peoples of Scotland.*

WAINWRIGHT, F. T. Editor. *The Problem of the Picts.* Edinburgh 1955

WAINWRIGHT, F. T. *Archaeology and Place-Names and History.* Routledge and Kegan Paul, London 1962

Gwyn Jones' *A History of the Vikings* was published after Chapter 4 was written. He agrees with Brøndsted in distinguishing between Ivar of Dublin and Ivar the Boneless.

CHAPTER 5

BARBOUR, J. *The Bruce.* Edited Mackenzie, W. M. Black, London 1909. Written c1376

CAMERON. (4)

DOWNIE, R. A. *All About Arran.* Blackie, London 1933

HOLMER, NILS M. *The Gaelic of Arran.* Institute for Advanced Studies, Dublin 1957

LAMONT, W. D. *The Early History of Islay.* Burns and Harris, Dundee 1966

MACBRIDE. (4)

MACKENZIE. (4)

MACKERRAL, A. *Kintyre in the Seventeenth Century.* Oliver and Boyd, Edinburgh 1948

MARTIN (2)

MITCHELL, D. *History of the Highlands and Gaelic Scotland.* Gardner, Paisley 1900

MONRO. (2)

CHAPTER 6

AITON, W. *View of the Agriculture of the County of Bute.* Glasgow 1816

Arran Sheep Mark Register. Allan and Ferguson, Glasgow 1899 Earlier editions undated

253

BIBLIOGRAPHY

BAUCHOP, R. Series of plans of the inhabited parts of Arran, 1807-12 NRA(Scot)0331, plans 1-68.

BURREL, J. MS *Journal, 1766-73*. NRA(Scot)0331

BURREL, J. MS *Journal, 1776-82*. NRA(Scot)0331
  Plan of the Island of Arran. NRA(Scot)0331, miscellaneous estate plans 7. c1773

CAMERON. (4)

Census enumerator's return, Arran. MS NRA(Scot)0331, box 8. 1801

COCHRANE, J. H. MS 'Review of the farms of the island of Arran at present in the Duke of Hamilton's own hands'. NRA(Scot)0331, box 8. 1784

HEADRICK. (1)

HUGHES, T. *Memoir of Daniel Macmillan*. Macmillan, London 1883

KENNEDY, REV J. Editor. *Memoir and letters of Rev Finlay Cook and of Rev Archibald Cook*. 2nd edition, Northern Counties Publishing Company, Inverness 1896

Lives of the Brothers Haldane. Bryce, Glasgow c1890

MACKENZIE. (4)

MACKILLOP, D. M. *Annals of Megantic County, Quebec*. Lynn, Massachusets 1902

New Statistical Account of Scotland, The. (2)

PATERSON, J. 'Account of the Island of Arran', *Transactions of the Highland and Agricultural Society of Scotland*, Vol XI. 1834

PENNANT. (2)

Statistical Account of Scotland, The. (2)

STEVENSON, W. MS 'Report to his Grace the Duke of Hamilton about Arran Estate matters'. NRA(Scot)0331, box 8. 1800

STORRIE, M. C. 'Landholdings and Population in Arran from the Late Eighteenth Century', *Scottish Studies*, Vol 11. 1967

STORRIE, M. C. 'Balliekine, Arran : Survivor of Two Revolutions', *Folk Life,* Vol 5. 1967

YULE, J. Plan of the Island of Arran showing mode of letting in 1814. NRA(Scot)0331, miscellaneous estate plans 5. 1814

CHAPTER 7

COCKBURN, LORD. *Circuit Journeys*. Douglas, Edinburgh 1889

DUCKWORTH, C. L. D. and LANGMUIR, G. F. *Clyde River and Other Steamers*. Brown, Son and Ferguson, Glasgow 1937

GREEN, R. Editor. *The Diaries of Lewis Carroll*. Cassell, London 1954

HEADRICK. (1)

INGLIS, J. C. *Brodick-Arran and the Great War 1914-1918.* Oliver and Boyd, Edinburgh 1919

INGLIS, J. C. *Brodick—Old and New.* Guthrie, Ardrossan c1930

LANDSBOROUGH, REV DR D. *Arran, A Poem in Six Cantos.* Edinburgh 1828

LANDSBOROUGHS. (2)

MACKENZIE. (4)

MACQUEEN, A. *Echoes of Old Clyde Paddle-Wheels.* Gowans and Gray, Glasgow 1924

MILNER, G. *Studies of Nature on the Coast of Arran.* Longmans, Green and Co, London 1894

MOORE, D. L. *Marie and the Duke of H.* Cassell, London 1966

NOEL-PATON, M. H. *Tales of a Grand-daughter.* Moravian Press, Elgin 1970

SCOTT, SIR W. *The Lord of the Isles.* Edinburgh 1814

SILLARS, J. *The MacBrides.* Blackwood, Edinburgh 1922

SILLARS, J. *Gavin Douglas.* Blackwood, Edinburgh 1923

SILLARS, J. *The Brothers.* Blackwood, Edinburgh 1924

SILLARS, J. *The Desperate Battle.* Blackwood, Edinburgh 1925

STIRLING, A. M. W. *Victorian Sidelights.* Benn, London 1954

TYRRELL, G. W. 'Economic Geology', *The Geology of Arran.* (1)

WILLIAMSON, J. *The Clyde Passenger Steamer.* MacLehose, Glasgow 1904

CHAPTER 8

A Handbook of Scottish Administration. HMSO, Edinburgh.

Census enumerator's return, Arran. (6)

Local Government in Scotland. HMSO, Edinburgh

MACKENZIE. (4)

MACPHAIL, I. M. M. *A History of Scotland,* Book 2. Edward Arnold, London 1956

New Statistical Account of Scotland, The, (2)

Statistical Account of Scotland, The. (2)

Third Statistical Account of Scotland, The. (2)

CHAPTER 9

Accommodation Register. Isle of Arran Tourist Association. 1968 and 1973

Census 1961 Scotland, County Report, Bute. GRO, Edinburgh 1964

BIBLIOGRAPHY

HALL, T. S. *Tramping in Arran*. Oliver and Boyd, Edinburgh 1928

Isle of Arran, The. Official Guide, Isle of Arran Tourist Association. 1974

JOHNSTONE, J. M. *Rock Climbs in Arran*. The Scottish Mountaineering Club, Edinburgh 1958

MEEK, R. *Hill Walking in Arran*. Chambers, Edinburgh 1963

Modernisation of Local Government in Scotland, The. Cmnd 2067. 1963

Peerage, Baronetage and Knightage. Burke's Peerage Limited, London 1949

Rates Statistics 1967/68. Association of County Treasurers in Scotland.

Rating Review. Institute of Municipal Treasurers and Accountants. 1968

STORRIE, M. C. and JACKSON, C. I. *Arran 1980-81: 2,021?* Scottish Council of Social Service, Edinburgh 1967

STORRIE, M. C. *Enumeration of the population of Arran in 1968*. Isle of Arran Council of Social Service. 1968

STORRIE, M. C. *Arran Population Enumeration. Report No 2*. Isle of Arran Council of Social Service. 1971

Third Statistical Account of Scotland, The. (2)

ACKNOWLEDGMENTS

The author gratefully acknowledges his indebtedness not only to those listed in the bibliography, but to the Lady Jean Fforde of Strabane and her factors Alan Newlands and John Nisbet for access to unpublished material from the archives of Arran estate, to M. H. Noel-Paton for access, prior to publication, of her *Tales of a Grand-daughter*, to Margaret Kelso and Tom Alexander for the loan of rare books, and to Allan Leach, formerly the Bute county librarian, for constant willing help during the writing of this book :

Also to the Arran District Clerk, the Department of Agriculture, the Director of Education for Buteshire, the Forestry Commission, and the manager of Torrylin Creamery, for their help in providing statistics :

To the Arran Society of Glasgow for permission to use line illustrations from Vol I of *The Book of Arran*; to J. R. C. Hamilton and the Edinburgh University Press for permission to copy their drawing of a vitrified fort from *The Iron Age in North Britain*; to Tom Huxley and the Nature Conservancy for permission to copy their drawings of the Arran service trees; to M. C. Storrie and Christine Elkins, the School of Scottish Studies and the Aberdeen University Press for permission to use maps from 'Landholdings and Population in Arran from the Late Eighteenth Century' and for the use of blocks :

To J. G. Scott of the Glasgow Museums and Art Galleries for much helpful advice and for the use of the photograph of the late Bronze Age ornaments found at Low Whitefarland; to Alexander Hamilton for the use of his photograph of old Lamlash; and to the National Trust for Scotland for photographs of the Scougal portrait of the Duchess Anne and of the drawing of Brodick castle before 1844 :

To Finlay Cook, Alastair Douglas, Alastair Kelso, John Henderson, Angus MacMillan, Donald MacNiven and Howard Walker, for information of a kind not obtainable from books or written records.

257

INDEX

Page numbers in italic indicate illustrations

INDEX

260

INDEX

INDEX